Contents

Preface		**v**
Acknowledgements		**viii**
Notes on Contributors		**ix**
1	**History and Recent Developments**	**1**
	Introduction	1
	Historical Overview	1
	Recent Developments	4
	Conclusion	15
2	**Resources for Reading**	**17**
	Introduction	17
	Choosing Books for the Classroom	19
	Big Books	27
	Core Books	28
	Books in Series	31
	Reading Schemes and Programmes	33
	Books in Other Languages	43
	Books Made by Children	45
	Environmental Print	47
	Information and Communications Technology (ICT)	47
	School Libraries and Bookshops	52
	Managing and Organising Resources	54
3	**Reading Routines**	**60**
	Introduction	60
	Everyone Reading in Class	61
	Reading Aloud to Children	63
	Shared Reading (Big Books) and Shared Writing	68
	The Class Reader	72
	Telling Stories	76
	Drama and Playing in Role	79
	Teaching Phonic and Graphic Knowledge	82

Group Reading/Guided Reading 94
Reading Partners 101
Reading to the Teacher 104
Working with Parents 109

4   Monitoring and Assessing Reading   **113**
Introduction 113
Informal Observation 114
Conversations with Children 115
Structured Semi-Formal Assessments 116
Formal Assessments 127
Frameworks for Assessment and Record Keeping 133
Glossary of Assessment Terminology 134

5   Meeting Individual Needs   **137**
Introduction 137
Assessment 141
Meeting Individual Needs In and Out of the Classroom 142
Parental Involvement 149
Conclusions 149

References   **151**

Index   **159**

Preface

Many students elect to enter initial teacher training because they are convinced of the importance of education and in particular of the importance of literacy. They themselves are successful readers and writers, and they see no reason why all young people should not have similar success. They know that literacy, and in particular the teaching of reading, is a topic on which everybody has an opinion, including the media, politicians, teachers, researchers, parents, and even the children themselves. They cannot fail to pick up the polarisation of people's views about the teaching of reading but, full of ideals, they believe that there must be a solution to these contentious issues and that there must be ways to turn all children into readers. If this description is one that you recognise, we have written this book for you because we want this idealism to remain while you learn how to teach and throughout your teaching career.

As students, you will go into many different classrooms where you meet a bewildering array of books, materials, approaches and practices. All sorts of schemes and programmes surround you; there are statutory *National Curriculum* requirements; there is the 'Literacy Hour' and its accompanying ring binder; there are practices accompanied by unfamiliar terminology that teachers assume you understand; there is a mass of record keeping; there are four-year-olds who can read and ten-year-olds who cannot. That early idealism you brought with you to university is still there but you are now wondering quite how to make sense of all that you see. You know that to be a good teacher you need to have a clear view of what it is you are doing, and why. You know that, if you are to feel in control of all the issues involved, you will need to have a deep understanding.

Keeping reading under control is what this book is about. Control in any area springs from a secure understanding of processes and enabling practices; control in teaching reading is no different. How do we teach children to read? We believe that there are four strands in the answer to this question and the book is structured around those strands. Firstly, to teach reading you need to understand how reading is learned. Research that has gone on over many years is informative here, and knowing how teaching approaches have come and gone over time helps you to keep a sense of perspective when thinking about new developments. This is what we discuss in Chapter 1. Secondly, in Chapter 2 we talk about the resources you need to teach reading. With so much potential reading matter for children, you need a rationale for choice and for the way in which you organise the books and materials. However good your resources, they will be ineffective if you do not have our third strand firmly in place: good classroom practices, through which reading is taught. We are calling these 'routines' and Chapter 3 introduces you to them. Fourthly, the role of assessment, addressed in Chapter 4, needs to be clearly understood as an enabling mechanism for identifying and planning appropriate teaching for all your pupils. Some of these pupils will be struggling, and in Chapter 5 we discuss the more targeted teaching that they will need.

The framework provided by this book is intended to give you a structure for teaching reading. We give you theories to think about, definitions of terminology, classroom examples to look at, practical ideas, ways of organising the children, ways of planning for reading, analyses of interactions between teacher and child, and suggestions for further reading. All of this will contribute to your feeling that you can control this vast area.

There is another kind of control, the external one provided by the *National Curriculum*, and, for some of you, by the *National Literacy Strategy Framework for Teaching* which gives students and teachers a baseline for work on reading. Throughout our book you will find references to both the *National Curriculum* and the *National Literacy Strategy* which we tie into the teaching and assessment described in the five chapters. What you cannot find in these official documents is debate, discussion, reflection and the fine-graining of what it all looks like in practice. It is these things which develop inner conviction and confidence which will in turn lead to good practice. Statutory control is one thing; ownership of your own understanding is, in the end, what gives you personal control.

Provision and practice for different age groups, boys and girls, for both monolingual and bilingual children and for children of varying abilities are described throughout the book but it is important that you do not skim through, seeking out reference to your current classroom experience only. As you will find out, reading is a complex process, not made any easier to understand by the fact that individual children go about learning in very different ways. What you will learn about beginners informs your teaching of older children; what you will learn about how older children tackle reading gives you insights into how to work with younger children. In addition, a range of reading behaviours is seen at every age and we help you to avoid assuming that age and stage are always the same.

Finally, it is our intention to talk about good teaching. The bitter and polarised discussions that have gone on about the teaching of reading have not served children and the teaching profession well. In our book you will see how it is not necessary for one approach to war with another and you will find examples of teachers working in many different and balanced ways in the interests of each and every child in their classroom.

In the children's book *A Cultivated Wolf* (Pascal Biet and Becky Bloom), a ravenously hungry wolf comes across a pig, a duck and a cow whom he would clearly love to eat except that he is mightily puzzled by the fact that all three are engaged in silent reading in the sun, claiming that they are 'cultivated animals'. The wolf is determined to read and write but his initial efforts do not impress the trio of farm animals. Ultimately, having progressed through school and various library books, the wolf buys his first storybook. He reads to pig, duck and cow, one story after another, 'with confidence and passion'. 'He's a master,' the animals declare and wolf joins this band of readers.

Teaching and reading with 'confidence and passion' would seem to us to say it all. It is our hope this book sets you on the path to reaching these goals.

Judith Graham and Alison Kelly
University of Surrey Roehampton
May 2000

PS Throughout this book we address students directly. However, there is relevance in all we say for newly qualified teachers, people who are returning to teaching and English/Language Coordinators and anyone concerned with and interested in the teaching of reading.

Acknowledgements

Judith Graham and Alison Kelly have been able to include accounts of teachers and children at work thanks to examples supplied by their students, their colleagues and classroom teachers with whom they have worked. In particular they would like to thank David Ashley, Rachel Hogarth-Smith and Louize Allen for their contributions to both editions, and Alison and Matthew Coulter, John Nolan and Lez Smart for contributions to the second edition. Grateful thanks also to Maggie Hancock who has provided essential help in researching and updating information and Laura Huxford for her advice.

In case of failure to obtain permission to include copyright material in this book, the editors and publishers apologise and undertake to make good omissions in subsequent printings.

Notes on Contributors

FIRST EDITION

Rebecca Bunting, Fiona M. Collins, Fiona Y. Collins, Judith Graham, Alison Kelly, Gillian Lathey, Liz Laycock, David Montgomerie, Pat Pinsent, Sue Smedley, Anne Washtell.

SECOND EDITION

Judith Graham, Alison Kelly, Liz Laycock (especially for Chapter 4), Anne Washtell (especially for sections on Phonics in Chapters 1 and 3).

Judith Graham is Principal Lecturer with interests and teaching commitments in all areas of literacy and children's literature. She is the author of *Pictures on the Page* (NATE) and of *Cracking Good Books* (NATE) and co-editor (with Alison Kelly) of *Writing Under Control* (David Fulton Publishers).

Alison Kelly is Senior Lecturer in Language Education and teaches on undergraduate, postgraduate, INSET and MA courses. She is co-editor (with Judith Graham) of *Writing Under Control* (David Fulton Publishers).

Liz Laycock is Principal Lecturer in Education and was coordinator of the Language Teaching Studies Department for six years. She is Programme Convenor of the Primary PGCE Programme and has particular interests in early literacy, narrative, the teaching of children with English as an additional language and the assessment of reading.

Anne Washtell is Senior Lecturer, contributing to all language and literacy courses. She is particularly interested in early literacy development, the development of phonemic awareness in children and supporting children with literacy difficulties.

Chapter 1

History and Recent Developments

INTRODUCTION

Go to any library and you will find scores of books on the teaching of reading. There have always been discussions and debates about how children learn to read and the best way to teach them. The sheer volume of literature on the topic can be daunting. In addition, these debates are often passionate and polarised, sometimes even vitriolic. The difficulty is that there is no one definitive all-encompassing theory or method, so one of the things all teachers of reading have to do in order to feel in control is to inform themselves. You need to have a balanced, historical perspective on the issues and you need to allow your developing understanding of the theories to inform your practice. You should also read, share and reflect upon accounts of theory and practice from other educationalists and teachers.

The controversies about reading relate to beliefs about what reading is, what it is that readers have to do and how reading is to be taught. As we shall show, these beliefs are tied up with broader understandings about how children learn which have changed across the years. The intention of this chapter is to provide a brief historical overview and then to look more closely at some recent significant developments.

HISTORICAL OVERVIEW

Alphabetic method

For many years people thought that reading was simply about seeing and hearing letters, sounds and words. This view leads to a particular kind of teaching where reading can be broken down into little bits to be taught in sequence. An early example was the 'alphabetic method' that was used in England in mediaeval times. In this approach, children learned the names of the letters of the alphabet and spelled out combinations of them. In museums, there are examples of seventeenth-century 'horn books', so called because they were constructed out of wood with a sheet of paper protected by a layer of transparent horn. These early reading books were not much bigger than a child's hand and could be tied on to the child's belt so that they didn't get lost. They usually comprised the alphabet, the Lord's Prayer (which was of course a very well-known text) and columns of syllables for the children to read. Apparently, horn books were also used in bat and ball games and we have reports of eighteenth-century ones made of gingerbread where the letters were gradually nibbled away!

The alphabetic method is still in use in some parts of the world. Judith Graham and Alison Kelly have each taught a child – one from Barbados and one from the travelling community in Ireland – who gave the letter names in each word, e.g. 'O-N-C-E', before reading the word accurately.

The phonic approach

In the mid-19th century the alphabetic method was challenged by an increasing interest in phonics (although it is interesting to note that phonic methods are to be found in an alphabet book published as early as 1570 (Avery 1995)). The difference between these two approaches is that phonics is about decoding using the letter *sounds* rather than names. There were strong debates about the efficiency of this method as the title of the primer, *Reading Made Easy in Spite of the Alphabet* (in Diack 1965), shows. Winston Churchill recalls learning to read with one such book called *Reading Without Tears*. He says that 'It certainly did not justify its title in my case . . . We toiled each day. My nurse pointed with a pen at different letters. I thought it all very tiresome' (Diack 1965 p. 30). These early phonic primers taught children through carefully graded sequences of sounds but, as we shall show, one of the difficulties with phonic approaches lies in the nature of the English language, which is not completely phonically regular. To overcome this, *Reading Without Tears* omitted irregular words while another, *The Pronouncing Reading Book* (1862, in Diack 1965), used different colours to show different vowel sounds such as the 'a' in 'apple', 'was' and 'are'.

A more recent initiative in 1960 attempted to regularise the sound–symbol system through the introduction of a so-called 'Initial Teaching Alphabet' (ITA). To the 26 letters of the alphabet, an additional 20 symbols were added. It was a short-lived initiative: a paucity of texts using ITA (and a lack of any environmental print) restricted the range of reading and children with reading difficulties found the transfer back to the conventional alphabet enormously challenging.

The 'look and say' approach

Another approach, 'look and say', is often described as being more recent than phonics but it too was being promoted in the mid-19th century. Unlike phonics, 'look and say' starts with words (or sometimes whole sentences) which children learn from flash cards before meeting them in a book. A contemporary advocate of this approach claimed that 'a child would learn to name any twenty-six familiar words much sooner than twenty-six unknown, unheard and unthought of letters of the alphabet' (Horace Mann 1838, quoted in Diack 1965 p. 42). Just as phonic approaches introduced children to sounds in a carefully graded way, so too with 'look and say', where key words, written on cards and held up by the teacher, were gradually taught and reinforced through books containing much repetition and carefully controlled vocabulary. As with phonics, traditional teaching of this method involved lots of rote learning, drills and whole-class work; such routines were well suited to the organisation of the large classes so typical of elementary schools from 1870 and gave teachers a sense of control in very difficult circumstances.

Both phonics and 'look and say' were taking hold at a time when behaviourism was a prominent and popular learning theory. This theory portrays the child as a 'clean slate' and sees new learning coming about as a matter of stimulus and response, the idea being that learning is goal-directed with appropriate behaviour being reinforced and inappropriate being ignored (Skinner 1953). Advocates of 'look and say' made claims for the centrality of meaning in their approach while supporters of phonics argued that phonic knowledge enabled children to 'attack' unfamiliar words. The 'look and say' emphasis on the whole word owes something to the Gestalt theory that stresses the importance of the 'whole' to which the 'parts' are subordinate.

The 'language experience' approach

Phonics and 'look and say' approaches, and sometimes a combination of the two, were dominant through to the 1970s and many of the reading schemes that were published during this long period reflect these views of reading. The idea of 'language experience', where the children's own experiences and language are the basis from which their first reading matter is constructed, is an approach typified by the *Breakthrough to Literacy Materials* (McKay 1970). These comprised personal banks of words and 'sentence makers' (stands rather like those used in Scrabble) from which the children constructed their own sentences which became their first reading matter. The publishers also produced reading books that made an attempt to present children with familiar language and situations. Some teachers continue to use *Breakthrough* materials today and find them especially useful for drawing children's attention to words and sentences.

Language experience theories came about in the 1960s and 1970s when there was a broadening of interest in looking at how a child learns to talk. With the advent of the tape recorder, researchers were able to listen to children over longer stretches of time and in more systematic ways than previously. They showed children to be much more active and creative in their learning than behaviourism acknowledged them to be, and went on to look at how teachers might build on these understandings about children's oral language to bridge their move into literacy.

'Whole language' approaches

As the name suggests, this approach (springing up as long ago as the 1940s in the USA) is characterised by a belief that language work in schools should not be broken up into component parts and learned separately. A whole-language teacher would use trade books rather than reading schemes, read aloud to children from quality literature and encourage lots of independent and own choice reading. There would be teaching of all possible cue-systems (see p. 5) for children to arrive at meaning from their reading. Children would work with reading partners and parents would be seen very much as part of the team. There would be generous time given to work on personal projects, plenty of opportunities to present and publish work, and teachers would try to replicate professional editorial practices so that, for instance, correction of errors would be a practice reserved for the stage of writing just prior to publication and always in the context of the child's work.

This way of teaching was a rejection of commercially produced packages and programmes. It was popular at a time when there was great support for child-centred education and certainly many teachers felt that children with special educational needs (SEN) and those learning English as an Additional Language (EAL) were helped through such an approach.

RECENT DEVELOPMENTS

Reading has always attracted research and new thinking and there is no exception to this in the modern era. Some ideas may well have been current or popular in the past and have been resuscitated. We will concern ourselves here with a few recent developments which we consider have had a considerable impact on our view of reading and its teaching. You will find these developments reflected in the *National Curriculum* (DfEE/QCA 1999a) and the *National Literacy Strategy* (DfEE 1998a).

New understandings about the reading process

The 1970s and 1980s saw a development of interest in the teaching of reading by an influential group of researchers known as psycholinguists, including Constance Weaver (1980), Ken Goodman (1973) and Frank Smith (1978). As you would expect from its name, the discipline of psycholinguistics brings together psychology and linguistics.

From psychology came work on memory, attention and perception that was helped by the development of machines to record readers' eye movements. This work was linked with the Gestalt theory that we mentioned earlier (about learning from wholes and not separate parts) and together they contributed to a more refined view of the reading process.

From linguistics came ideas (for instance, those springing from Chomsky's work on how creatively children generate language) that children implicitly know a great deal about how language works as soon as or even before they begin to speak and certainly before they begin to read. They may say 'I'm spoonfulling my cornflakes in,' but they will not say 'In my cornflakes spoonfulling I'm,' unless they're just mucking around, with language as much as with their cornflakes. They use this knowledge to form expectations about meaning from speech around them but also from written language when they start to meet it, as long as it is in meaningful contexts. Children can make deductions about the written words 'Toys' or 'Books' if they are in a department store where toys and books are displayed beneath these labels.

The joining of psychology and linguistics led to a broader view of reading than had been seen before. Words and letters are still important; all predictions have to be checked against the actual print on the page but the model of reading now includes other information that children bring to reading. This model, based on the idea of 'cue-systems', shows what children need to draw on and pull together when they read; the term 'orchestrate' (Bussis *et al.* 1985) has been used to describe this process and it does seem to us to be a useful term. There are three cue-systems:

1. *Semantic*, in which readers draw on meaning both from the text itself but also from what they know of the situation they are reading about, from life experience and from other texts. A child who knows that 'ice creams *melt* in the sun' is unlikely to miscue and read that 'ice creams *meet* in the sun'.
2. *Syntactic*, in which readers draw on what they know of language and grammar (spoken and written) to predict what is coming next. A child who knows that what ice creams do in the sun is *melt* is unlikely to miscue and read that 'ice creams *meal* in the sun' as she implicitly knows that a verb needs to fill that slot.

3. *Grapho-phonic*, in which readers use what they know of sound–symbol correspondences, visual knowledge of letter combinations and sight vocabulary. Thus, a child
   meeting 'melt' for the first time could blend its four constituent phonemes (sounds)
   together: 'm' – 'e' – 'l' – 't'.

Some teachers also find it useful to think about a fourth cue-system sometimes
referred to as 'bibliographic'. For this, children are drawing on what they know about
written texts; for instance, if they are reading a fairy story they will not need to bring
into play what they know about indexes and glossaries, information they use for
reading non-fiction texts. For younger children this is also about knowing the way
around a book, where to start and so on.

More recent models (e.g. Adams 1990) make a clear distinction between graphic (i.e.
visual) and phonic (i.e. auditory) cues and, as we shall see below, these cues are
represented separately in the *National Curriculum*.

From the psycholinguistic model, there developed a process called 'miscue analysis'
which was and is a most useful 'window on the reading process' (Goodman's term,
1973). Through analysing children's mistakes when reading aloud, we can see reading
strengths and weaknesses and whether children are over-dependent on single
strategies. For instance, they may depend on what they know about meaning and
predictable language and they may not be checking their assumptions by looking at
words and letters and using what they have been taught about sound/symbol
correlation. Conversely, they may be over-dependent on decoding and neglect to use
the context of the book to help them. We look in more detail at miscue analysis in the
chapter on Assessment.

One of the criticisms levelled against the psycholinguists was that they failed to spell
out what their theories meant for people in the classroom. Work at the Centre for
Language in Primary Education (Barrs and Thomas 1991) drew from the psycholinguists and from Bussis *et al.* (1985, see below) and has developed and clarified the
psycholinguistic model so that it has become more user-friendly for teachers in
classrooms. CLPE use the terms 'big shapes' and 'smaller units'. 'Big shapes' refer to the
'larger overarching textual structures . . . and the way these structures are reflected in
the rhythms and tunes of written language' (Barrs p. 6). The smaller units comprise the
words and letters which children have to attend to and know about if their reading is to
be accurate. Children use all this information and need to know explicitly about both
these aspects of the reading process. It is through the classroom reading routines (see
Chapter 3) that teachers teach them.

The main focus of the helpful research undertaken by Bussis in the 1980s was
reading (though it also looked at other curriculum areas) and the researchers' findings
have important lessons for us. What their longitudinal study found was that children
have different learning styles – that they go about their learning in different ways. Some
children responded to the 'big shapes' in reading and were much more concerned with
keeping the story going fluently than with complete word-for-word accuracy. These
children read for meaning and would predict with confidence. Others were much more
reluctant to guess and were preoccupied with the smaller units, with getting the words
right using a step-by-step approach. Two interesting findings come from this: firstly, as
long as the children were given appropriate teaching experiences which stressed all

facets of the reading process, they made progress in reading whatever their preferred learning style. Secondly, these attitudes were not confined to reading. A child who favoured the 'big shape' in reading would be the one to get out all the bricks and experiment with construction tasks, while the child predisposed towards the 'smaller units' would be more interested in the detail and taking things methodically. A reception class teacher confirmed this for us: 'One thing I've noticed particularly is the actual difference in the types of reading . . . the big shapes and small shapes. There are those [children] that have the tune and there are those who are looking at the words and that is so distinctive, and you can see it in everything they do'. Within families, the differences can be visible too. Judith Graham's two daughters were 'impressionists' in their early days of reading; her son was more interested in the details of the print and went as far as reading the page numbers aloud as the pages were turned.

Early literacy

Views of the reading process have been considerably influenced by insights about children's very earliest moves into reading. A New Zealand researcher, Don Holdaway (1979), looked carefully at the interplay between text, adult and child in bedtime story routines and revealed the ways in which these routines 'set' the child up for literacy. As children are read to, they learn about books: about their structure, their characters, their language, the way a story keeps going. Above all, they learn about the enjoyment and intimacy that comes from the sharing of a book. (In 'Shared Reading (Big Books) and Shared Writing' in Chapter 3 we have a fuller discussion of how this research was turned into classroom practice.)

Another important contribution from this research was the observation of 'reading-like behaviour' in very young children. Holdaway records retellings of favourite texts by children as young as two and these 'readings' show how such young readers are already grasping the 'big shapes' of reading. They confidently retell the stories using book language and they hold the overall shape of the narrative. They use the illustrations and their recall of earlier readings by adults to arrive at an approximation of the text. They may not be able to decode a single word and, in some cases, they may not even realise that the black marks tell the reader what to say, but some of the conditions for becoming a reader have been laid down.

Many researchers claim that this reading-like behaviour is 'playing' at reading and that such play fits in with the importance of play in general. Children who have had good experience of play, particularly make-believe play, seem to find the entry into reading relatively straightforward (see Clark 1976). After all, entering a cave created by a sheet thrown over a table or sailing a boat manufactured from a cardboard box with a pillowcase sail is not very different from entering the imaginary world of *Can't You Sleep Little Bear?* (Waddell and Firth) or *Where the Wild Things Are* (Sendak).

As well as reading-like behaviour, there is also 'writing-like behaviour', though the terms you are more likely to come across to describe children's early written marks are 'early writing', 'emergent writing' or 'developmental writing'. (No one describes it as 'scribble' any more.) Children see that adults make marks on paper for all sorts of purposes and they imitate these purposes in their play. They also make marks for the delight of it, and research (e.g. *National Writing Project* 1989) shows that these marks move gradually towards the script of the culture. The child of Arabic parents will make marks taking on the characteristics of Arabic writing; the writing from the same child, if s/he is growing up in this country, may also reveal the impact of seeing the script of the English language all around and the writing may be a mixture of both scripts. This early mark making is evidence that children pay attention to the 'smaller units' of written language (see above) and the very literate environment in which we live is a great help. Children can 'read' 'MacDonalds' at the age of two, Tom can identify the 'T' that starts his name on the pavement where BT is laying cables and Madeleine can see that 'Made in England' has its opening letters in common with her name and she may reflect upon the different pronunciations.

We need to point out that the entry into reading, as we have described it above, is to some extent culture specific. Researchers such as Hilary Minns (1990) and Shirley Brice-Heath (1983) have shown us that literacy practices vary in different cultures; in some, for instance, the oral tradition is stronger than that of reading aloud. A child's 'approximation' of the text, which is what we see in reading-like behaviour, may cause anxiety in some families that the child is 'getting it wrong'. Perhaps there is an expectation that the child does not interrupt a reading or talk about how the book relates to her own life. Similarly, play opportunities may be restricted so that the child does not 'escape' sufficiently to her own world. Children's marks on paper may be thrown away. It is only recently that the value of these early attempts at writing have been recognised and pored over with interest and delight by teachers and researchers. In our classrooms, the way we go about the teaching of reading could thus seem very strange compared with home practices and you will need to take that into account, perhaps talking with parents (see 'Working with Parents' in Chapter 3) and certainly providing make-believe play opportunities and consistent and frequent interactive reading and writing sessions.

This research into children's early moves into literate behaviour offers a complex picture of what it is to become a reader. It challenges the idea, common at one time, that you could not teach children to read until they demonstrated their 'readiness' through various perceptual tasks. You may still come across the notion of 'reading readiness' but we now know that children are learning many lessons about reading long before they can decode or encode in writing.

Children learning English as an Additional Language (EAL)

The last two decades have seen considerable progress in our understandings about the ways in which young children whose first language is not English can best be supported in learning to talk, read and write in English. We know, for instance, that the withdrawal units of the 1970s, which gave such children English lessons through repetition and decontextualised exercises, did not offer a rich enough context for language learning. We know (Wiles 1985) that such children do learn a lot about the new language through the following:

- interactions with peers;
- the provision of activities with a practical framework which allows the child to make sense of what is going on (e.g. work with circuits in science, shapes in maths);
- activities where language is repeated in meaningful ways (e.g. in games: 'It's your turn now');

- many opportunities to hear, share and retell (maybe using props) stories with strong plots and predictable, maybe repetitive language, such as 'Run, run as fast as you can, you can't catch me, I'm the gingerbread man' (see Hester 1983 for many practical ideas for developing stories with bilingual children).

We also know more about the role of the mother tongue and the importance of sustaining it for the child's cognitive development (Mayor 1988). For children to feel confident in the classroom they need to know that their home language is accepted, valued and celebrated in the classroom. The visibility of different languages and scripts through the environmental print and books you provide make an important contribution to this (see Chapter 2).

But we also know of some of the difficulties faced by bilingual children learning to read. Using all the cue-systems together and as fully as a monolingual child is likely to do will be very hard for EAL children learning to read in English. For many children, something as obvious as the domestic scenarios painted by Sarah Garland and Shirley Hughes in their picture books will strike no chords. So using context cues will be difficult. Equally syntactic cues can present difficulties. As monolingual children's ears are attuned, they know what to expect in terms of likely word order, of course, but they also know which words typically go together. For instance, expressions like 'bread and butter' and 'ride' a bike (rather than 'drive') are extremely easy to read because the words collocate. Bilingual children do not bring such culturally acquired knowledge nor do they bring such secure idiomatic confidence to their reading although they learn and confirm such expressions through reading (see Gregory 1996). Lastly, in terms of grapho-phonic processing, for children whose first language uses a different script, there is further new learning to be done in order to become familiar with a totally new set of symbols. These understandings underpin points that we make later in the book.

Gender and reading

Gender inequalities have long been a concern of educators, but primarily with regard to the achievement of girls. However the 1990s saw the emergence of worrying statistics about boys; OFSTED reported both a 'persistent vein of low achievement' and, among boys, negative attitudes towards reading (1993 p. 127). Accounting for this trend` is complex but some commentators (e.g. Millard 1997; Barrs and Pigeon 1998) argue persuasively that the very act of reading is seen as gendered, as a female preoccupation. Research suggests that there are more women readers (especially of fiction) than men; there are more women teachers than men in primary schools and it is mostly mothers who read with their children. It is not surprising that young boys receive a particularly gendered view of who does the reading.

One striking difference between boys and girls reading that you may have noticed is the preference for non-fiction that boys show. This preference needs to be acknowledged and valued if boys are to happily extend their reading into areas less to do with facts and more to do with affective responses.

Throughout the book we will be considering ways in which the needs of all readers can be met and you will find examples of good practice that takes into account the particular perceptions of boys towards reading.

Texts

You can tell a great deal about the current view of reading if you look at the texts that are used to teach reading – the 'reading books', 'reading schemes' or, more recently, 'reading programmes'. The horn book with its alphabet and syllables was superseded by texts such as *Petherick's Progressive Phonic Primer* (1913, in Beard 1987) which required children to blend sounds (as in 'o-f of, o-r or, o-n on, o-x ox'). These texts, and some of the early ones that used a 'look and say' approach, are predicated on a view of reading that is about decoding letters and sounds.

Several factors have had an impact on the texts that are used with children now. For a start, we know much more about the role of the text itself in the reading process. Margaret Meek's booklet, *How Texts Teach What Readers Learn* (1988), describes the reading lessons to be gleaned from the child's interaction with the author and/or illustrator and she shows how this works with a book like *Rosie's Walk* by Pat Hutchins, where the fox following the hen is not mentioned in the written text. *Handa's Surprise* (Browne), a picture book set in Kenya, is in the same tradition as *Rosie's Walk*. Handa sets off from her village, basket on head, to make a present of fruits to her friend Akeyo. Each fruit is stolen by an animal but Handa is blissfully unaware and so, it would seem, is the narrator. But we, the readers of the book, can see the drama unfolding in the illustrations and anticipate Handa's approaching anguish. (You must seek out the text to discover the happy resolution that is again to be read only in the pictures.) Meek claims that books like these teach children about layers of meaning, about irony and about viewpoint, and she suggests that it is the interactions children have with such texts that lay the foundations for the reading they will encounter in later years (see 'Choosing Books for the Classroom' in Chapter 2 for much more on this).

Another concern is with equal opportunities and again we explore this more fully in the 'Choosing Books' section. For now, it is important to understand that in the late 1970s and through the 1980s teachers became increasingly aware of the impact some of the materials used in schools could have on the self-esteem of children from ethnic minorities and on girls, who seldom had central or significant roles in books. Such awareness also pervaded concerns in the late 1990s but, as stated above, now it is boys whose self-image worries us and we are debating issues around the selection of texts that respect boys' interests.

Reading schemes from the 1970s and 80s were particularly criticised on both equal opportunities issues and also for their language which emerged as stilted because of the graded introduction of words and sounds. Such language sounded like nothing children had heard before and made it difficult for them to draw on what they already knew of language to help them read.

This concern with the language of the books reflects a wider concern: all books should allow children to exploit all the cue-systems as fully as possible. In the 1980s new reading schemes tried to take some of these recent understandings on board by using more natural language, giving attention to more meaningful plots and relevant themes, and trying to address equal opportunities issues through, for example, the inclusion of more characters from ethnic minorities: all this without losing sight of teaching graphic and phonic skills – a tall order! (See 'Reading Schemes and Programmes' in Chapter 2 for more information about some of these.)

There was also some disquiet about the rigidity imposed by the use of just one scheme, and one criticism of some of the early reading schemes was that they created a so-called 'reading ladder' with only a narrow progression of books to be worked through. Such a structure can work against the development of children's choosing skills and can also restrict the range of books they read. It was partly in response to this difficulty that the idea of 'individualised reading' was first developed in the late 1960s by Cliff Moon. The intention was to provide children with broad bands of books that were within their reading grasp. In a rationale for this method of organising books, Moon explained that we have not only to match book to child according to his or her interests but also that we have to take account of what he calls the 'readability of texts and reading skill, competence and fluency of readers'. *Individualised Reading* (which continues to be published yearly) offers lists for 12 stages of books intended to serve the primary age range. Moon is cautious about assigning ages to stages and is insistent that the bandings should be used flexibly so that, in his words, 'it is teacher guidance only and not . . . a restriction on a child's choice of book'. Typically, books are colour coded and you will sometimes hear this approach described as 'colour coding'. It is an organisational device still used by many schools although some prefer to work with fewer levels.

Some teachers were so concerned about the ways in which they perceived reading schemes as narrowing children's choices that they stopped using reading schemes at all and chose to use so-called 'real books' instead. Two primary school teachers wrote influential booklets about this. Jill Bennett, an infant school teacher, published *Learning to Read with Picture Books* (1979), an annotated booklist of picture books that she used instead of a reading scheme. The booklist is organised under three headings: 'First Steps', 'Gaining Confidence' and 'Taking Off' and these categories continue to be useful to some teachers in organising their books and giving a sense of control over progress. More recently, Liz Waterland's *Read with Me* (1985) described how she changed from using reading schemes to 'real books'. It is an account whose focus tends towards the 'big shapes' of reading and was written somewhat in reaction against approaches that focused exclusively on the 'smaller units'. Some critics felt that she did not provide sufficient detail as to how such an approach might be structured to meet the needs of all learners. She responded to this criticism in later editions.

The 'real books' approach suffered because it became associated with certain assumptions which were not necessarily part of its well-intentioned origins: that reading can be learned 'osmotically' without direct teaching; that phonic teaching is not necessary; that all books that are not part of a scheme are 'good' (and, vice versa, that all reading scheme books are not); and that reading can only be taught *either* through reading schemes *or* through 'real books'. Huge public controversy about these issues led to a number of government-initiated surveys (HMI 1991; House of Commons Select Committee Report 1990; Cato and Whetton 1991) which found that very few teachers believed in or operated according to any of these erroneous assumptions. What the surveys did find was that effectively taught reading was due to coherent and well-understood school policies which were properly implemented by the head, the member of staff with responsibility for language and the classroom teachers. The surveys also found that adherence to just one method, whatever the method, was almost unheard of but that where it did occur it could be detrimental to the children's progress.

To a large extent this section has been concerned with books but at the opening of the 21st century, texts come in all shapes and forms: reading from the screen is becoming as commonplace in classrooms as reading from paper. Information and communications technology (ICT) is probably changing the forms that literacy takes faster than any other development. (See section on ICT in Chapter 2.)

Phonics and phonological (including phonemic) awareness

One significant recent development in the area of phonics has been in our understanding of the contribution that phonological and phonemic awareness can make towards success in reading. This is a complex area and we will take some time here to explore definitions, research and issues. We will look at the practical classroom implications in Chapter 3 where you will also find a glossary of key terms (pp. 91–3), some of which we will use in this section.

As we have discussed in the opening of this chapter, phonic approaches first became popular in the 19th century. Traditional phonic approaches placed great emphasis on teaching at the level of sounds (phonemes). Typically, such approaches would use 'synthetic' methods of teaching that can be characterised as aiming 'to teach all the letter–sound correspondences in written English as phonic 'rules'. Children then blend together the letter–sound correspondences in unknown words, and derive a pronunciation for them' (Goswami 1996 p. 6).

What do we mean by 'phonics'? It is not 'phonetics', nor 'phonemes', nor 'phonology', all of which are explained in the glossary in Chapter 3 (pp. 91–3). At its simplest, it is the relationship between letter symbol and sound, so when we read aloud the word 'man' we are able to blend its constituent sounds – 'm', 'a', 'n' – and when we want to write the word 'man' we can segment the word up and hear the three sounds and represent them with three appropriate letters. The linguist David Crystal (1987) explains that 'phonic approaches are based on the principle of identifying the regular sound–letter relationships in a writing system, and teaching the child to use these to construct or decode words'. *National Literacy Strategy* materials published to support phonic teaching state that phonics comprise 'the skills of segmentation and blending, knowledge of the alphabetic code and understanding of the principles which underpin how the code is used in reading and spelling' (DfEE 1999b p. 4).

So, when children are first introduced to phonics it is usual to teach them to hear and identify individual vowel and consonant speech sounds (phonemes) and enable them to recognise the symbols used for these sounds (graphemes). What is the relationship between phonemes and graphemes? A significant number of words in the English language have a direct correspondence between how we hear the word and how the word is represented in print as the example above, of 'man', shows. If the whole of the English language maintained this consistency then the teaching of phonics would be straightforward. But, as we shall show, the English language is not completely phonically regular, so children have to learn that the phoneme/grapheme match is not always clear-cut in many of the words that they are likely to meet, even in the earliest stages of reading. Try out a few words for yourself to test this point. Say the word 'out' to yourself. What sounds can you hear? Many people hear the central sound as 'w'. Try the same thing with the words 'any' and 'supper'. You may have noticed that when children try to spell words like these independently they rely on the sounds they think they can hear, resulting in logical but incorrect spellings such as these written by the child who was 'sent to bed with owt eny supa'.

The difficulty is that there are at least 44 identifiable vowel and consonant phonemes in the English language. However, there are only 26 letters in our written alphabet to represent these 44 sounds. At face value, this presents a problem as there are simply not enough letters to go around. The solution to is to make some letters 'double count'; the same individual letter may be pressed into service to represent different sounds. For example, the letter 's' in 'soft' makes a completely different sound from the 's' in 'was'; 'girl' and 'giraffe' both have to use the same letter, 'g', even though the initial sound is different in both words. More ingeniously, we represent some sounds by combining two or more letters together. Let us look at the word 'shop'. On their own 's' and 'h' are individual phonemes but when they combine they form a new individual phoneme, 'sh', because the alphabet does not have one letter to represent 'sh'. Try segmenting the word 'shop' out loud and you will find that it consists of three phonemes ('sh'-'o'-'p'). Its written representation of course is with four letters ('s'-'h'-'o'-'p'). This insight about sound–symbol relations is a challenging but fundamental lesson for children to learn. We can have a neat one-to-one phoneme/letter match as in 'man' and 'animal' but, equally, as we have seen with the word 'shop', we may not.

Despite these difficulties and apparent inconsistencies, phonic knowledge is an important strand in the child's repertoire of strategies for reading and it is a *National Curriculum* requirement that children should be taught how to use phonics. There are children who seem to learn to read without any formal phonics lessons although they undoubtedly reflect on phonic features, if only privately. But most children will need much more explicit teaching. The difficulty is that work on sounds and letters can be very abstract. What is important, and this applies to whatever reading skill you are focusing on, is that the child does not lose sight of the fact that reading is a purposeful and meaningful activity and that there are small and large shapes to attend to.

We turn now to phonological and phonemic awareness. Phonological awareness is an umbrella term to describe sensitivity to speech at all levels. Phonemic awareness, a branch of phonological awareness, refers to alertness specifically to sounds at the phoneme level. Children have to learn how phonemes correspond to their written form, graphemes, and, in order to do this successfully they need to develop the ability to hear and distinguish sounds in their heads. For example, a single change of phoneme or grapheme can produce a quite different word with a very different meaning. Say the words 'cat' and hat'. Which phoneme has changed? Now, read the same words and, not surprisingly, you will notice that while the '-at' part of the word stays the same, the grapheme 'c' in 'cat' has changed to an 'h' to form 'hat'.

Recent research has shown us that children's awareness of the phonemic structure of spoken words is a strong indicator of future success in learning to read and progress in spelling. Recent British research (Bryant and Bradley 1985; Goswami and Bryant 1991) looked closely at how children develop phonemic awareness. These researchers centred their attention on children's sensitivity to rhyme and alliteration as indicators of children's growing phonemic awareness. A longitudinal study revealed that children who had scored highly on an initial rhyming test progressed successfully in their read-ing and spelling. The tests were also given to a group of ten-year-old 'backward readers' (Bryant and Bradley's term). Significantly, the results of these tests indicated weaknesses in the children's sensitivity to rhyme.

Why is this research so important for us as teachers? First of all, as we have just described, there is a clear link between the early development of sensitivity to rhyme and progress in reading. For many children this sensitivity develops informally through exposure to nursery rhymes and playground rhymes long before they go to school. Secondly, children with good rhyming skills can make links between one word and another known as 'rime analogies'. For example, they are able to use the spelling–sound information in a word such as 'light' as a clue to help them read a new word that shares the same spelling pattern such as 'fight'. Beginning readers find using rime analogies supportive because the correspondence between the spelling sequences that represent the rhymes and their sounds in spoken words is more consistent than the correspondence between single alphabet letters and individual phonemes. By analysing words in this way, it seems that children are distinguishing between what are known by linguists as 'onsets' and 'rimes'.

The onset is the opening consonant or consonant cluster of a word or syllable and the rime is the vowel sound and any following consonants. So for the word 'sand', 's' is the onset with 'and' as the rime. In 'string', 'str' is the onset and 'ing' is the rime. What the research has shown us is that, as they begin to learn to read, children draw on their sensitivity to rhyme and find it easier to analyse or 'chunk' words in this way.

You may well be thinking that knowing about onsets and rimes is all very well, but surely children ultimately need to be aware of and understand about how sounds are represented by letters. Usha Goswami (1995) makes the connection for us in this way: she believes that children use their awareness of rhyme to make rime analogies that help draw their attention to phonemes. For example, you may have noticed the plea-sure that children gain from playing with a rime such as 'ook' and thinking of all the words that can be made by changing the initial sound, such as 'book', 'shook' and 'crook'. Playing in this way isolates the individual phoneme that is changing each time. You will find several children's books, such as those by Colin and Jacqui Hawkins, that enable children to turn half pages that reveal the changing onset. We also know that nursery rhymes can be used to help children increase their understanding of phonemes and graphemes as many have 'near miss' rhymes such as 'dame' and 'lane' or 'fourteen' and 'courtin'. By listening to these near rhymes and seeing them in print, perhaps through the use of an enlarged text, children learn about phonemic and graphemic contrasts.

The other way in which children develop phonemic awareness is through their independent attempts at spelling. Marilyn Jager Adams (1990) has studied the relation-ship between children's hypotheses about spelling and their growing understanding of phonics, and suggests that the two areas are closely related. Her study, and that of Goswami and Bryant (1991), points out that early attempts at spelling are a further crucial element in developing children's phonemic awareness. It is through their spelling attempts, which involve the act of segmenting the word and trying to represent its phonemes, that the relationship between individual alphabet letters and individual sounds becomes self-evident to children. It is therefore important that children are encouraged to hypothesise how words might be spelled and are provided with oppor-tunities to discuss the construction of their 'invented' spellings.

Ways of dividing words into chunks and seeing analogies between words are often called analytic approaches. These approaches differ from the one sound/one letter of the traditional synthetic 'c' 'a' 't' approach. (Look at the glossary on pages 91–3 for definitions of these terms.) There are arguments between proponents of these analytic and synthetic approaches, but you will find that the *National Curriculum* and the *National Literacy Strategy* show evidence of both analytic and synthetic methods. What has been added to the traditional synthetic approach is an emphasis on the importance of segmentation activities that provide the children with early experience of hearing the phonemes.

Government initiatives

Government control of the teaching of reading has never been tighter. The year 1988 saw the publication of the first version of the *National Curriculum for English* that laid down the content of the curriculum. It has been followed by two further versions (DfE 1995 and DfEE/QCA 1999a). *The National Literacy Strategy* (DfEE 1998a) both expanded in detail on the content of the curriculum and prescribed how it should be delivered. Desirable Outcomes for Children's Learning (SCAA 1996) outlined expectations for nursery and reception age children. This document was then superseded by Early Learning Goals ((DfEE/QCA 1999c) which, in its turn was absorbed into the much fuller Curriculum Guidance for the Foundation Stage (QCQ/DfEE 2000). For teachers in training, a National Curriculum comes in the form of *Circular 4/98, Teaching: High Status, High Standards* (DfEE 1998b). In the section below we consider each of these initiatives starting with that aimed at the youngest children.

Curriculum Guidance for the Foundation Stage (includes Early Learning Goals)

The document lays out expectations for 'Communication, language and literacy'. The intention is that children will have met these by the end of their reception year, having started on them at the age of three. With regard to reading you will find goals that contribute towards young children's understanding of both the 'big shapes' (e.g. retell narratives; use language to recreate roles; listen and respond to stories) and the 'smaller units' (e.g. hear and say initial sounds; link sounds to letters). Useful 'stepping stories' (illustrated by small multi-coloured footsteps on the page!) provide helpful indication of activities and progession.

The National Curriculum (NC)

The *National Curriculum* (DfEE/QCA 1999a) for English is structured in the same way as the other core and foundation subjects so it starts with the 'Programmes of Study' that specify what the children should be taught. These are followed by the 'Attainment Targets' that describe the standards children should be meeting and are arranged in 'level descriptions of increasing difficulty'.

In common with the other programmes of study for English, reading requirements are listed under the headings of 'Knowledge, Skills and Understanding' and 'Breadth of Study'. We look at 'Breadth of Study' in 'Choosing Books for the Classroom' in the next chapter, and you will see that there is an expectation that children will become acquainted with a rich array of different genres, both fiction and non-fiction.

Under 'Reading Strategies' in the 'Knowledge, Skills and Understanding' section for Key Stage 1, you will see the influence of some of the research we have discussed above. For example, the work on cue-systems and phonological awareness is reflected in the requirement that children should be taught to use phonemic awareness, phonic, graphic and grammatical knowledge as well as contextual understanding. You will see too that understanding and responding to literature are clearly indicated in both key stages. The sections on 'Language Study and Variation' develop children's understanding of text types, literary conventions and literary language.

The National Literacy Strategy (NLS)

The National Literacy Strategy Framework for Teaching (DfEE 1998a) expands on the content of the *NC* Programmes of Study. For example, it adds considerable detail to the *NC* 'Breadth of Study' section in its lists of suggested genres to be read and written term by term; the *NC* requirement for teaching phonemic awareness and phonic knowledge is amplified in the *NLS* by a breakdown of the order in which phonemes should be taught.

The introduction to the *NLS* offers a reading model which uses the metaphor of 'searchlights' which shed their light on the reading process: 'grammatical knowledge'; 'word recognition and graphic knowledge'; 'knowledge of context' and 'phonic (sounds and spelling)'. Note how this model splits up the grapho-phonic and retains the semantic (context) and syntactic (grammatical) cue-systems.

What is innovatory about the *NLS* is its prescription for delivery: a dedicated hour a day for literacy with sections devoted to text, sentence and word level work. With its emphasis on comprehension, text level work allows for the development of contextual/semantic understanding. Sentence level work, which focuses on grammar and punctuation, is the context for a grammatical/syntactic emphasis, while word level is where teaching about graphic and phonic aspects of reading goes on.

Circular 4/98, Teaching: High Status, High Standards (4/98)

Circular 4/98 (DfEE 1998b) lays down the statutory requirements for courses of initial teacher training. As well as requirements for teaching the *NC* to trainee teachers, *4/98* specifies subject knowledge that teachers need at their own level. The rationale here is that sound teaching requires very secure subject knowledge. For instance, you cannot teach the features of fables, myths and legends unless you are clear what their distinguishing features are, any more than you can help children spot phonemes in a word if you do not know the difference between a phoneme and a cluster.

As well as requiring a grasp of technical terminology (see glossary in Chapter 3, pp. 91–3), *4/98* also expects students to understand the spoken and written language systems of English under three headings: Lexical, Grammatical and Textual. You will find that sections in *Reading Under Control* on the reading process (Chapter 1), choosing books (Chapter 2), the teaching of phonics (Chapter 3), assessing children (Chapter 4) and meeting individual needs (Chapter 5) all contribute to this knowledge.

CONCLUSION

Research into the teaching of reading and its practice is never static. It will be evident from this chapter how complex and subtle the reading process is and how vital it is to avoid over-simplifying descriptions of how we read and how we should teach reading to others. It is as if the search for the one foolproof method has been a preoccupation ever since writing systems emerged. What we can say with certainty is that this quest will continue. The important thing is not to be daunted by the volume of research but rather to see it as ultimately helpful to us in giving children the very best possible teaching.

Further reading

Barrs, M. and Pigeon, S. (eds) (1998) *Boys and Reading.* London: CLPE.

Barrs, M. and Thomas, A. (eds) (1991) *The Reading Book.* London: CLPE.

Beard, R. (1987) *Developing Reading 3–13.* Sevenoaks: Hodder and Stoughton.

Edwards, V. (1998) *The Power of Babel, Teaching and Learning in Multilingual Classrooms.* Stoke-on-Trent: Trentham Books.

Millard, E. (1997) *Differently Literate: Boys, Girls and the Schooling of Literacy.* London: Falmer Press.

Chapter 2

Resources for Reading

INTRODUCTION

When you enter a primary classroom, you are usually met by an abundance of materials, artefacts, print and images. Not for the classroom the white walls and uncluttered spaces of a modernist home or company foyer. The good teacher, in her efforts to reflect the interests and lives of her 30 plus children, not to mention her effort to cover the full range of the curriculum, uses walls, racks, shelves, trays, boxes, screens, tables, the ceiling and the floor to contain and exploit the available resources. Teachers need to make their selection of resources based on as much information as possible and students need to appreciate and assess the resources they encounter with a full awareness of their purposes and relative usefulness. In this chapter, we will be giving a guide to, and a rationale for, those resources that are commonly found in classrooms that specifically relate to the teaching of reading.

It is an important chapter, as the selection, organisation and management of these resources are critical and complex aspects of teacher effectiveness. But resources are not the whole story and this chapter is complemented by the next on 'Reading Routines' where we look at the teaching contexts for reading, mediating and using these resources.

There is a bewildering array of skilfully marketed materials and books available and teachers have to perform a kind of juggling act between those and what they currently know about children, learning and the reading process. If, as we discussed in the introduction, children learn to read in different ways and if, as we saw, reading involves the orchestration of different strategies, then it follows that children need to be reading a range of texts. There is a very sound insistence on range under both the 'Knowledge, Skills and Understanding' and 'Breadth of Study' headings in the *NC* and we find there a useful recognition that different types of text demand different types of reading. For instance, ways of reading information books will differ from reading fiction, as you will see below.

Books in all their varied forms are perhaps the most immediately obvious resource that one encounters in the classroom. Initially, it is necessary to make categories that enable both children and teacher to find different types of book. The sections that follow consider the need for a central collection or 'Core' of books that meet the requirements of developing and fluent readers. It would be convenient if we could state that as long as children have a set of a dozen sure-fire titles, their entry into reading and their interest in reading will be assured, but it is not as simple as that. Children have different interests and vastly differing prior reading experiences so the same books cannot be equally significant to every child. What we can be sure about is that among a core of books should be a range of genres – non-fiction as well as fiction and poetry – a range of narrative and linguistic complexity, and a range of illustrative styles. These and other issues relating to a core of books are considered in depth below.

Among the books found in classrooms, there are usually many that have a similar appearance and which are often shelved separately. These will be one or other of the many reading schemes found in the vast majority of classrooms in this country or they may be books which belong in a series, published in identifiable format though not usually sharing the other distinguishing features of a reading scheme. We look at books in series below and we give an account of some of the most commonly found reading schemes. We believe that knowing how such schemes are structured and comprehending their underpinning philosophies will give all students and teachers more control over this area of the teaching of reading.

In another part of the classroom, possibly keeling over a little under their own weight, will be Big Books, enlarged versions of titles found in regular sizes and specifically marketed materials including non-fiction. These have been seen as central to the teaching of reading by many teachers for many years and are now an indispensable resource during the shared reading slot of the Literacy Hour. Big Books are also discussed below.

In many classrooms there will be books originating in other languages and there may also be translations of familiar English works. With these parallel texts may be dual-language texts where an additional language is overprinted on to the original English version.

Resources often overlooked because they are not commercially available, are the books made by the children themselves. The interest which children take in home-produced books has to be taken seriously and in classrooms where book production is habitual there is often a high level of literacy.

For many young children their first experience of print will be from the environment, from cereal and sweet packets for instance, or the many artefacts arising from current TV, film and sporting heroes. Such environmental print has been shown (Hall 1987) to play a significant role in young children's understanding about literacy and there should be examples of it in the classroom too.

Words and letters – on the walls, in boxes and tins – are part of the teacher's repertoire for supporting the development of children's alphabetic and grapho-phonic knowledge. Children can be introduced to the alphabet from a selection of the many available friezes and books as well as through rhymes and songs. There may be flash cards and wall charts focusing on words, vowels and consonants and the ways in which they can be combined. In many cases such materials will be part of a reading scheme (see p. 33). Games, either commercially produced or teacher-made, are often used to supplement both the above.

Non-fiction texts should be prominent in the class as their contribution to the literacy development of children is as important as that of fiction. The *NC* and the *NLS* give equal status to both types of texts.

Undoubtedly, in many classrooms the screen is important these days. The internet plays an increasingly significant role as both a source of information and as a means of communication. In classrooms can be found not only videos of certain texts to help teach reading, but also CD-ROMs, which aim to amuse while they teach. Literacy teachers make use of TV schools programmes which aim to support young readers.

Some programmes share with CD-ROMs the highlighting on screen of appropriate words and phrases; others invite children to identify letters, to predict, to sing along and to join in. Such programmes can be a stimulating and unifying class literacy experience. Programmes for older children also play an important role in encouraging reading and stimulating the exploration of deeper issues. Finally, there is the cassette tape. These audio tapes are usually sold with an accompanying book but often teachers, helpers, parents and children make their own recordings of favourite books, of the opening page or pages of a book or of a version in another language. As long as playback equipment is kept in a good state and listening opportunities created, the contribution of the cassette tape in all these forms can be considerable. All of these resources are discussed in the section on 'ICT' below.

CHOOSING BOOKS FOR THE CLASSROOM

Range considerations

All teachers aim to create autonomous readers: children who are capable of making personal and informed choices from among the wide range of books available. In countries where books are scarce, there is probably little choice and children may read and reread the few titles that they and their teachers can get their hands on. In this country, there are thousands of books for both the emerging and the fluent reader and thus teachers have a challenge and a responsibility in that their initial choices will dictate what children read, at least within the school walls. What we say in this section is intended to make selecting books for use in school a task that you feel you can approach with confidence.

The *NC* has always acknowledged the importance of offering range and the *NLS* expands amply on its broad categories. Most schools will have criteria for book selection, possibly written into their language policies, and of course the more people who can read, discuss and comment on the suitability of books the better. If you feel confident that your books have been chosen with care, you will have gone some way towards meeting your responsibility as a teacher of reading and you will feel that everything is more under control.

It ought to go without saying that we want to introduce children to as wide a range of reading as possible. There are children who love poetry and those who are indifferent to it, but none should be deprived of the chance to experience it. And this applies to all other genres. That is not to say that the youngest children are to struggle through newspaper editorials or Shakespeare's soliloquies but there are plenty of texts, from comics to letters to instructions to songs, which children want to read and which widen their understanding of the functions of literacy and prepare them for the wealth of text types which they will meet as they grow older.

A workable *NC* document cannot hope to convey all the issues to do with selection of books in the classroom. Here are a few further points about texts that amplify the brief sections on 'Breadth of Study' in the *NC*:

• Children develop favourite authors and favourite illustrators, and these authors and illustrators seem to develop children as readers. Teachers need to provide many titles by popular authors. Enid Blyton, Roald Dahl and J. K. Rowling convince children that they are readers; on completion of one book, children cannot wait to find the next or indeed to reread.

- Children's feelings are involved when reading. Teachers should be seeking out affecting texts at all levels. The predicaments, sometimes terrifying, that characters in traditional tales fall into, make for real stories and real involvement on a scale that whets the appetite for more. Suspense, making the heart beat faster and the pages keep turning, is a quality lacking in some older reading scheme stories. (See also comments below on humour.)

- The role of the story on cassette and the video or film of the book should not be underestimated. As we know, children demand and need more retellings of stories than we can ever give them so this resource should not be neglected. We have a section on these aspects in this chapter (pp. 47–52).

- If all the children we teach are to believe that books speak to them, we need to give much more thought to the range and quality of what we offer. For instance, sensitive representation of black people is now more the norm; there is no excuse for giving space to books with negative or token characters or stereotypical illustrations. Similarly, there is a need to check that the books we share show girls who can be strong and brave and clever and that boys, equally, can be liberated from conforming to these expectations at all times. The section on equality issues (pp. 23–4) explores this topic at greater length.

- Humour, comics and novelty books have a role to play in becoming a reader. There is no doubt that the interactive nature of some novelty books forms an ideal transition from the toy to the book for the youngest readers, and that all children return to books that make them laugh and to comics that are part of the group culture of the classroom. Teachers should not despise these ways into reading.

Subject matter

Fiction

Story is significant to all of us, but particularly to children for whom it is a basic way of appreciating and supporting understanding of the world (Wells 1987). It is very important that we satisfy this hunger and thus the best texts for reading aloud to young children are usually narrative texts. We are all interested in human behaviour (or in animals who behave in recognisably human ways) and the satisfaction of seeing a story develop is the strongest incentive to go on listening or reading. In addition, narrative texts usually rely on clear story lines including, for instance, a resolution that brings the story reassuringly full circle. These story shapes are quickly recognised by children and give them a feeling of familiarity and competence as well as developing the knowledge base needed for effective use of the semantic (contextual) cue-system.

Most writers are very careful with the language of their books, especially in picture books where each word counts and is going to be read by teacher, parent or child scores of times. From Year 4 the *NLS* expects children to explore figurative language in their reading and writing and you may find that, once you have selected your books according to range and challenging subject matter, you need to look again to ensure that you have included books which offer rich images, simile, metaphor, personification and alliteration. Texts by authors such as Joan Aiken, Kevin Crossley-Holland,

Geraldine McCaughrean and Jill Paton Walsh are rewarding in these respects.

When selecting books for your classroom you will also want to take a careful look at content as well as structure and language. Stories which focus more on domestic themes need to be interspersed with something more fantastical. So a Jacqueline Wilson title could be followed by one by Philip Pullman. Across a year children need to have met stories with boy and girl main characters, set in this country and abroad, in real and fantasy worlds, in present and past times and so on. The key is balance.

Poetry

Poetry is an area that, traditionally, has been neglected but it is much rarer these days to find teachers and student teachers who 'never touch poetry'. The fact that it is a statutory requirement in the *NC* has helped to rouse those who might otherwise have avoided poetry. In addition, the detail provided by the *NLS* with regard to the different forms of poetry that children are to be taught gives teachers a clear sense of direction. Also there has been a realisation that children's natural affinity with, and pleasure in, rhyme and rhythm should be exploited both for its own sake and because of its clear contribution to literacy (see Chapter 1). But perhaps more than anything a more informal and child-friendly strain of poetry has been published in the last 20 years or so which, along with hugely popular poet visits to schools, means that children have tasted poetry's delights and that teachers are not so nervous of the genre. Poets such as Michael Rosen, Gareth Owen, Kit Wright, Allan Ahlberg, Jackie Kay, John Agard, Grace Nichols, Roger McGough and Brian Patten have opened up the world of poetry for a new generation of children and made the genre attractive to boys, perhaps for the first time. Teachers have been able to explore this varied output and then to approach the work of other, perhaps more demanding, contemporary poets such as Charles Causley, Ted Hughes, Seamus Heaney and James Berry. It is likely that classical poetry has always found followers among certain teachers and pupils but the net is probably cast much more widely now that familiarity with newer poets has created confidence and enthusiasm.

The following list suggests what kinds of verse to look out for in terms of range:

- nursery rhymes
- finger rhymes
- contemporary and classical poetry
- poetry from around the world
- long and short poems
- some for declamation, others for quiet individual reading
- some rhyming and some not
- a variety of forms, e.g. haiku, sonnets, rhyming couplets, four-line verses
- poetry by children.

Plays

In this short section, we are only considering the area of scripted plays. Reading a play together is one of the most interdependent forms of reading aloud (and is thus well suited to the group reading activities we describe in Chapter 3). The *NLS* expects that children will read (and write) scripted plays in Year 3 and in schools where children meet good play scripts early, there is a chance to witness and appreciate a dramatic and exciting side of literature. Experiencing how a story can come alive in a group reading or, if the play reading develops, in a performance, is likely to benefit the reading of all narrative texts, which must be fleshed out in our imaginations. Teachers concerned about boys' attitudes and progress have found that play readings can be one successful way of promoting motivating contexts to read.

When looking for play scripts, the quality of the narrative is the first priority and if you know the story in its original format (for instance Jeff Brown's short novel *Flat Stanley* or the traditional tale *Stone Soup* by Tony Ross), you will probably find the play scripts (in these cases in the old, but still excellent 'Take Part' series by Lane and Kemp) to be of equal quality. There are many plays within reading schemes and programmes; make sure you think they are well written enough to be worth having multiple copies.

Children need a lot of help in the early stages of reading from play scripts regarding the conventions to be observed (e.g. not reading the stage directions aloud, following the story rather than looking ahead to see where your lines come in again). With your support, the activity becomes extremely popular and makes a clear contribution to literacy levels.

Non-narrative texts

We know that story is important for young children and that most early texts are stories, and even non-narrative texts for the young tend to include narrative elements. Nevertheless, we also all know many children, particularly boys, who have an equal hunger to possess information texts and, in truth, neither the narrative nor the non-narrative mode should be neglected. The *NC* and the *NLS* require children to be reading fiction and non-fiction from the outset and there is a specific role for the teacher in teaching the children how to use non-fiction texts (see Chapter 3 where we stress the importance of letting children hear you read aloud from information texts so that their different 'tune' is heard). There are also some important factors to take into account when choosing non-fiction:

- Does the contents page help children find the section they want?
- Does the index work in terms of full coverage, useful categorisation etc?
- Is the glossary written in language that children can understand?
- Is the page layout balanced between image and text, so that one extends and supports the other?
- Is the general design attractive to the child reader? Is it colourful and up to date? Does it make use of sub-headings to break up the text?
- Are the facts accurate as far as can be determined? Are they presented without undue bias?
- Are new words clearly explained in context as well as in the glossary and repeated frequently?
- Are readers helped with words which have one common and one specialised meaning?
- Is it recognised that, because there is no supportive narrative structure, vocabulary might need to be simpler than in narrative texts?

- Is it recognised that long sentences are not necessarily harder than a string of shorter ones?
- Is there variety in the prose, perhaps supplied by dialogue or case studies or perhaps through alliteration, simile and metaphor, and rhythmic prose?

Equality issues

Media sneering at 'political correctness' is currently widespread but to join in with it and to act as if unfair representations have no influence would be a very unwise course for a teacher or student to pursue. There are extremes of political correctness of course, such as the censorship of long-established traditional material, but what we are advocating here is to do with ensuring that, as you read and select books for children, you have a raised awareness of the ways in which stereotyping and omission can leave children feeling that reading is not for them. Some books can marginalise some children and you want to be a teacher in whose class all children are readers. To have reading under control in this sense is to feel confident that your selection of books conveys no offence to minority groups, no unnecessary stereotyping of girls or boys and no unexamined assumptions about age, class and race.

It is perhaps useful to think of making selections of books that offer reading 'equality' under the following three broad headings.

Traditional tales

Often it is traditional tales that present girls and women in passive roles with boys and men being brave and having all the adventures. The move now is away from the 1970s' initiative to rewrite these stories, having Red Riding Hood for instance kill the wolf herself, and more towards unearthing the 'forgotten' traditional tales that were ignored in the 19th century by such collectors as the Brothers Grimm. James Riordan and Alison Lurie have made good collections of such tales.

In addition, there is a rich seam of 'new' tales where traditional expectations are upset to amusing effect. Tony Ross and Babette Cole create books of this type that are very popular with children. Children will enjoy rewriting traditional tales themselves once they have had exposure to enough examples of the genre, and of course the full enjoyment of Allan and Janet Ahlberg's books or those of Jon Scieszka and Lane Smith depend upon a grasp of the traditional stories that are quoted or subverted. It is also important that you find stories from across the world. The fact that Disney has made films of the more well-known European traditional tales means that a story such as *The Sleeping Beauty* is better known than the powerful stories of Anansi or ancient tales from China, India, or even North America. A recognition that there is a rich worldwide store of tales needs to be evident in your classroom.

Some boys may have been deterred from reading folk and fairy tales if they are convinced that they are about pathetic princesses and besotted suitors! You may find that tales from non-European cultures appeal more to boys and there is no doubt that many myths and legends, with their beasts and heroes, are more immediately robust and are tales with which boys may want to identify more rapidly.

You may want to make links with the popular stories that children see on television and read in related material and comics. Much of this popular literature is quite sexist, racist, classist and violent and a thoughtful teacher will discuss some of these issues with her class.

Families in all their diversity

Books for children have only recently, and then by no means universally, revealed that their authors and illustrators realise that we live in a world of many races and varied family groups. We do not want books written self-consciously to present this plurality nor do we want a comprehensive coverage in every book but, rather, good stories which naturally and in an unforced way give our children a sense of themselves having a place in a diverse world. *Starting School* (Ahlberg) follows children from various cultural backgrounds as they all start in the same reception class. *Since Dad Left* (Binch) explores a child's coming to terms with his father's alternative lifestyle. For older children, the picture books of Charles Keeping and the novels of writers such as Bernard Ashley, Malorie Blackman and Anne Fine reflect an appropriately mixed society.

Exposing and exploring assumptions

You might imagine that fiction which challenges conventional assumptions would mostly be for older readers. However, picture books by author/illustrators like Anthony Browne are written for a younger audience willing to see the world in a different light. His *Voices in the Park* contrasts two families, revealing that it is adults, rather than children, who perpetuate class difference. *Piggybook* is an exploration of male chauvinism which, while delighting, makes children think. The stereotyping of boys is wonderfully managed in the picture book *Jump!* (Magorian and Ormerod). *Nobody's Family is Going to Change* (Fitzhugh) also raises issues of stereotyping, and novels for older children such as *Kiss the Dust* (Laird) or *Gulf* (Westall) are skilful explorations of war and its effects on minority groups. The careful research done by these authors gives their books the authentic feel of other cultures and countries as well as accurate and full information. Translated books are also powerful ways into other cultures.

Literature by itself cannot change society but it can help change thought processes, without which society cannot change. It can help children to experience vicariously what it is like to be a member of an otherwise alien group and to develop positive attitudes. For all our children, the feeling that the author knows we exist, that we are like his or her characters in some way, is a powerful incentive to pick up a book and stay the course. The author may then, if he or she wishes, take us beyond our own lives and allow new horizons to open out.

Matching the child to the book

There are no short cuts to the art of putting the right book into the child's hands at the right time. A child who does not want to read will reject everything, and we know how difficult it is when a child insists on choosing a long 'chapter' book which s/he really cannot tackle but wants to be seen reading. Then there is the child who is unwilling to take any risks and wants to keep returning to the same books. An equally painful scenario is where children, who do not want to be 'shown up', race through books from a reading scheme to keep up with their friends.

There are three things to disentangle here – range, personal interest and motivation – and an appropriate text choice for the reading stamina of the child. In order to help, you need to keep records of what the child has read before, to have read a great deal yourself and to have found some way of remembering what you have read so that you can access it usefully. Some of the categories that we have used above may act as an aid to memory though, of course, if you keep a card index as you read, you can riffle through it, which helps you and reassures your pupil. Also, as the previous section pointed out, you need to have organised your book collection so that the books are easily accessible.

This section has described and developed the 'Breadth of Study' requirements of the *NC*. The planning that you do across different routines (see Chapter 3) can ensure that children are meeting as full a range as possible across the school year. This has to be balanced alongside the child's personal interests, particularly when the child is reluctant to read. Children's interests, embedded as they generally are in current popular culture, may or may not coincide with ours or those of the *NC*. But if we ignore them totally we are in danger of jeopardising a potential site of reading growth and this may affect boys more than girls. The role of magazines, comics and books based on popular culture needs consideration here and you might want to negotiate with the children as to where, when and how there is a place for these (on specific days of whole-class reading for instance; see 'Everyone Reading in Class' in the next chapter). Individual time spent with children (see 'Reading to the Teacher' in the next chapter) is an excellent context for finding out about the child's out-of-school interests and reading habits. You may well discover that the most reluctant reader in school turns out to be an avid consumer of comics or 'Point Horror' books.

Then there is motivation: the motivation to choose which must be allied with knowing how to choose a book. Again, it is through reading routines that we teach children how to choose books. Sections on routines such as 'Everyone Reading in Class' and 'Reading Aloud to Children' in Chapter 3 show how you can make important points about authors, illustrators, the blurbs on book covers and other conventions. All this information helps children towards making their own choices. In addition, teachers claim that you can get children to start reading again by offering a book which:

- is new so the child will be the very first one to read it;
- you are very informed and enthusiastic about;
- you think has a main character rather like the child in front of you;
- is by an author or illustrator whom you know the child likes;
- is considerably shorter than the book the child read last;
- is in the area of the child's known interests;
- is 'more for older children but I think you're probably ready for it';
- other children are enthusiastic about;
- has scared you but which you think the child will be brave enough to read;
- is going to appear (or has appeared) as a film;
- you are considering for reading to the whole class or to a younger/older child.

Possibly hardest of all is ensuring that a book matches the reading stamina of the child, that the text is one that s/he can realistically tackle. This is not to say that children should never be allowed to choose books that appear either too easy or too hard for them; on the contrary, returning to old favourites and browsing through more challenging books is to be encouraged. The former confirms children as readers and the latter shows them what lies ahead. But they also need to be tackling texts that will push them forward a bit and this is particularly tricky. It may be that the challenge lies in the length of the book, or the complexity of the plot or, with a younger reader, it may lie in the need to ensure ever more accurate decoding. If you are working with a reading scheme or colour coded system you will have a ready-made structure and a sense of progression that may seem reassuring. However, you will need to inspect this structure closely so that you are sure that it is appropriate for the children's needs and that it is predicated upon a sufficiently broad view of reading to allow for both individual learning styles and *NC* requirements. The danger here can be that you are lulled into a false sense of security as the child moves up the ladder and that you lose sight of the individual needs of the child so that his or her capacities for choice are stifled. This is where careful monitoring of the child's reading strategies and choices will help (see section on 'Assessment' in Chapter 5).

However, there is no doubt that structure is important and that there are significant points in children's reading development where you will need to choose books for them with enormous care. The move into decoding print, for instance, is a delicate one that needs books with supportive, predictable and meaningful language. Some teachers report on the success of early books from the 'Oxford Reading Tree' and 'Story Chest' reading schemes for children at this stage, while other teachers rely on their own selection of books which they guide children towards.

In the final analysis, if your classroom is one where: the initial selection has been made with care; children's interests and choices are reflected and respected; children's progress is attentively monitored; access is easy and discussion of books takes place frequently, you should have time and incentive to match child with book and you should experience great pleasure when your pupil says, 'It was really good Miss'.

Further reading

Kropp, P. and Cooling, W. (1993) *The Reading Solution*. Harmondsworth: Penguin.

Pinsent, P. (ed.) (1992) *Language, Culture and Young Children*. London: David Fulton Publishers.

Powling, C. and Styles, M. (eds) (1996) *A Guide to Poetry 0–16*. London and Reading: Books for Keeps and the Reading and Language Information Centre.

Stones, R. (ed.) (1999) *A Multicultural Guide to Children's Books 0–16+*. London and Reading: Books for Keeps and The Reading and Language Information Centre.

Boyz Own (reading list with needs of reluctant inexperienced boys in mind) available from Books for Students, Bird Road, Heathcote, Warwick, CV34 6TB.

Books for Keeps – The Children's Book Magazine, School Bookshop Association Ltd.

Websites

Make Friends with Books   http://www.anholt.co.uk
Worm Works   http://www.wormworks.com

BIG BOOKS

Everything is relative of course and there are tiny books for children, bigger books and very big books but what we are talking about here are enlarged books, which may be as big as 60 x 45 cm but are more often around 30 x 36 cm or 50 x 36 cm. Numerous publishers produce them and they are nearly always called Big Books.

They provide a major resource for the shared reading slot in the Literacy Hour but have been used with young children for many years. These books started to come into nursery and infant classrooms in the early 1980s. (We must not forget, however, that teachers themselves had been making large-scale books for their classes for a long time and that many still do.) Don Holdaway (1979) powerfully describes teachers at work with large-scale books. These teachers reproduce the experience of the single child/adult reading encounter in which the child can see the print as clearly as the illustration. The enlarged text means that children at the back of a class of 30 can always see the print, and that the teacher can draw attention to features of print within the context of a story heard and seen by all the class. No published Big Books were available at that time and all Holdaway's examples are of books made by the teachers themselves. The books include poems, songs, fiction and non-fiction and children's own work.

Publishing companies were quick to see a gap in the market and Scholastic Publications (who were Holdaway's original publisher), Arnold Wheaton (original publishers of 'Story Chest') and Oliver and Boyd (whose Big Books are called 'Storytime Giants') all produced large-scale texts. Sometimes these were originals, such as *Hairy Bear*, *The Hungry Giant* and *Mrs. Wishy-Washy* ('Story Chest'); and sometimes a text, which appeared in conventional size in the first place, proved extremely popular and so was reprinted in large size. *Not Now Bernard* (McKee), *Oscar Got the Blame* (Ross), *Each Peach Pear Plum* (Ahlberg) and *The Lighthouse Keeper's Lunch* (Armitage) come into this latter category.

You will find that publishers tend to use texts where the stories are traditional, rhythmic, predictable and include much patterned language and intrinsic repetition with which children quickly join in. Many books make a great effort to vary and play with the print size to make it distinctive and indeed there is evidence that children are attentive to print which grOWS or Shrinks or changes in some way. Books that rely on a complex interplay between text and illustration such as the ones mentioned above (and *Handa's Surprise* mentioned in Chapter 1) obviously lend themselves to enlarged text format as the whole class can then see the game that author and illustrator are playing. There's an ever-growing selection of non-fiction titles as well.

Take Teresa Heapy's *Korky Paul, Biography of an Illustrator* which provides a lively mixture of graphics, photographs and accessible text. It comes complete with contents page and index and its non-patronising tone, as well as the use of Paul's own distinctive illustrations, mean that it could be used with both older Key Stage 1 children as well as in Key Stage 2. With the advent of the Literacy Hour, the Key Stage 2 market has grown with teachers exploiting the strength of books such as *The Three Little Wolves and the Big Bad Pig* (Trivizas and Oxenbury).

Many publishers now produce packs of small-size versions of Big Books so that children can reread the familiar text in a more manageable form on their own. Big

Books are obviously more expensive than regular-sized books, but in terms of the opportunities that they provide for inducting children into the mysteries of print and of providing whole-class and class-unifying experiences, they are invaluable. Once you have seen a teacher successfully teaching reading in a Literacy Hour using a Big Book, or indeed used one yourself, you will see what an effective resource Big Books are. If your classroom has none, borrow or make your own and then make careful and considered use of them. There is clear evidence of their contribution to improving the literacy of young children and they are particularly important for those children who do not have sufficient one-to-one reading experiences. 'Shared Reading (Big Books) and Shared Writing' in the next chapter provides more information on ways of working with these books.

Further reading

Clark, H. *et al.* (1999) *Once Upon a Time: Big Books for the Literacy Hour at Key Stage 1.* Available from: Hertfordshire Libraries, Hatfield, AL10 8XG.

Holdaway, D. (1979) 'A Fresh Start: Shared Book Experience', in *The Foundations of Literacy.* Sydney: Ashton Scholastic.

Madeleine Lindley Ltd publish a yearly list of Big Books (available from Book Centre, Broadgate, Broadway Business Park, Chadderton, Oldham, OL9 9XA). From this company also can be obtained Brown, M. and Williams, A. (1995) *Eager Readers: A Whole Language Approach to Literacy in the Primary School Through Using Big Books.* Bristol: Giant Steps.

CORE BOOKS

The idea of a core of books in classrooms is very simple, is found in many primary schools and arises from what we know of very early reading behaviour. We know how children begin to 'read' by speaking the words of a book while turning over the pages of a much-heard and well-remembered book, perhaps using the illustrations to trigger memory of the story. At first there may be little one-to-one matching of words spoken to words written – indeed, there may be only the haziest idea of how writing works – but most teachers and parents recognise this pretend-reading behaviour and at the very least find it amusing. Hopefully, we also recognise it as an important stage in learning to read. If there is an audience for the child's recital and one that is appreciative, so much the better. But even if children have no audience or only an audience of toys, the feeling of fluency, of book language tripping off the tongue, is immensely gratifying and comforting and children begin to see what reading can be like. Knowing that, among all the books in the classroom, there are some they can 'read' is very reassuring.

The books that children choose for this 'pretend' reading are the ones that teachers and other adults have read to them so often that they are remembered 'by heart'. Very occasionally, a child may listen to a book once and the impression created is so strong that it can be recalled for reasonably 'close' private readings from just this one hearing. We know a nursery child for whom John Burningham's *Aldo* was this significant book. Most children however require several readings for the story to be confidently recalled.

The Core books are the ones the teacher has chosen because, from experience, she knows that children like them. Year after year, children uncannily select the same books with which to give themselves their private reading lessons. So teachers have capitalised on this tendency and formalised the whole procedure. Student teachers will want to familiarise themselves with the Core books that are commonly found in schools and reflect on their common qualities. However, the whole idea of Core books is more than a list of guaranteed titles, as the account of procedures and extending activities that you will find in Chapter 3 makes clear. (Incidentally, the particular qualities that appeal to children make frequent rereading bearable for you as an adult. 'Bearable' may strike you as no great recommendation, but for a book read aloud possibly hundreds of times in a teaching career that may be praise indeed. We are sure that there are teachers who have read *My Brother Sean* (Breinburg and Lloyd) or *But Martin!* (Counsel and Dinan) more than a thousand times and who would still claim that their magic is not quite threadbare. But the teacher's needs are not really the issue here. It is the qualities of the book for child hearers that are important.)

The following qualities characterise the Core books that teachers use. Under each of the headings, we give three examples, broadly suitable for nursery, Key Stage 1 and Key Stage 2.

Significant stories

Whether the story is about animals, toys, children or adults it needs to be emotionally true for all children – girls and boys, black and white – and to make contact with experience, feelings and interests. The child's world needs to be reflected; the story needs to matter or to have some tension.

- *Dear Zoo* (Campbell)
- *Pumpkin Soup* (Cooper)
- *The Patchwork Quilt* (Flournoy and Pinkney)

Prediction opportunities

Children love to predict what is about to happen or to play in their minds with what could happen. Amazingly, even when they know absolutely how the story turns out, they continue to enjoy the anticipation. It is as if they feel that they are one step ahead of the narrator.

- *Jasper's Beanstalk* (Inkpen and Butterworth)
- *All in One Piece* (Murphy)
- 'The Pudding Like a Night on the Sea' (in *The Julian Stories*, Cameron)

Books with secrets

The simple device of concealing something under a flap makes certain books very alluring to children. Not all novelty books are successful but when the flaps, holes or movable parts are an integral part of the narrative the resulting book has a lasting attraction for the child.

- *Maisie Goes Swimming* (Cousins)
- *The Very Hungry Caterpillar* (Carle)
- *Leonardo da Vinci* (Provensen)

Work for the reader to do

Readers are flattered by authors and illustrators into believing that they have insider knowledge and we all know that flattery bonds us to the flatterer. If this sounds complex, look at the Ahlbergs' books and see how they take their readers' knowledge of traditional tales and rhymes for granted.

- *Each Peach Pear Plum* (Ahlberg)
- *The Jolly Pocket Postman* (Ahlberg)
- *The Stinky Cheese Man and Other Fairly Stupid Tales* (Scieszka and Smith)

Illustrations

(a) In some books the illustrations contribute very clearly to a sense of time or place. The written text can focus on different things (characters' thoughts, feelings, etc.) while the illustrations give all we need to know about period and background.

- *A Dark Dark Tale* (Brown)
- *The Christmas Story* (Wildsmith)
- *Sir Gawain and the Green Knight* (Hastings and Wijngaard)

(b) Often the secrets of a book are found only in the illustrations and then the child reader feels that the narrator has not noticed them. That makes us feel very clever, and again this is a feeling that we all like and we return to the book that makes us feel good. Sometimes there is a more open invitation to search the illustrations for the secrets and at other times there is subtle illustrative detail that, if you attend closely, deepens the meaning of the book. Children are good at attending to illustrations.

- *Once Upon A Time* (Prater)
- *You'll Soon Grow Into Them Titch* (Hutchins)
- *Gorilla* (Browne)

Memorable language

These are books that have language that rhymes, that is rhythmic, and that is repeated in patterned ways. Children also respond to alliteration, onomatopoeia and other language devices, for example, 'I'll bim, bam, bash 'em' (*Hairy Bear* in the 'Story Chest' series). Books with dialogue, books with natural sounding language and books for older children that do not sound babyish are important.

- *We're Going on A Bear Hunt* (Rosen and Oxenbury)
- *My Cat Likes to Hide in Boxes* (Sutton and Dodd)
- *Prowlpuss* (Wilson and Parkins)

The use of Core books needs careful planning across the years in a primary school to ensure progression but also to provide for some overlap, so that the security of the known book (mentioned above) can support those readers who need it. You will be using Core books in many of the routines that we describe in the next chapter; the following points will help to maximise their effectiveness:

- Each year group should have sets of Core books with perhaps four or six copies of a title in each set so that children can read together or to minimise problems if several children want the same book.
- There needs to be a way of marking these books so that they, or at least some of them, are kept always in the classroom.
- Core books, if they are marked distinctively, can be kept with other books in the book corner. They neither need to be seen as 'learning-to-read books' nor as being too different from other classroom books.
- Children need to become familiar with these books and all adults in the classroom should be aware that frequent reading aloud is the one way of effecting this. (Tapes are useful but a poor substitute.)
- Children should not be forced to read these books but if you choose with care there should be no problem in them developing favourites. Try to allow choice.
- Books need to be introduced to the class with enthusiasm. Often a little anecdote or a personal connection helps the class to focus.
- The books want to be related to activities but not swamped by them.

Some schools have extending activities to accompany every Core book in the same plastic folder. A 'Core book pack' sometimes includes a bilingual version, a Big Book, a tape, miniature versions and a video if one exists. In the later years of primary schooling, and especially when there are children for whom reading is still difficult, the activities should make rereading the books essential for the work to be completed. Making a map of the story, for instance, requires close reading and attention to sequence. A group of inexperienced readers from a Year 4 class made a game with dice based on the Core book *Oi! Get Off Our Train!* (Burningham). Some fluent Year 6 readers spent time meticulously annotating a map and cross-section of Hogwarts, Harry Potter's school.

Core books are proving a very important resource in the teaching of reading. They give a sense of security and familiarity which helps children feel that they have got reading under control. The subtlety of the texts (if they have been well chosen) makes them books to return to, and therein lies their usefulness.

Further reading

Ellis, S. and Barrs, M. (1997) *The Core Book: A Structured Approach to Using Books Within the Reading Curriculum.* Accompanied by *The Core Booklist* compiled by Lazim, A. and Moss, E. London: CLPE.

Laycock, L. (1998) 'A Way into a New Language and Culture', in Evans, J. (ed.) *What's in the Picture?* London: Paul Chapman Publishing.

BOOK IN SERIES

Books written in a series format fall roughly into two categories. In one group are those that are written about the same characters and are of the same genre. The popularity of the character(s) means that the books are often marketed as 'Meg and Mog' books (Helen Nicoll and Jan Pienkowski), or 'Spot' books (Eric Hill) or 'The Famous Five' books (Enid Blyton); in other words not by title but by the characters whom readers have grown to know and love. The second category comprises books that are marketed as a series by a publisher but which are not always by the same author. These will have the same colour covers and overall design and are usually the same length. They also often have the same characters appearing in several books. If you choose books from a series for your class collection it is important that you read them all and do not just rely on sampling a few; we know of teachers who have been upset to find a quite racist book among a generally successful 'Cartwheel' series.

In the first category, you will find books that may not have been originally planned as a series. For the very youngest children, the 'Large' family (of elephants) appeared first in *Five Minutes' Peace*. The book was so successful that Jill Murphy followed it with *All in One Piece* and then *A Piece of Cake*. Similar popular demand brought David McKee's Elmer the patchwork elephant back in a new story, and we met Martin Waddell and Barbara Firth's two engaging characters Little Bear and Big Bear in *Can't You Sleep Little Bear?* which has, to date, been followed up by two further titles. For Key Stage 1, Titch (Pat Hutchins) appears in several titles, Treehorn has his fans in such books as *The Shrinking of Treehorn* (Heide and Gorey) and Julian and his brother Huey are found in several books (e.g. the recent *Julian, Dream Doctor*) by Ann Cameron. At Key Stage 2, books such as Laura Ingalls Wilder's *Little House in the Big Woods* and J. K. Rowling's phenomenally popular 'Harry Potter' series (which, at the time of writing, has had three published with four more to come). 'The Famous Five' or 'The Babysitter Club' are books children find themselves with no particular promoting by the teacher.

All these are popular because children enjoy reading about the same characters; they feel comfortable with the style of writing and the familiar format of the books. The child knows what to expect; it is easier to enter a 'secondary world' when you've been there before. This idea of a 'secondary world' comes from Tolkien (1964) who explains that readers are 'sub-creators' who suspend disbelief as they read. So newly fluent readers encountering their third or fourth Harry Potter book will already have created their own images of the dreadful Dursleys and the evil Snape and they know they can cope with the style of writing. This means that they can slip easily into the book and come away from it with the confidence to want to read another one. Children at this stage often enjoy reading through a series and recording their progress. Indeed the collecting can become a competitive craze. Publishers have realised this and will often put a number on the spine so that children can see at a glance which ones they need to add to their collection. The problem is that the child may get 'stuck' on the series rather than moving on to try other genres and authors. Thus it is up to you to monitor the range of books that the child is reading (see Chapter 4), both in and out of school, so that you can decide when to intervene and suggest another series, genre or author.

The second type of series is sometimes used to complement reading schemes. Again, we can usefully suggest titles for different ages. In the nursery there is the 'I Can Read' series which includes *Frog and Toad* (Lobel) and *Little Bear* (Minarik and Sendak) which become favourites if read aloud to children; at Key Stage 1 the 'Happy Families' books (Allan Ahlberg and various illustrators) and the Dr Seuss 'Cat in the Hat' books are very popular. For older children, there is an increasingly strong range of series books on the market, including 'Jets', 'Spirals', 'Banana Books' and 'Superchamp

Books'. The last two all have named authors, such as Dick King-Smith and Penelope Lively, and are aimed at newly fluent readers. They have hardback covers, are slightly smaller than a paperback and have proved to be hard-wearing. The first page tells the reader about the story and there are coloured illustrations throughout to give guidance to the inexperienced reader. They lend themselves very well to group reading situations (see 'Group Reading/Guided Reading' in Chapter 3). Spirals books are more commonly found in secondary schools for pupils who are daunted by longer novels. They are short novels written in chapters about teenage-friendly subjects and, as such, are useful to use with Year 6 children as an alternative to longer novels.

Further reading

Campbell, A. (1998) *Outstanding Sequence Stories: A Guide to Children's Books that Carry the Reader Forward.* Librarians of Institutes and Schools of Education ISBN: 0901922323.

Daniels, J. (1996) 'Is a Series Reader a Serious Reader?', in Styles, M. *et al.* (eds) *Voices Off: Texts, Contexts and Readers.* London: Cassell.

Fry, D. (1985) 'Chapter 5 Karnail', in *Children Talk about Books: Seeing Themselves as Readers.* Milton Keynes: Open University Press.

Watson, V. (2000) *Reading Series Fiction: from Arthur Ransome to Gene Kemp.* London: Routledge.

READING SCHEMES AND PROGRAMMES

In Chapter 1 we talked about the background to many of the reading schemes and programmes that you will find in schools today. Her Majesty's Inspectorate (HMI) and OFSTED, in pre-*NLS* days, found that reading schemes formed a significant part of the resources used by most teachers in the teaching of reading. What reading schemes offered to teachers was the chance to take children through a series of structured readers and they were most often used in one-to-one reading. As opportunities for one-to-one reading fade in the face of the *NLS* focus on shared and guided reading (see Chapter 3), there is less demand for structured reading schemes and more for Big Books and sets of books for guided reading.

The intention of this section is to provide an introduction to some of the most commonly used schemes. This should give you some insight into the materials that you find in your school. We will use the term 'reading scheme' for convenience but you will find that some are called 'programmes'.

As we said in the first chapter, this is a controversial area that has been distorted by misinformation. Most schools do in fact use either one or a selection of schemes and the most successful schools use these flexibly without sticking dogmatically to any one approach. It is also essential that reading schemes are used with *NC* requirements in mind (interestingly, the *NC* does not mention them). Many of the most recently published schemes will allow you to teach the 'Reading Strategies' required by the Programmes of Study; however, you may need to look quite carefully to see how far any one scheme will fulfil the 'Breadth of Study' expectations. Those teachers who use a judicious mix of reading scheme books and children's literature are likely to be most successful.

An issue here is how you organise the books (see 'Managing and Organising the Resources' on p. 54). Some schools integrate reading scheme books with children's literature using Cliff Moon's 'individualised reading levels' (see p. 10) or a version of them. Others keep reading scheme books in the book area but separate from other books; obviously this is practically expedient and it does have the advantage of giving them equal status. Keeping reading scheme books completely separate can lead to some confusing messages for the children about views of reading; they may, for instance, come to believe that the only reading that counts is that done from these 'separate' books. Again, the most successful use of such books seems to be where they can be confidently used alongside your other resources and are seen to be integrated into your reading routines (see Chapter 3). It should be possible to select books for shared reading and reading aloud from both reading scheme books and children's literature. As with all children's books there are issues of quality to be considered here, and one useful question to ask when choosing a book is 'Does it read aloud well?'

With regard to the information in Tables 2.1 to 2.8, you can rely on all schemes having a teacher's handbook. In addition, most schemes include a good range of supplementary materials. These are likely to include: enlarged texts, cassette and video tapes, workbooks, CD-ROMs, games and puppets. Where we have used the term 'eclectic' (under 'Underlying Method') it means that the scheme claims to support children's reading development through a variety of methods and approaches. Typically these include a phonic approach, developing a sight vocabulary, the use of motivating subject matter and language that reads fluently. Some of the schemes show quite explicitly how they link with *NC* and *NLS* requirements and you will find that the recently published ones are particularly clear in demonstrating these links.

Further reading

Perera, K. (1993) 'The 'Good Book': Linguistic Aspects', in Beard, R. (ed.) *Teaching Literacy Balancing Perspectives*. Sevenoaks: Hodder and Stoughton.

Title	Publisher	First published	Latest edition	Age range
Letterland	Collins Educational	1973		3–7

Organisation/structure
Early Years Programme: develops phonological awareness; introduces letter shapes and sounds and establishes correct letter formation.
Programme One (4–5): reinforces grapheme/phoneme correspondences for a-z; introduces digraphs 'ch', 'sh' and 'th'; word endings '-ff', '-ll', '-ss', '-ck', '-ng'; strategies for segmenting and blending.
Programme Two (5–7): teaches long vowel phonemes, vowel/consonant phonemes (e.g. 'ar', 'ew', 'ow'), consonant digraphs ('wh', 'ph', 'ch'), suffixes ('-ed', '-ing', '-ful', '-ly') and other spelling strategies.

Underlying method
Phonics-based literacy programme involving characterisation of letter sounds through pictograms.

Range of books
Teacher's Guide; *15 Minute Phonics*: whole-class word level activities; *Making Words: Onsets and Rimes*: split page books; range of Big Books; workbooks, videos, games; *Letterland At Home*: materials for home use.
The publishers emphasise that *Letterland* is a phonics teaching programme intended for use alongside other reading materials.

Special features
Letterland's originator, Lyn Wendon, devised the materials for children with reading difficulties. Publishers claim that the multi-sensory, interactive approach is appropriate for such children.

Comments
Teacher: 'It introduces children to vowels and consonants. The trouble is that some children say that the letters are "Dippy Duck" and "Clever Cat" rather than "d" and "c". I wonder whether this holds the children up.'
Primary adviser: '*Letterland* has become very popular and is clearly a major weapon in the battle for literacy.'
6-year-old boy: 'The alphabet is where the letters are and the letters are how you read; if you don't know the letters you can't read.'
9-year-old girl: 'I really enjoyed these. They were helpful in learning.'
Teacher: 'The publishers are absolutely right; *Letterland* books should only be used with other texts. On their own you couldn't meet *NC* requirements with them.'

Table 2.1

Title	Publisher	First published	Latest edition	Age range
Bangers and Mash	Longman	1975	1994	5–7, but also older struggling readers

Organisation/structure
Numbered books from 1 to18 which become progressively more difficult. Supplementary books 1a, 2a, etc.

Underlying method
Aims: 'to introduce children to phonics by a graded presentation of the main sounds of the language in interesting and amusing stories'. Letter combinations and words listed at the end of each book.

Range of books
Story books about a family of chimps with two children: Bangers and Mash. Big Book available for every level. Teacher's book revised to take account of *NLS*.

Special features
Could be useful for KS2 struggling readers who need phonic support but who will still find the books appealing.

Comments
6-year-old boy: 'They're my favourite books because they're about chimps. I got a whole box for my birthday.'
Reception teacher: 'I must admit I don't like them much but the children are really hooked on them. I think it's because they're funny, they're a set, they're red, the print is clear and the pictures are exactly what's in the text so the children's guesses are close. They like recognising the "B" and "M" for "Bangers" and "Mash".'
Y6 teacher: 'If these books are used carefully I can't see anything wrong with them. The only problem would be if the children were only reading these! I use them as part of a colour coded scheme and they're fine.'
Language coordinator: 'In our multi-cultural school the chimps in these books would have caused some racist name-calling.'

Table 2.2

Title	Publisher	First published	Latest edition	Age range
All Aboard	Ginn	1994	1999	KS1 and 2

Organisation/structure
16 graded stages.
KS 1: 216 titles with 6 strands: pattern and rhyme; characters (Sam and Rosie); non-fiction; poetry; plays; traditional tales.
KS 2: core of literature.

Underlying method
KS1: focus on rhyme, alliteration and patterns of language, sight vocabulary.
KS2: higher order reading skills and information retrieval.

Range of books
KS1: see strands above: all have guided reading notes linked to *NLS* objectives; genre sets of 3 Big Books, 2 poetry anthologies with Teacher's Resource book; *Phonics Handbook and Sight Vocabulary Handbook* with games and activities.
KS2: core of novels, short stories, poetry, plays, non-fiction (with contributions from well-known authors); colour sets of OHTs (one per year linked to NLS objectives); Big Books: novel, short stories, 2 poetry anthologies, 2 non-fiction.

Special features
The scheme's structure is well linked to *NC & NLS*. Younger children will empathise with the experiences of Rosie and Sam.

Comments
A student reports from her class teacher that *All Aboard* is 'more contemporary' and she liked the non-fiction readers which were illustrated with photographs.
Teacher 1: 'Wonderful illustrations which really grab the children's interest.'
Teacher 2: 'It's exciting to have such a good range of material for Key Stage 2 children.'

Table 2.3

Title	Publisher	First published	Latest edition	Age range
New Reading 360	Ginn	1994	1999	KS1 and 2

Organisation/structure
12 levels. 1–8 develop core vocabulary, Little Books consolidate this.
9–12 provide structured framework for developing reading skills. Pocket Books complement these.

Underlying method
Structured progression: levels 1–5 build sight vocabulary, further developed in 6–8.
9–12 help children gain fluency and develop 'higher order reading skills'.

Range of books
1–8: fiction and non-fiction; plays; Pocket Books (level 5 onwards) are short novels.
9–10: 3 anthologies, short stories and novel.
11–12: 3 anthologies, novel, plays and Pocket Books.
Also: Big Books, support books for guided reading, software for KS1, wordless books, large format anthologies for KS2 shared reading.

Special features
Lower level books are much more engaging and supportive for struggling readers than the original Ginn books.

Comments
Teacher: 'We treasure our structured reading scheme.'
8-year-old girl: 'I really like the Pocket Books, especially the one about the cat in Egypt.'
Head teacher: '*New Ginn 360* is a great deal more attractive than original Ginn. It includes stories, poetry and plays from well-known authors in the form of Pocket Books.'

Table 2.4

Title	Publisher	First published	Latest edition	Age range
Cambridge Reading	Cambridge University Press	1996	1999	N–Y6

Organisation/structure

Nursery/Reception: *Preparing to Read* (PTR): traditional tales, nursery rhymes, alphabet resources.

Reception: *Beginning to Read* (BTR): books offered in strands (e.g. pattern and rhyme, phonics).

Year 1: *Becoming a Reader* (BAR): 54 books.

Year 2: *Towards Independence* (TI): books arranged in genre strands.

Years 3–6: Independent Reading A and B; Extended Reading A and B.

Underlying method

Teaching of 'reading skills, phonics and sight vocabulary, in the context of highly motivating books'.

Range of books

PTR/BTR: traditional stories, rhyming texts, fantasy, domestic realism, counting books, non-fiction texts by a variety of authors and illustrators.

BAR/T1: contemporary, fantasy, traditional, autobiographical, poetry and rhyme and information books.

Same characters appear in several books. Well-known writers and illustrators used.

Special features

Much reinforcement; integrated phonics programme; some use of well-known authors and illustrators; extensive Early Years provision; KS2 has separate text, sentence and word level Teacher's books.

Comments

Teacher: 'An up-to-date scheme that's taken on board most of the latest understandings about children and books and the teaching of reading. The handbooks contain wise words about classroom management and reading with children, with an emphasis on enjoyment and meaning. I wouldn't use the limited and monotonous worksheets.'

Nursery World: 'This is a reading scheme with books which look as if they have been approached as real books. The standard of illustration is high; the entertainment factor is considerable and the blurbs on the back are aimed at children.'

Table 2.5

Title	Publisher	First published	Latest edition	Age range
Story Chest	Kingscourt	1981	1996	3–11

Organisation/structure
KS1: Stages 1–7
KS2: Stages 8–20

Underlying method
Eclectic with an emphasis on the importance of enjoyment and motivation.

Range of books
Stages 1–7: story, rhyme, plays.
Stages 8–20: folk tales, fantasy, real life, plays, non-fiction, poetry, rhyme books.

Special features
Range at KS2 is very wide. Authors are identified and profiled in KS2 range. Formats are very varied.

Comments
10-year-old girl: 'There's something about this (from Focus 2) that says it's a teacher's guide or something. I wouldn't be interested to read it.'
9-year-old girl (about *The Storm*): 'It's not really a story, just a piece of writing.'
6-year-old boy (about *Cornelius Cobb*): 'This is exciting.'
5-year-old girl (about *The Hungry Giant*): 'I like the hungry giant's bommy knocker.'
Teachers: 'I really like the early ones. Lots of rhythmic predictable language in good stories.'
'The range for older readers is great.'
Language coordinator: 'The Big Books remain some of the best on the market in terms of illustration and memorable language. The early books vary in quality. The range of genres, formats and authors in the later books is excellent. We especially like features such as the author notes in some of the stories.'

Table 2.6

Title	Publisher	First published	Latest edition	Age range
Oxford Reading Tree	Oxford University Press	1985	New materials published regularly	4–11

Organisation/structure

Central idea is of a tree with different branches that present different aspects of reading, e.g. phonic branch: 'woodpeckers'. There are 16 stages: trunk books followed by stages named after birds.

Underlying method

Eclectic.

Range of books

In early books heavy dependence on single partnership of author and illustrator but a variety of other contributors appear elsewhere.

Some wordless books in Stage 1. Stories are varied often with a humorous twist. Collections of poetry. Big Books available. Also includes non-fiction 'fact-finders' reading books, and phonics strand 'Rhyme and Analogy'.

Special features

Photocopiable worksheets and workbooks.

Guided reading cards and sets of books.

Comprehensive Teacher's Guide with practical activities.

Lots of dialogue in stories.

Comments

Teachers: 'The children love the stories especially "The Magic Key". It's one of the better reading schemes.' 'It's very popular, the kids like it, it's been very successful.' 'The layout is not very exciting; they could, for instance, have used speech bubbles.' 'The books get poorer later on.' 'I use the early books with my struggling readers.'

Principal lecturer in education: 'It provides a rich variety of material to suit the different emphases which individual teachers and schools may have towards the teaching of reading. Because of the abundance of published texts, it affords good opportunities for the involvement of parents in their children's reading.'

Table 2.7

Title	Publisher	First published	Latest edition	Age range
1,2,3 and Away	Collins	1966	1996	3–7

Organisation/structure
Stories with built in progression, workbooks, Teacher's Handbook and video.

Underlying method
Stories use carefully controlled vocabulary and sentence structure. Simple sentences are introduced and repeated.
Supporting resources develop sub-skills of word recognition and decoding.

Range of books
Pre-readers in two progressive strands, Introductory Books, Blue Books, Green Books, Red and Yellow Books.
All stories are written by the same author – Sheila McCullagh.
All narrative.

Special features
Ongoing theme of village where story characters live.
Range of support materials (including video and wooden figures) help develop reading skills and understanding.
Teacher's Handbook has a pull-out flow chart suggesting a route through the scheme.

Comments
Student teacher: 'I remember these books very well. I used to love Roger Red-hat, Billy Blue-hat and Jennifer Yellow-hat.'
Teacher: 'Children either find security in the characters and stories which continue throughout the scheme or quickly grow tired of them. I find the stories very old fashioned. I think it's something to do with the controlled vocabulary.'
10-year-old: 'I don't think the ones for younger children are very interesting. I know you have to repeat everything but it could be about more interesting things than windows and doors and colours. The ones for older children are much better.'

Table 2.8

BOOKS IN OTHER LANGUAGES

All children, no matter what languages they speak themselves, need to learn that English is only one of the many languages that are spoken and written in the world. We can help them to understand this by providing books written in a wide range of languages, including, of course, those spoken by the EAL children in the class. It is not always the case that speakers of a minority language are readers in that language, but the features of the written scripts will often be familiar and the psychological importance of seeing a book in your own language in the classroom or school library is considerable.

The majority of books which are in other languages are folk-tales, picture story books and books about the domestic routines of everyday life. There are few information or reference books. The main types of books in other languages are described below.

Single language books

Single language books can be divided into two categories. There are books from the country of origin that you can find if you visit a foreign country or in bookshops here which specialise in importing books. Two problems arise: firstly, if you do not know the language you will have to rely on others' help or use your instincts, based only on appearances; secondly, the content quality of some books may not be appreciated if they are poorly printed.

There are also books originally published in English, the rights to which the publishers sell on so that foreign publishers can print them in their own languages. There is still a slight problem here in that unless you know the language you will not be able to judge the quality of the translation without help. The recognition of familiar books is less of a problem, especially with picture books where you recognise the illustrations. Eric Hill's 'Spot' books, for instance, have been translated into a vast number of languages from Arabic to Vietnamese. The following well-known titles also appear in many languages.

Nursery

How Do I Put it On?	Shigeo Watanabe
Peace at Last	Jill Murphy
Ben's Baby	Michael Foreman

Key Stage 1

Where the Wild Things Are	Maurice Sendak
Not Now Bernard	David McKee
Noisy Nora	Rosemary Wells

Key Stage 2

The Boy who Cried Wolf	Tony Ross
The Visitors who Came to Stay	Annalena MacAfee and Anthony Browne

Dual language books

Dual language books also divide into two categories. There are books that have been designed and published with the aim of giving equal status to both languages so that each language is given a proper space in the text and is printed in type of equal size and weight. Usually, both author and translator are acknowledged. You may not be able to judge the quality of the translation without help but the story in English can of course be evaluated.

The second category comprises those books that were originally published only in English. A certain amount of the print run will be held back to be overprinted in other languages. This is sometimes fine but more often leaves an ill-designed page and an impression of the second language being subsidiary. The problems are of course immense if the original picture book is read from left to right (as in English) and its translation is into a language such as Urdu which starts at 'the back of the book'. Only very bland pictures will 'work' and the resulting books are often very dull in appearance. The point at which the stories cross over is the only time the illustrator can produce a detailed and relevant picture.

You will find that there is resistance to the idea of dual language texts in some classrooms. The problems are often in the area already mentioned, that of not being able to judge the quality of the translation. Also, the particularity and spirit of the original version may be quite lost. Publishers do not often pay translators particularly well so probably they only get what they pay for.

There are other problems, equally important. You have only to think for instance of *I Want my Potty!* (Ross) being overprinted (as it has been) into languages such as Vietnamese or *Ben's Baby* (Foreman) into Hindi to see that not every story originating in this country will be understood and culturally acceptable in another language. Even folk-tales and their morals and messages are not automatically appreciated in every culture though there is probably less risk here. Having said that, we know many children who are fascinated to glimpse such strange stories told in their own language and who, far from being offended and alienated, are quite delighted.

Another problem is that children and their parents frequently read only the English text (that is 'what they are in school for') and so one wonders for whom the other language is there. Closely connected with this is the realisation that in fact the dual language text does not exist in any real sense outside school. We do not need two sets of print that say the same thing. The dual language text is rather an artificial genre, created for teaching rather than reading purposes.

There are fewer problems with the use of single language stories but of course this means buying two or more versions of the same story and this is not cheap. The poor production of some imported books and perhaps of some school/LEA or locally produced books means that the texts may be seen as demeaning and/or lacklustre by the children. If there is personal involvement in production, amateur publishing is less of a problem.

In the end you must ask yourself why you want dual language books in your classroom. The books probably make only a very small contribution to literacy in English as very few children who are literate in their own language use dual language texts to increase their literacy in English. The books probably make little contribution to literacy in the home language either. But there is, as stated above, an important message that other languages are recognised and given status and, for monolingual children, there are opportunities to increase the awareness of other languages. These points alone make the expenditure on books with languages other than English justified.

For a useful list of publishers who produce books in other languages you could contact a specialist bookshop such as Heffers Children's Bookshop, 20 Trinity Street, Cambridge, CB3 3NG, England.

BOOKS MADE BY CHILDREN

He saw space books, race books,
setting-your-own-pace books,
slow books, fast books,
show-them-to-your-class books.
And finally he said,
'I like every one,
but none seems quite right.
So the best book of all
for me will be . . .
the one that I write.'

(Extract from *The Best Book for Terry Lee* by Virginia Loewen and David Pearson.)

This is a Big Book which would be an excellent way in to making books in the classroom as well as being an engaging rhyming story about a boy's reading and all the reading choices that he finds in the library.

In many classrooms child-made books share shelf-space with commercially produced books. These are often some of the most popular and well-thumbed books of the collection; they really live for children who either know the authors and illustrators because they are their classmates or enjoy the pride of authorship themselves.

Bookmaking can enhance children's appreciation of books as artefacts and also increases their commitment to reading and response to literature. The books they have made themselves are often the books that make a difference and that they remember for a long time.

The *NC* expects that pupils 'write extended texts' (KS1) and 'discuss and evaluate their own and others' writing' (KS2) and creating a book can help children do just that. Working through from drafting stages to final publication helps children actively engage with the whole process. They begin to recognise some of the decisions that authors and illustrators have to make and by understanding the control writers and readers can have over print, they cease to find it intimidating.

You can encourage children to examine published books to discover the complexities of layout: choice of print size and font, art techniques used in illustration, and the relationship between pictures and text in picture books. The positioning of illustrations on the page and choice of artwork becomes increasingly sophisticated as children's bookmaking experience expands, and your provision of imaginative examples of children's book illustration or picture book art (Fiona French, Quentin Blake, Anthony Browne) will inspire innovations in the children's own work. The functions of endpapers, book jackets, dedications, title pages, copyright, blurbs, ISBN numbers and bar codes can also be discussed so that children's own books incorporate as many of the features of the 'real thing' as possible. They will gain an understanding of the publishing industry as well!

However, bookmaking can be daunting so it is important to remember that you do not have to produce a beautiful hardback book every time. A piece of written work and illustration can be mounted on folded card, which gives 'publication' status to a piece of work. An overall school policy helps. One school decided to promote bookmaking and allocated classroom assistant time for producing 'book kits' which were centrally stored. These comprised ready-cut pieces of folded card, sugar paper and the where-withal for making more complex hardback books. Such kits can provide a short cut but sometimes you might want the children to undertake these aspects themselves (a useful technology exercise). A school policy can also help in defining the kinds of books you might be making with different age ranges. Here is a list of books that we have seen made by the children from different classes in one school:

Nursery   Simple sewn books based on children's dictated stories.
Reception   Class book containing thank you letters to a storyteller who had visited the
            school.
Year 1   Concertina photo book based on farm visit with captions written by the
            teacher after shared writing with the class.
Year 2   Snail-shaped story books (based on class project on mini-beasts).
Year 3   Hardback books made by each child about the Romans (class topic).
Year 4   Enlarged book entitled *Karate Cat*. A rap story based on *Curtis the Hip-Hop
            Cat* (Gini Wade) written as class shared writing.
Year 5   Miniature books about superheroes.
Year 6   Spiral-bound books written by a group of children about how to use the
            computer. One book written for nursery and one for teachers.

Another way of managing bookmaking is by involving parents. Many schools have organised workshops so that parents can write, illustrate and publish stories based on family anecdotes or incidents, thus creating delightful additions to the school's stock of reading material. In some cases bilingual parents or children can write in their first language, or provide a translation so that a book initially written in English may reach a wider audience of readers outside school.

Realistically, you cannot be making books with your children all the time. The format of the Literacy Hour itself does not provide enough time to see a book through from start to finish but valuable work can be done in both the shared and guided slots on planning and writing the content. You will need to make time outside the Literacy Hour to see the process through but be assured that none of this is time wasted.

Further reading

For details of how to make these and other types of books consult any of the following:

Brilliant Publications (1993) *How to be Brilliant at Making Books*. Brilliant Publications,
    PO Box 143, Leamington Spa, CV31 1EB.
Johnson, P. (1993) *Literacy Through the Book Arts*. Sevenoaks: Hodder & Stoughton.
Johnson, P. (1996) *Words and Images on the Page*. London: David Fulton Publishers.

Johnson, P. (1998) 'Making Picture Stories: children illustrating their narrative texts', in Evans, J. (ed.) *What's in the Picture?* London: Paul Chapman Publishing.

ENVIRONMENTAL PRINT

Young children's first significant encounters with print may well be with cereal packets on the breakfast table or wrappers from their favourite sweets. Here they will spot letters from their names (the most important 'string' of letters for very young children) and then they will look out for more examples. Skilled early years teachers exploit and develop this budding interest in print by making sure that there are plentiful examples of it in their classrooms.

You may want to collect examples with the children either in a scrapbook or on a display board, focusing on a particular grocery item (such as cereal or biscuits) and asking the children to bring in packaging. You can then use these examples to discuss similarities and differences, to spot particular letters, the name of the item, brand names and so on. Or you could start from the letters themselves in your work on phonics. So, in teaching the phoneme 'm', you could display Mars and Malteser packets, MacDonalds place mats, an empty Marmite jar and anything else the children bring in or you find. Or children could make their own personal collections with letters from their names.

The role play area is a useful classroom context for collecting environmental print in 'real life situations'; so the home corner can have kitchen ingredients and a shop will abound with items for sale as well as notices on the wall about special offers, opening hours and rules ('No smoking or dogs!'). The children can suggest what these might be and either use real examples or design their own. A Year 1 garden shop included a notice warning customers, 'Mind the wet floor'. For the same shop the children made packets of seeds to sell and designed paper bags with a special logo.

Labelling the classroom can provide another source of environmental print. It is not necessary to use single name labels such as 'door' or 'bin' but rather the kind of labels that children will meet in the real world: 'Please don't slam the door!' and 'Please don't put half-finished drinks in the bin'. You will of course use simple labelling for name cards, plan chests full of different papers and the children's own trays.

As with all the resources mentioned in this chapter, your role is to keep these literacy aids alive and to ring the changes. You need to stay alert to their usefulness and make sure they have not become wallpaper!

Further reading

Committee on Primary Education (1982) *Mr Togs the Tailor: A Context for Writing.* Edinburgh: Scottish Committee on Language Arts in the Primary School.
Hall, N. (1987) 'Environmental Print', in *The Emergence of Literacy.* Sevenoaks: Hodder & Stoughton (in conjunction with UKRA).

INFORMATION AND COMMUNICATIONS TECHNOLOGY (ICT)

As we said in Chapter 1, technological advances have the potential to change the face of literacy teaching. At the time of writing, schools vary enormously in terms of resources they provide, particularly with regard to computers. Children vary too: some will arrive in school confidently able to navigate their way round a computer whereas others will be novices. Whatever your situation, this is an exciting time with new developments emerging by the minute.

However, in this time of rapidly expanding technology, we need to remember that, however enticing a video, a CD-ROM, or a website may be, its use can only be as good as the considered learning intentions of the teacher for her class. ICT can enhance good teaching; it cannot replace it.

Videos

Videos of children's books are very useful adjuncts to the teaching of reading. Apart from the tradition which seems to have grown up of annual showings on television of picture books such as Raymond Briggs' *Father Christmas*, John Burningham's *Granpa* and Antonia Barber and Nicola Bayley's *The Mousehole Cat*, there are very many videos of award-winning children's picture books produced by such companies as Watchword Storytime Library (the old Weston Woods firm) and these are well worth investigating. The claim that 'children will want to read the original books' really does seem to be borne out and in some cases (e.g. Quentin Blake's *Patrick*) the video is made with only music on the soundtrack, so the discovery that, because the story is familiar, the words in the book are easy to read is highly motivating. It works the other way round as well of course; the book may be known first and the video can provide opportunities for bonding further with characters and a re-acquaintance with the written text and its 'tune', so important in the early stages of reading. Video films of longer texts are used widely in junior and secondary schools for simple pleasure and for literature teaching, and are certainly worth the effort of dragging the TV into your classroom or the class to the TV room. We cannot ignore the fact that television is a common cultural medium and that children talk about their television viewing constantly. Their competence in this area is well developed; for instance, the abilities to fill in textual gaps, to link episodes, to retain significant clues are all literary abilities developed by television but needed for book literacy also. In class, a group activity where you compare your own visualisation with the film-maker's interpretation is the start of advanced literary criticism.

TV programmes

Schools' programmes on television always include a presentation or dramatisation of a children's book. In the year 2000, teachers could have built some of their literature teaching around such books as Ted Hughes' *The Iron Man*, Mairi Hedderwick's *Katie Morag and the Tiresome Ted*, Anne Fine's *Bill's New Frock*, some Anancy stories, Aesop's fables, Shakespeare, poetry selections and popular fiction. For the youngest children, programmes such as Rat-a-tat-tat (Channel 4), Storyworld (ITV) and Words and Pictures (BBC) encourage children to join in with highlighted portions of text on the screen or with songs and letter-recognition games. The very simple stories are chosen to cover a range of literary structures, with repetition, patterning and rhyme aiding involvement and the stories lending themselves to prediction activities. TV programmes come with activities booklets and many of them also come with software packages.

Cassettes

The resource that most teachers do ensure that they have in the classroom is the cassette and the tape recorder. Tapes of books are invaluable for the listening that is so necessary to new readers though, of course, tapes can never replace the committed and responsive reading from a real live person. But their use has certainly meant that children hear continuous, uninterrupted text when they want to and many a parent reports that tapes at bedtime or in the car are invaluable.

In some classrooms a listening space is incorporated into the book area; in others it is separate (or non-existent). Certainly the provision of some taped books complements your book collection well. Look at the range of tapes you have and make sure they reflect the overall range of your books, including children's home languages. Again, there is a role here for older children to plan and set up such an area. They can decide what should be included, design tape packaging, make notices inviting children to read along, even make tapes themselves (maybe for younger children or their 'Reading Partner', see Chapter 3). They can also join with you in making class rules for maintaining the listening area. These might include things like remembering to rewind the tapes and replacing tapes and books in plastic wallets. The children will come up with what is needed. Obviously well-maintained tape recorders and headphones make all this much more classroom-friendly.

In one classroom, we have seen carefully structured listening in groups with headsets around a tape recorder where children have listened to and then worked on activities connected with *Amazing Grace* (Mary Hoffman and Caroline Binch). The teacher had obtained help from a parent to make a recorded reading of the story from the Bengali edition of the book so that the children (all Bengali) could listen in Bengali and in English. They discussed the tasks in their own first language and then worked on one of writing a review of the school performance of *Peter Pan*. The taped versions meant a great deal to these children and they often listened to them voluntarily in their free time. There are now many outlets for tapes-and-books but it is not too difficult to produce your own. Recording the opening pages of a longer book often eases children into text; it is always at the beginnings of books where we have most uncertainty to overcome. Children are also keen to make recordings and if they are good readers these tapes, too, can provide a useful resource. Finally, teachers will often use tapes of songs and display the words in the listening corner. Young children will soon start pointing to the print as they sing along.

Reading from the screen

CD-ROMs

In order to feel in control, teachers need to know about computer developments in the teaching of reading. This can be quite a daunting area as the market is expanding rapidly and we are being pressed to purchase software of all kinds to enhance our teaching. There is no doubt that much of this software is of enormous help to us but, having said that, there are some claims by the producers of the new media in terms of their contribution to literacy learning that need inspecting quite critically.

You will find CD-ROMs for teaching reading can be usefully grouped into those that deal with the smaller units (letters and words) and those that deal with the big shapes (texts and language). Among those that deal with smaller units there is a CD-ROM in the 'Living Books' series called *Dr Seuss's ABC*. The popularity of the Dr Seuss books is such that this CD will draw teachers and children to it. It sets out to teach initial sounds only and proceeds by asking questions such as 'What begins with "c"?' and showing us a camel on the ceiling. It comes with noisy sound effects and lively graphics but, unless you fast forward, the pace is very slow, even for beginners. There are other problems also, not least of which is that the American accent gives children in the UK difficulties with vowel sounds e.g. 'boogie' comes with a short vowel sound compared with the long vowel sound in the UK. In addition, American vocabulary such as 'bug', 'closet', 'ditty' may be unfamiliar. These vocabulary items and others are not likely to be in the experience of a four-year-old at whom this CD seems to be targeted.

Working with big and small shapes comes in the form of *Nursery Rhyme Time* (Sherston), suitable for the early years. In this delightful CD children can choose to sing along with, play with and hear read aloud any one of about a dozen nursery rhymes which they can select by clicking on an easily readable picture icon. Lively cartoon illustrations reflect a multi-cultural world and the English voice-over is easy on the ear.

A CD-ROM such as *Arthur's Teacher Trouble* (Mercer Mayer) works more with the big shapes of reading. The programme presents this well-known children's book and invites the children to listen to the story in one of three offered languages. Having heard the story, the child then has the opportunity to click on different features of text and illustration. The programme is fun but the aspects children most enjoy are the animation of the illustrations and, while you can't usually activate these until you've been read to and seen the text highlighted, it is doubtful that this sort of programme on its own, any more than *Dr Seuss's ABC*, could teach reading.

CD-ROMs seem to us to hold out a great deal of promise in providing information texts and a CD such as *Oxford Children's Encyclopedia* (OUP) aimed at 8–13 year-olds uses videos and animation to make difficult concepts accessible to children. The video clips are short but of high quality so that, for instance, you might be able to watch a butterfly emerging from its pupa, feeding and mating, all in the space of two minutes. It is easy to navigate your way round this CD which has enormous classroom potential.

CD-ROMs can be highly motivating for children. They provide an ideal opportunity for independent work (for example after the whole-class Literacy Hour slot) and can be used to consolidate and extend skills taught in previous sessions. The children can be sure that, whatever their mistakes, the programme will not be judgemental but will encourage them. So if you attempt a spelling test in a programme such as *Hyphen Hall* (Aircom) and only score 5 out of 20, there is no negative comment, just a chance to see the correct spellings. CD-ROMs lend themselves particularly well to collaborative work and provide a context for productive talk during their use and reflective talk when children are reporting back (maybe in a plenary session) and moving from what has been a visual and verbal experience to a purely verbal description.

You may find that these programmes throw up some management problems. Some take a long time (over an hour in some cases) to view; some programmes make 'escape' very hard as you find yourself trapped in yet another spelling test; they may emit disconcerting noises and they may provoke noise from the operating pupils who can become competitive and rather excited.

The Internet/World Wide Web/Cyberspace

The internet is the 'biggest collection of information in the world: nothing can match it' (Grey 1999 p. 6). It takes the form of innumerable websites. These typically use words but also graphics, animation, sound and video to provide information. Hyperlinks allow cross-referencing between pages so that any area of interest can be pursued almost indefinitely.

Because the 'net' is not easy to vet and is so vast, a need arises for a specially tailored internet service that is safe for school use. You can do this yourself by creating gateway or portal sites into which you put selected items in a chosen area or you can use one of the many 'safe' sites Internet Service Providers are establishing. The *National Grid for Learning (NGfL)* provides such a service. On these sites, material has been suitably focused, limited and 'filtered' for its audience so that children who access them will not be able to reach unsuitable material.

The *NGfL* is at the heart of current developments in this country. With its *Virtual Teachers' Centre (VTC)* it holds enormous potential for teachers and children. To give just one example: there is a site currently being developed about using children's literature in history; it contains teacher-written reviews of books that could be used alongside teaching of the different history study units, providing a resource that could be used by you and your children.

The fact that the internet works by way of its hyperlinks – its web of connections – means that children who enter the net can go off in any direction. While this is clearly exciting and fosters independence, it is also potentially frustrating for you as a teacher and ultimately for the child as they will not necessarily gather the information they originally set out to discover. There is no doubt that we, as teachers, have a definite role in structuring and focusing children's access to the net and ensuring that they are taught the necessary research skills associated with typing in their key words, evaluating the material that comes up, rejecting the irrelevant and only printing what is needed. In this respect, our teaching needs the same focus and sense of purpose that any task concerned with information retrieval needs.

As well as using the internet as a source of information, children can add to the net themselves by contributing to a school website. School websites fall into two categories which have different audiences and purposes: there are sites that are intended to attract customers to the school and that function rather like a school prospectus, and there are web browser display boards which, rather like classroom walls, display examples of work. You can buy software packages such as *Web Workshop* (Iona Software) to help you set up such a site. These provide exciting opportunities for communications between schools: the incentive to write to others far away and know that there can be an instant response is stimulating and motivating. Many children will find the whole experience improves both their reading and writing. We know of one site where the children are encouraged to write poetry that is sent to partner schools. Children in these schools read and respond to the poems – either through their own writing or through art work. The international possibilities are enhanced by such networks as the *European SchoolNet* and the *Commonwealth Electronic Network*. Leask and Meadows provide an inspiring account of children across the world exchanging Christmas customs (2000 p. 31).

but remember that, as with all resources for reading, what we want for our children an attitude of critical inquiry, a questioning of both the information and its conveyance. One Year 5 class reflected with their teacher on the pros and cons of 'snail mail' and 'e-mail'; among the points they made was the fact that you do not feel compelled to answer a traditional letter as immediately as you do with e-mail and that 'you can keep letters'.

Further reading

Ager, R. (1998) *Information and Communications Technology in Primary Schools.* London: David Fulton Publishers.

Byrom, G. (1998) 'If you can't read it then audio-read it', Reading **32**(2).

Grey, D. (1999) *The Internet in Schools.* London: Cassell.

Medwell, J. (1996) 'Talking Books and Reading', *Reading* **30**(1) (and see **32**(1) for follow-up report).

Thomas, B. and Williams, R. (1999) *The Internet for Schools.* Plymouth: Internet Handbooks.

Websites

Yahoo! search engine to find different school websites.

National Grid for Learning http://www.ngfl.gov.uk

http://www.teem.org.uk (for teachers' evaluations of software).

http://www.listening-books.org.uk (1,000 titles on tape for children age 7–15 including titles for those with literacy difficulties).

European SchoolNet http://www.eun.org

Commonwealth Electronic Network http://www.col.org/cense

SCHOOL LIBRARIES AND BOOKSHOPS

One of our concerns as teachers of reading is to raise the status of books. This is achieved not just through a well-organised classroom collection, important though that is. The school library and bookshop can also play a significant role and all three contexts can be enhanced by visits from authors and illustrators.

Most schools have a central library. It is another environment in which children can learn to value, enjoy and use books. In some schools, classes are timetabled for weekly slots; in others, use of the library is more informal. There will probably be a member of staff who has responsibility for the library and s/he can give you invaluable support in resourcing your teaching. You will need to consider carefully how you will use the library as part of your teaching of reading. It is another useful source of books and can supplement classroom topic work or provide a collection of books around a particular genre or author. Incidentally, many local libraries will let you borrow a small collection of books for half a term and some local education authorities have a Schools' Library Service which may offer advice and books on long-term loan.

There are specific things that you can teach in the library. Most libraries use the recognised Dewey classification system (or a simplified version of it) and you can start teaching children how to use this. You will need to think carefully about making such teaching appropriate for your age range so that you ensure progression across the school year. In one reception class children had weekly sessions in the library with a classroom assistant. They were given task sheets such as 'Find a book about zebras'. The emphasis was very much on understanding the system, with the assistant asking questions like 'Why is it important to put books back in the right place?'. These five-year-olds were all clear about procedures; they were able to find the item on the reference system, locate its number and find it on the shelves. A London teacher describes how children in Year 1 and 2 classes 'became so interested in the categorisation system that they did a whole assembly on how the Dewey system worked!' (Johns 1992/3). Children from a Year 6 class worked in groups to produce library guides for three different audiences: the nursery, teachers new to the school and children in the earliest stages of learning English.

The library is also a context in which you can model and develop appropriate behaviour around books. This includes both 'social' behaviour in libraries as well as more specific skills such as browsing and choosing books. Louise Johns describes how one class wrote a 'Library Song' about things you can and cannot do in the library. When you induct children into using a library you are also leading them towards the adult world of reading with all that that means about feeling independent, being able to make your own choices and knowing that you are a real reader. The confidence that children gain through induction into the school library should enable them to make trips to their local libraries where many projects and special holiday schemes operate which help maintain children's reading habits and progress over the holidays.

With regard to choosing and browsing it is useful to watch a new class and see how comfortable they are with making choices. Do they really browse? Do they head straight for the books they know they like (maybe the 'safe' ones, a series perhaps)? What skills do they show in 'sampling' books (e.g. reading the blurb, reading the first few pages)? Do they seek out particular authors/genres (e.g. information books)? Your observations will help you to assess your children's understandings and to plan accordingly. You might, for instance, discover that a class, generally inexperienced in sampling books, benefits from your modelling and talking very explicitly about how you go about sampling. You could set up a library activity in which you ask the children to sample at least two books by a new author and to report back.

Libraries are a context in which children can learn what it feels like to be an experienced reader. One characteristic of mature or experienced readers is that they own books and this is where the school bookshop can have a role. As teachers and student teachers you will already have a collection of books you would not be without; you can be a significant model for the children and should share the joys of ownership with them. ('Everyone Reading in Class' is one forum for this; see Chapter 3.) Saving for books, having regular opportunities to browse through new book collections, having another adult with whom to talk about reading – these are some of the benefits of a school bookshop. The importance of updated stock cannot be overemphasised; when the books connect with the children's interests, with contemporary popular concerns, with current TV programmes and films, you have all the more opportunity of drawing children into the world of books.

Visits from authors, poets and illustrators can make a significant contribution to children's enthusiasm and motivation. The excitement for children of hearing 'real' authors talk about their work can generate tremendous personal commitment to their books. You do need to prepare for this: bookshops should stock up on the author's work; children should be encouraged to read as many of the author's books as possible; a display can be mounted and questions for the author prepared. When such visitors bring in manuscripts and talk about the process of publication there are important benefits. The children's own bookmaking (see p. 45) gets a boost and there are important lessons about the role of the author and the printed word itself. When children realise that authors are fallible writers like the rest of us, that they have to research, edit and rework, and that they sometimes get stuck, then the processes of writing and reading become more transparent and accessible.

Further reading and useful sources of information

Fincham, L. (1996) 'Authorising Your School', in *Books for Keeps*. **97**.

'Libraries in Schools', in *Language Matters* 1992/3 **1**. London: CLPE.

The School Library Association (SLA), Liden Library, Barrington Close, Liden, Swindon SN3 6HF. Tel: 01793 617838. SLA run an annual summer holiday reading scheme; this operated in 1999 (under the name of 'Reading Safari') in 85% of local authority libraries.

The School Bookshop Association, 6 Brightfield Road, Lee, London SE12 8QF. Tel: 0181 852 4935.

Authorbank Directory, The Children's Book Foundation, Book House, 45 East Hill, London SW18 2QZ.

Specialist children's bookshops such as 'The Lion and the Unicorn' (19 King Street, Richmond, Surrey TW9 1ND. Tel: 020 8940 0483; e-mail: theRoar@lionunicornbooks.co.uk) are well worth visiting for the model they offer of ways of presenting books and for the advice they can give about books and authors.

MANAGING AND ORGANISING RESOURCES

The final section of this chapter is about controlling all the resources we have mentioned, making them manageable for you and the children, and giving you a rationale for doing that. It is a section that must be read in conjunction with the rest of the book. You can have the best-organised resources in the world but they will only help in the teaching of reading if they are properly and efficiently mediated by you. Nevertheless, their organisation and manageability is an important part of the structure that you give to the teaching of reading and of your feeling of being in control.

So start by making a detached survey of the classroom in which you are working and consider the messages it gives about the status and desirability of reading. Try reviewing both the provision itself and the children's use of the resources. Look, for instance, at the book area and consider not only the range of books on offer but also how inviting it is for all the children and how far they actually use it.

Books

If we are concerned to promote children's skills in choosing books then their accessibility is hugely significant. Children may go to libraries and meet classification systems there, but it is important that the foundations for using these systems are laid in the classroom. Organising and categorising the book corner can be an extremely productive exercise and one that is most usefully done with the children. (It can also provide useful information about the children's understandings: in one reception class a group of children classified the books according to shape and size so all the square ones went together!) Do not feel you have to pigeon-hole every book; some broad categories will be enough. You can define some of these and ask the children for theirs too. One Year 3 class used the following teacher categories: information books, specific information books around the class topic, poetry, short stories, novels. Then the children looked at the picture books and suggested their categories: books that make us laugh, favourite books, books in Urdu, and animal stories. These were displayed in inexpensive plastic baskets from a supermarket and labelled by the children. As we discussed in Chapter 1, some schools use colour coding as a way of organising their books. Others have found the old *National Curriculum* (1995) range headings useful for sections of their book areas but you may find these changing to meet the *NLS* or new *NC* (1999) headings.

You will need to think about where you keep reference books and consider having a permanent section for these. More difficult though is managing more ephemeral non-fiction material (e.g. newspapers, fliers, brochures, current advertisements etc.). Some teachers find a separate box, tray or even notice board useful for these. In some schools, all reading scheme books are integrated with children's literature. You may prefer to keep these separately. You may also wish to keep your sets of books for guided reading (see Chapter 3) separately; your school may have a central storage point for these so they can be shared between year groups.

The example that follows shows how teachers in one primary school organised their book corners. Unless the category was obvious (e.g. hardbacked books) the books were marked with a shape, letter or coloured sticker to help the children find and put them back in the right baskets or shelves.

NURSERY

- rhyming story books
- nursery rhyme collections (including finger rhymes)
- enlarged versions of short rhymes
- alphabet books
- picture books
- Big Books
- information books
- wordless picture books

RECEPTION

- 1 Very repetitive
- 2
- 3
- 4

} 4 broad categories covering beginners, gaining confidence, taking off and slightly beyond.

- 'favourites' (with repetitive parts)
- alphabet books
- rhymes/poetry
- all hardback picture books
- sets of books for shared reading
- box of Big Books, both published and teacher/children made (along with easel and pointer for class and group shared reading sessions)

YEAR 1

- categories 1–4 as above
- 'favourites'
- alphabet books
- rhymes/poetry
- longer/harder to tackle paperback picture books
- short novels (e.g. Picture Puffin 'read alones')
- some picture books organised under 'favourite authors'

YEAR 2

- very repetitive
- gaining confidence/books with repetitive parts
- books for those 'taking off' with reading
- alphabets, rhymes, poetry
- longer/harder to tackle paperback picture books
- hardback picture books
- short novels
- longer (and more difficult) novels
- sets of books for group reading

YEAR 3

- 'quick read' picture books (1)
- 'quick read' picture books (2)

} Two broad readability categories

- longer/harder to tackle paperback picture books
- hardback picture books ('longer read')
- short novels (paperback)
- longer (and more difficult) novels (paperback)
- hardback novels and collections of short stories
- poetry and rhymes
- sets of books for group reading (including plays)
- non-fiction books
- books written by children

YEAR 4

- 'quick read' and 'longer read' paperback picture books
- hardback picture books/novels
- short novels
- longer (and more difficult) novels
- short story collections
- poetry
- sets of books for group reading (including plays)
- non-fiction

YEAR 5

- 'quick read' and 'longer read' paperback picture books
- animals ⎫
- funny ⎬ categories for novels decided
- adventure ⎪ by children
- magic/ghosts ⎭
- short story collections
- poetry/anthologies
- sets of books for group reading
- non-fiction

YEAR 6

- 'shorter read' paperbacks and picture books
- adventure ⎫
- ghosts/magic ⎬ categories for paperback novels
- humour ⎪ chosen by children
- animals ⎭
- hardback novels arranged in alphabetical order
- short story collections
- poetry
- sets of books for group reading
- non-fiction

(Adapted from a list from the ILEA IBIS team, 1988)

You will note that, although this model preceded the *NLS* and the *NC*, it provides broad categories into which the finer detail of the *NLS* can be slotted.

Kinder boxes, plastic baskets and sloping shelving will all help with the presentation of these categories and you will need to work hard initially to ensure that the children understand and maintain the categories. You might find it useful to devise a set of class rules with the children for the book area. All this is about more than a tidy book corner; it is also about demonstrating the range of authors and genres, developing children's understanding of these and helping the children to make informed choices. Nigel Hall's suggestion (in conversation, 1992) of a collection of 'Books that Wolves would like to read' demonstrates how one can take categorising on to even more subtle levels. In organising this collection, the children had to respond critically to the text, reading the books from a predatory wolf's point of view. A book such as *The Cultivated Wolf* (Biet and Bloom) might well involve the children, as they try to categorise the book, in animated talk on how the wolf changes from a predatory loner at the start of the book to a cultivated member of the community at the end! So organising books is not just about range and accessibility; it can include teaching and learning about such things as evaluation and narrative viewpoint.

You can draw attention to specific themes, books, authors, poets or illustrators by setting up special displays. If these are to be effective and more than just window dressing they need to be brought alive for the children both through their involvement but also through your planning.

A nursery class had been reading books about bears and the resulting display was not only of all their teddy bears but also of at least two dozen books about bears. The children had particularly liked *Can't You Sleep Little Bear?* (Waddell and Firth) and it was not long before a dark cave appeared in the corner of the classroom with a little bear within. At the entrance to the cave was a notice 'Please take the torch and a bear book and read to little bear'.

A Key Stage 1 class were learning about pulleys and the teacher read them *The Lighthouse Keeper's Lunch* (Armitage) in which the keeper's wife devises an ingenious pulley system to get her husband's lunch to him, avoiding the greedy seagulls. The class constructed a lighthouse and pulley and this became the focus of a display of books about sea creatures.

In one Key Stage 2 class the children were asked to nominate their favourite author, giving reasons for their choice. Then they voted. Some of the authors they chose included Charles Keeping, Dick King-Smith and Anne Fine. A special display was set up with books begged and borrowed from other teachers and libraries and also bio-graphical information about the author (Books For Keeps authorgraphs or John Carter's book listed below are useful sources for this). The children researched the author and made a poster or flier for their display. They also redesigned the cover of their favourite book. The teacher's planning for her read-aloud programme included books and extracts from the display. This did not include all the books but enough to whet the children's appetites and invite them into reading other texts by the author.

In another school children took it in turns to nominate their 'Top Ten' books; you can extend this to include books from home as well as school since this can give you useful insights into your children's reading choices. If you do this, though, you will need to be ready to deal with issues that arise from some of the books associated with contemporary popular culture (see 'Choosing Books for the Classroom' in this chapter).

Highlighting poetry is usefully done through a 'Poet's Corner'; in one class this included a 'poetry request board' where the children used 'post-its' to request both a poem they wanted read aloud and its reader (see 'Reading Aloud to Children' in the next chapter). Carefully worded notices can also convey useful messages:

We have at least five anthologies in our book corner and lots of picture books that are written in verse. Come and browse! We've got:

A Caribbean Dozen   eds John Agard and Grace Nicholls

Classic Poems to Read Aloud   ed. James Berry

Talking to the Sun   eds Kenneth Koch and Kate Farell
(This has got paintings in as well from the Metropolitan Museum of Modern Art)

A World of Poetry   ed. Michael Rosen

The Utterly Brilliant Book of Poetry   ed. Brian Patten
(Read it – it really is brilliant!)

The books need to be accessible to the children and to be displayed in a context that is attractive and inviting. The idea is that children will want to go and browse, share a book with a friend, get lost in a book on their own or listen to a book being read aloud. You might find it useful to ask yourself if you would want to sit and read in the book area. Try it sometime. Cushions, carpet, lamp and comfortable chairs all contribute to an inviting environment, although you might find that you need to set up a rota for which group gets to sit there! You can get free publicity posters from publishers and could also start to make your own collection of pictures of readers, images from books, or maybe information about films of children's books. This is an ideal opportunity to make sure that you are including representations of readers that challenge stereotypes; we know that boys' interest and motivation in reading is more vulnerable than that of girls so the more images they can see of boys and men reading the better. We have seen posters of the English football team reading displayed in one classroom. In one nursery book area pictures from publishers' catalogues were effectively displayed at eye level. You may be constrained by space and money but even the smallest collection of books can be invitingly displayed in a limited space.

Finally, you need to think about the actual access the children have to the books. All too often the very realistic constraints on space mean that book areas are used for a great deal more than reading: taking the register, class-sharing times, shared writing, construction activities, whole-class ticking off . . . the list is endless. What is important is that you take stock of all this and make sure that reading is firmly built into your planning for use of this area so that it is not just a place to go and read 'when you've finished your work'. You might, for instance, devise a rota with the class whereby groups take it in turns to be in the book corner during 'Everyone Reading in Class' times (see Chapter 3). This can be very effective, especially when combined with that group having access to the 'Favourite Books' collection. The trouble with favourites is that everyone wants to read them!

Further reading

Campbell, R. (1995) *Reading in the Early Years Handbook*. Buckingham: Open University Press.
Carter, J. (1999) *Talking Books*. London: Routledge.
Chambers, A. (1991) *The Reading Environment*. Stroud: Thimble Press.

Chapter 3

Reading Routines

INTRODUCTION

In the last chapter we looked at the resources you need for teaching reading. The care with which you choose and organise these will be wasted if they are not underpinned by the systematic use of regular reading routines. By 'routines', we mean the regular activities and organisational strategies that teachers employ to teach reading. For example, the routines of the child reading to the teacher and of the teacher reading to the children at the end of the day are ones which have been going on in most classrooms for decades.

Before the advent of the *NLS*, such routines provided a way of structuring a programme for the teaching of reading whatever the age range and whatever the particular constraints or possibilities of the classroom setting. Now that many schools have adopted the notion of a dedicated hour for literacy, superficially things look rather different. Many of the routines that have always shaped the effective teaching of reading, but which were scattered through the week, are now to be found within the daily Literacy Hour. For example, you will find that the established practice of reading with children using Big Books (shared reading) is a well respected and central routine in the hour. However, other equally important routines, such as sustained reading aloud by the teacher, do not feature in the hour and have to jostle with other curriculum demands during the rest of the day. As we shall argue below, all of these routines can make significant contributions to the teaching of reading and you need to be able to articulate their importance, whether they are prioritised by the *NLS* or not.

Planning and organising for reading

As we write, with the *NLS* in place in most schools and a proliferation of published materials to aid delivery of the Literacy Hour, the sort of advice that we would have given to students and teachers about planning for reading could seem to be less immediately relevant. However, there are sound reasons that demand that you understand the principles that govern wise planning.

Essentially, you need to decide which routines should feature in your timetable week in and week out. Shared reading, 'Everyone Reading in Class' and the teacher reading aloud are examples of such routines. Others, such as telling stories or working with a class reader are more likely to feature as a blocked unit of work running over a number of earmarked weeks. Planning for reading may also occur in activities where reading is being taught in conjunction with another curriculum area. In history, for instance, you can plan that children will spend time reading and extracting information from copies of census material and other primary sources; in science you can plan for them to read the instructions that come with a battery. Whatever the context, your planning for any of these routines must include what you want the children to learn and how you will assess it (see Chapter 4).

As well as planning what you want the children to learn you also need to think about how best to organise them. In an inspection report on the teaching of reading in a number of inner-city primary schools, OFSTED noted that 'the best planning ensured that there were regular sessions for individual, group and whole-class work with clearly defined objectives and approaches,' (1996 p. 23). The *NLS* structure respects OFSTED's conclusion about planning in these respects except that there is no provision for individual work within the hour. In the sections below you will find examples of teaching in whole-class, group and one-to-one settings.

EVERYONE READING IN CLASS

Various acronyms are used to describe periods of quiet reading undertaken by the whole class, and in some cases by the whole school, including teachers and support staff. Among the more common are:

USSR: Uninterrupted Sustained Silent Reading
ERIC: Everyone Reading In Class
SQUIRT: Sustained Quiet Uninterrupted Reading Time.

Why?

A quiet reading routine, properly implemented, can provide opportunities for children to get 'lost in a book', and is another context for highlighting issues about choosing and enjoying books. Because the children are required to read quietly and with concentration for a specific period of time it is a routine that can encourage reading stamina which the Literacy Hour does not encourage. When the whole class (or in some cases the whole school) stops for the sole purpose of reading, then important messages are given to parents and children about the status of reading. A quiet reading time allows all children to read independently at their own pace, to behave like real readers who do such things as stopping to reflect, skipping passages, reading back to check and even reading ahead to cheat!

Real readers also read silently and another benefit of this routine is for children to experience what such 'reading in their heads' is like. Some children seem to make the transition from reading out loud to silent reading very easily while for others it is not so seamless, and it is therefore important that planning for reading includes the opportunity to practise such a skill. You may see these children engrossed in a book but still voicing the words. Sometimes a gentle nudge to 'try reading in your head' is all that is needed, but they must have peace and quiet for this to be viable.

How?

Of all the routines that we describe in this chapter, quiet reading is the most vulnerable to misuse. You have to plan with extreme care and think about what you want the children to learn. It is not a time for you to catch up on marking or displays while the children idly flick through randomly chosen books. You will need to work hard in setting up this routine, in conveying your expectations for the children's behaviour and in maintaining its purpose and structure. Do this well and you are providing yet another valuable context for the teaching of reading.

Different schools may schedule different periods of time for quiet reading. Such periods are usually short – between 20 and 30 minutes – and are regularly timetabled, sometimes on a daily basis and sometimes on a weekly/twice-weekly basis. How you structure the session will vary according to the age range and needs of your class. The following example shows how one school structured whole-class reading times for three different age groups.

Nursery

There was a ten-minute slot when the whole nursery group assembled on the book corner carpet to share books. Of course this was seldom a very quiet time but it was a time when the children experienced what it felt like to be reading alongside other people. In addition, although the overall emphasis was on collaborative book experience, the children were already being inducted, albeit on a tiny scale, into the idea of reading on their own.

Key Stage 1: Year 2

In the rest of the school, the half-hour period after the lunch break was set aside for quiet reading. In this Year 2 classroom the teacher avoided everyone descending on the book corner at once by sending the children group by group before lunch to choose three books from the book corner, one of which had to be the book they were currently reading with the teacher. As the children selected their books, the teacher commented on aspects such as the authors or genres they were choosing and also on any positive strategies that she saw the children using (e.g. skimming the contents page of an information book, looking at the blurb on the back of a novel). This class took it in turns to sit in the book corner at quiet reading time with the cushions and favourite books.

When the children came in from the lunch break they were expected to go straight to their places and start reading. The teacher structured the half hour so that they spent the first 20 minutes reading silently and on their own, but could quietly share with their neighbour for the last ten. At the beginning of the autumn term the session lasted just 15 minutes and it gradually built up to the full half hour. At the end of the session there was a short discussion during which children were encouraged to share any good poems, best bits of stories, or problems they had encountered (e.g. words or concepts they did not understand). As with the choosing of books, the return was carefully organised with the teacher complimenting children on the care they took to return books to their rightful places.

Key Stage 2: Year 6

In the Year 6 class the teacher followed a very similar procedure to the one above but the expectation here was that most children would be tackling 'chapter' books and that the period of individual sustained reading would be even longer and quieter. Because the procedures of choosing and returning books had been established so successfully lower down in the school, the practical aspects worked very smoothly. As well as reading from longer novels, the teacher encouraged children to read from different genres each week. The range might include poetry one week, an information book related to ongoing history work the next and a folk-tale during the third week. When a class reader was being used some children might choose to reread bits the teacher had already read aloud or even read ahead (although you would have to decide with the children whether this was appropriate or not; see 'The Class Reader' in this chapter).

Your role as teacher in the quiet reading session needs clear definition. It is an opportunity to model what experienced readers do, so it is a time when you too can be reading, thus demonstrating the different kinds of texts you read, the importance of reading for you and what quiet, absorbed reading looks like. Your own contributions to discussion after the session can show the children your commitment and enthusiasm as a reader and begin to reveal to them the important part that reading plays in your life. Because the majority of primary school teachers are women this still leaves unresolved the problem of ensuring that the children also see models of men reading. It is partly for this reason that some schools have adopted the practice of involving the whole school community in this communal reading time. It reminds us how much of a social activity the business of becoming a reader is.

Practically, it is not always realistic to spend the whole session on your own reading and what many teachers do is to model some reading themselves (maybe for the first five minutes or so) and then read with individual children (see 'Reading to the Teacher' in this chapter). The important thing is to make clear how highly you rate this time and that it is for enjoying and valuing reading. You may want to spend some time with the class establishing a code of conduct for these sessions; as with all your teaching it is very important that the children know why you have silent reading times and what you hope will be learned from them. You may find that you spend the first few sessions shaping and enforcing a clear and secure structure for the children. Do not worry; it is time well spent.

The success of this routine is partly dependent on the structure that you provide for it but it also relates to other issues that we looked at in the previous chapter concerning the range and organisation of the books.

Further reading

Campbell R. (1990) *Reading Together.* Milton Keynes: Open University Press.
Fenwick, G. (1999) 'Reading Silently', in Goodwin, P. (ed.) *The Literate Classroom.* London: David Fulton Publishers.
Southgate, V. *et al.* (1981) *Extending Beginning Reading.* London: Heinemann.

READING ALOUD TO CHILDREN

Why?

Reading aloud to children has been one of the most commonplace activities in the primary classroom. For many years, teachers in early years settings have read and shared picture books with their children; teachers of older children have read aloud from longer texts which may or may not be illustrated. At the heart of this routine is children's active listening; the intention is not that children's eyes should be on the print but that, rather, their ears and brains should be engaged.

Reading aloud is a central means for introducing children to texts of all sorts, as it exposes them to each genre's distinctive language. As children meet an ever-widening range of books and authors, so their potential for personal choice is enhanced. For very young children the language they hear read aloud may be their first exposure to written English, which is different from spoken English in many and varied ways. Take the classic story opening 'Once upon a time there was . . .' and you immediately know that this is not how people talk. The patterns and tunes of book language have to be learned and reading aloud is when they are taught. For children learning English as an additional language, listening to fluent reading provides essential information about how their new language works. In addition, as texts are usually written in Standard English, this is when children can appreciate and operate the distinctive structures for themselves. This is true of aspects other than the language; twists of plot and subtle characterisation are more likely to be taken on board when the physical act of reading itself has been taken over, maybe temporarily, by a more experienced reader. It is an example of learning within the 'zone of proximal development' (Vygotsky's description) where 'what a child can do with assistance today she will be able to do by herself tomorrow' (Vygotsky 1978 p. 87).

The following extract from a read-aloud session in a reception class shows young children being empowered to make meanings from a complex text. For half an hour the teacher read aloud to the children from an original version of *Alice's Adventures in Wonderland* (illustrated by Anthony Browne). She sustained their interest and ensured their engagement through her questioning, through the space she gave for the children's own ideas and by relating difficult concepts in the book to their current understanding. The children were working on 'Flight' in science and had just made parachutes; when the teacher asked the children about the story so far one child gave the following succinct summary:

> She saw a bunny with a watch in his pocket and then . . . and then she saw it and she was bored with that sister telling stories with no pictures in, and the bunny went down the hole and he went quick cos he didn't have a dress cos he's a boy and . . . and Alice went down with her dress like a parachute.

The teacher read lengthy passages of text, stopping to discuss points she considered needed clarifying for the children. For instance, at the point where Alice shrinks she asked:

Teacher   Can you answer this important question? If you were very very very small what would everything look like?
Child   . . . things would look bigger than you.
Teacher   If you were small what would I look like?
Child   Big giant.
Child   I got the video of *Honey I Shrank the Kids*.
Teacher   What did the grass look like?
Child   Thorns.

This fragment clearly signals the children's understanding and involvement with a more challenging text than any they could tackle single-handedly. The teacher helps them make the necessary conceptual links, encouraging them to draw from both story experience ('big giant') and contemporary concerns (*Honey, I Shrank the Kids*).

Older children also benefit from hearing more demanding texts being read aloud. These induct children into more challenging forms of language (fiction and non-fiction alike) and indeed they will be able to enjoy and accommodate far more complex language than they can manage on their own. A Year 4 teacher was reading *A Fairy Tale* (Ross) and was particularly keen that the image found within 'a yellowy light tickled the black clouds' should not be lost on the children. He made sure that he included it verbatim in his summary of the story which he gave at the start of the next session and children started to comment on the use of language in the book as a whole. In these ways reading aloud shows children what lies ahead for them in books. This is especially important for inexperienced readers who may only be able to tackle quite limited texts but who badly need the enrichment this routine can provide. It can give them a sense of the 'big shapes' of the text, of a fluency with sustained text that they may not be able to achieve on their own.

Finally, the way we read aloud to children can offer them a model for developing their own style in reading aloud. We can demonstrate how to bring the story to life through, for instance, our use of intonation or the way we read dialogue. (See below for some suggestions about ways in which the routine can provide a useful context for developing this for the children.)

How?

As mentioned above, reading aloud as we have described it is not intended to happen in the Literacy Hour. This leaves teachers with a problem as they have to find time to accommodate the routine in among countless other curriculum demands. If you believe it to be as important as many teachers do, then you should arrange specific times for this routine in your weekly planning.

First of all think about timing: is story time always at the end of the day? Does it have to be? Are there other times that would be more appropriate? One teacher tells of the dramatic effect that reading an enormously popular class novel from 9.00 a.m. every morning had on her class's lateness! Certainly, children are often at their most receptive early on and, while a late story time can be a successful and bonding way of ending the day with a class, other times do need to be given some consideration. A common pattern in several early years classrooms is to have three daily read-aloud sessions using three books at each one, making a total of nine in all. It works like this: one book is very familiar to the children, another is one to which they have been recently introduced, and the third is new to them. In this way, their repertoire of known books is constantly expanding but in a very carefully structured way. It does, of course, have resource implications but teachers can be enormously resourceful themselves, using and exchanging existing classroom collections flexibly and supplementing these with library loans. With older children read-aloud sessions may be less frequent (perhaps two or three times a week) though if a teacher knows that the pace of a novel needs to be sustained then she will plan more frequent sessions accordingly. In addition, much reading aloud goes on at other times: the teacher may read aloud an introductory paragraph from an information book, or may share a child's writing with the whole class in order to demonstrate a point or encourage the others.

What do we read to the children? If we are to use this routine as an opportunity to increase the range and richness of the children's literary experience, then we need to give careful thought to the choice of books and authors. This should be done using the guidance about 'Breadth of Study' in the *NC* and 'Range' in the *NLS*, but also with a view to balance across a school year and, if appropriate, relevance to ongoing classroom work. The range of genres of writing deserves special attention; you should include reading aloud from non-fiction texts in your planning for this routine.

Once you have decided what you are going to read, you will need to plan the session itself. Decide what the main text for the session is but have something in reserve in case you end early. If you are using a longer book, think about how much you will read and make sure you end at a place which will make the children want to hear more. If the author does not end the chapters on cliff-hangers then you may need to decide on where suitably tense stopping places are. Whether it is a picture book or novel, you will need to read it through first so that you can anticipate any difficulties, for example with complex or specialist vocabulary or where dialects are used. You could discuss such things when you are introducing the book. Some students are tempted to simplify difficult words for children but you need to think carefully about this. As we have said, children can manage far more difficult language when it is being read aloud and very often the embedding context of the overall narrative gives the difficult words meaning. We underestimate the power of the text and the children themselves if we make assumptions about what is simple and what is hard. With longer novels, cutting whole sections is a different matter and there may be times when you decide to do this. You might, for instance, be introducing an impatient and lively class to a classic novel and decide to cut some description in order to get to the main action. But do it with care, tell children that you have done it, and why, and make sure you summarise it for them. Often you will find they go back and read it themselves anyway! If you find you are cutting out too much then you have probably made an inappropriate choice and the children will need wider reading experiences before they are ready to take on a text of this type.

Expectations about behaviour should be thought about and discussed with the children. Enthusiastic interruptions worry some teachers and can disrupt the flow of the story. The point here is that children are 'meaning makers' (Wells 1987) and they will make active personal responses to texts as they connect the reading both with their own experiences and with other texts they know. A reading of *This is the Bear* (Hayes and Craig) may call up the children's own stories about their teddy bears or about being lost, but may also lead them to think of other stories by Sara Hayes or to remember *Dogger* (Hughes). Typically, very young children will want to make these connections straightaway, leading to the lively and interactive sessions you will see in many early years classrooms. As children become more experienced readers, they will be able to internalise and hold on to such links and you will find it easier to sustain the reading. Anticipating points which invite response can help here. For instance, children are always desperate to contribute their own plans for trapping the Iron Man (in Ted Hughes' powerful book of the same name), so much so that one teacher reports an 11-year-old rushing up to draw his suggested trap on the blackboard. Talking with the children before you read and asking for their ideas goes some way towards pre-empting this. It is partly a matter of personal choice, but it is also to do with the demands of the text (try reading John Burningham's *Would You Rather?* without interruptions!) and the needs of the class. We have seen teachers of all age ranges working most effectively with a 'no interruptions' rule and there may be times when you feel the momentum of the story is at risk and you want to insist on this.

The way you open and close reading aloud sessions conveys important messages to children. 'Topping and tailing' can help children become more aware of ways of choosing books and of responding to them. We can introduce a new author and maybe include some autobiographical detail; Dick King-Smith for instance, was both a farmer and a primary school teacher before he turned his hand to writing animal stories for children and your class will find this sort of information very interesting. A reading or rereading of a favourite folk-tale can be the opportunity to draw children's attention to some of the features of the genre (e.g. to the 'rule of three' whereby things in folk-tales typically cluster in threes: wishes, events or characters). You can spend some time 'warming' a non-fiction text, maybe through a chart or diagram, before you start reading from it. 'Topping and tailing' are also times when we can remind children of the ways in which we choose books, by reading the blurb or looking through chapter headings or maybe sampling a few pages. These are all things that need to be made explicit to children.

Who reads aloud? Primarily we are talking here about the teacher, particularly if we are to maximise the benefits of listening to a more experienced reader. However, there are other possibilities. For instance, older children can read aloud to younger classes, and this is where the earlier point about the teacher offering a good model of reading aloud is salient. In one class there was a 'Read Aloud Request Board' to which the children pinned their requests for a particular poem, short story or picture book that they wanted to hear. They also nominated a reader. Helen Bromley (1996) has written an account of the enthusiastic way in which children in her early years class took on the idea of 'reading out'. Children often read in unison, in twos, threes or fours, so inexperienced readers could participate with confidence. A 'reading out box' was set up and the children would put books in here, labelled with a post-it, that they wanted to read. All these ideas give children the chance to practise reading aloud in a meaningful context with a real audience. These experiences are rather different from the most usual experience that children have of reading aloud, on a one-to-one basis with the teacher, and one of the benefits that Bromley comments on was the positive peer assessments children made of each other. She emphasises that her role in reading aloud was still important, for all the reasons that we have stated above, but you will certainly want to pay attention to the benefits of involving the children in this way.

We conclude this section by offering you a checklist that students have found helpful in planning for this routine.

READING ALOUD TO CHILDREN
A CHECKLIST
SELECT – PLAN – PRACTISE – DELIVER!

1. SELECT your book (don't leave it till the last moment!). Use the Programme of Study ('Breadth of Study') or *NLS* ('Range') to ensure variety. You will also need to think about the children's interests, ongoing work and cultural backgrounds.
2. Write a PLAN for the session. This should include:
   (a) any resources needed to accompany your reading, e.g. cut-outs of food and a

caterpillar for Eric Carle's *The Very Hungry Caterpillar*, or a map for a novel such as *The Great Elephant Chase* (Cross);

(b) how much you plan to read in a session (if it is a novel), ensuring it is a long enough chunk (e.g. a chapter or two). Read the text through with care so that you can anticipate any conceptual or vocabulary difficulties;

(c) how you intend to introduce the book, e.g. a discussion of other books by the same author that the class may have read;

(d) what kinds of points for discussion you want to raise with the children, e.g. do caterpillars really enjoy slices of salami?

(e) how you will conclude the session, e.g. predicting what might happen next in a novel;

(f) having something in reserve (e.g. finger rhymes for younger children; some poems for older children) in case you finish with time to spare.

3. PRACTISE reading the book aloud. If it's a picture book, you will need to try reading *and* showing the pictures – not as easy as it sounds!

4. DELIVER your plan! If you have planned carefully you should enjoy the session and feel sufficiently relaxed to cope with the unexpected.

Further reading

Barton, B. (1986) *Tell me Another: Storytelling and Reading Aloud at Home, at School and in the Community.* Portsmouth, NH: Heinemann.

Pennac, D. (1994) *Reads Like a Novel.* London: Quartet Books.

Teale, W. H. (1984) 'Reading to Young Children: Its Significance for Literary Development', in Goelman, H. *et al.* (eds) *Awakening to Literacy.* London: Heinemann.

Trelease, J. (1984) *The Read-Aloud Handbook.* Harmondsworth: Penguin.

SHARED READING (BIG BOOKS) AND SHARED WRITING

The routines of shared reading and shared writing are absolutely essential in order to show children the very heart of the process of reading. We must never forget how closely children observe adults; so many lessons about reading and writing can be taught through the modelling and demonstrations that we give.

Why?

Shared reading

Shared reading is the routine of using a Big Book with a group or class of children (see 'Big Books' in Chapter 2). It is a routine that was more commonly found in the early years of schooling but, as is discussed below, it has become a familiar routine throughout the primary years and forms a central plank of the Literacy Hour. The teacher leads the reading, pointing as she goes, with the children joining in. What is it that she can do that is impossible or difficult with a regular book?

- she can share the book with a larger group than usual and they can all see the print;
- there is a greater feeling of being drawn into the story: the 'large screen' experience makes for greater involvement;

- each member of the class has a chance to join in (with refrains, etc.) and make responses because each can see the print clearly;
- teaching points that the teacher wishes to make about print can be linked to examples seen by all;
- the teacher can use a finger or pointer to indicate: where she starts reading; left-to-right directionality; spaces between words; punctuation; paragraphing; speech layout; repeated words; capital letter use; the relation between illustration and text; non-fiction conventions such as the contents page, the index, the glossary or how diagrams are labelled.

The routine was developed in New Zealand in the 1970s by teachers working with Don Holdaway (1979). Holdaway had looked at the benefits of the bedtime story in setting children up for literacy and wanted to reinvent this homely routine for the larger classroom context. Hence the enlarged text, or Big Book, which allows a group of children to have the same intimate access to the book as is possible at home.

The benefits of shared reading are many. It ensures children are getting regular reading practice (a useful antidote to any lingering anxieties about daily reading). It can be used to make explicit phonic, graphic, semantic and syntactic strategies. It encourages rereading and is particularly helpful for inexperienced readers and EAL children who can have a strong sense of involvement in the reading without feeling personally pressurised. Shared reading has a place in Key Stage 2 classrooms as well where it clearly supports the older inexperienced reader but it is of benefit for all the class. The range of published enlarged texts for Key Stage 2 is growing at a pace and teachers of these older children are also making good use of all types of texts photocopied onto overhead transparencies, of home-made books and children's own writing. A teacher of a Year 4 class wanted her pupils to interview their grandparents about their schooldays; she put an enlarged photocopy of a magazine interview on the OHP and the class discussed its features before setting off on their task.

Shared writing

In the routine of shared writing the teacher and children compose a piece of writing together with the teacher 'scribing' on a board or flip chart easily visible to the whole class; s/he takes the transcriptional strain. It is important to distinguish this from children's dictated writing where the teacher transcribes exactly what the child says. In shared writing the emphasis is on joint composition. We include a discussion about shared writing in a book about reading because it is here that the teacher can demonstrate how the written word is produced. She can show how ideas can be captured, modified and revised in print. She can use it to teach children about how writers have an audience in mind, about how different types of writing require different types of organisation, and about how letters represent sounds and can be combined into words. It encourages collaboration and can be used to generate material that has a particular significance for the class: accounts of class outings, for instance, or a letter to a special visitor. Like shared reading, shared writing is a particularly supportive routine for inexperienced and EAL readers as it gives them evidence of how we can encode, structure and alter texts.

How?

Shared reading

We discussed the range and origins of Big Books in Chapter 2. For shared reading, as well as your Big Books, you will need an easel and pointer and as many small versions of the Big Book as possible. If available, an OHP will give you opportunities to use an even greater range of texts. If you are not implementing a Literacy Hour, daily sessions should be timetabled and you will need to plan these in terms of the books you use (to ensure range) and the skills you intend to teach.

For one of the best introductions to practical ways of developing this routine, Chapter 4 of Don Holdaway's *The Foundations of Literacy* (1979) is unbeatable. He gives detailed descriptions of how teachers in New Zealand made and introduced their own enlarged versions of children's favourite books. After initial sessions spent enjoying the story as a whole, he explains how they developed the 'Shared Book Experience' to encourage the children's attention to the print. He talks, for instance, about the importance of pointing and he describes 'masking devices' that the teachers devised in order to draw attention to particular aspects of print. First and foremost, you are modelling the pleasure and rewards to be gained from the overall reading of a text. Then the important thing is to decide what you want the children to learn; maybe you know that some children need support with some features of print (e.g. directionality, certain initial phonemes, punctuation). Or you might want to address broader issues related to response and choice (e.g. 'What other books do we know by this author?', 'Which part did you think was best?').

Because so much can be taught through this routine there is always the danger of trying to do too much in one session. Decide on your objectives and stick with them. A Year 1 teacher told us of trying to do so much with a single text that one child finally pleaded, 'Please miss, could you get on with the story?'.

The teacher below is encouraging her reception class to inspect rhymes. They are reading together from a Big Book and they have stopped at the word 'hedgehog':

Teacher	(1)	Hedgehog, look, it says 'hog'. 'Hog' and 'bog'; they sound the same.
Children	(2)	Hog and bog, hog and bog . . .
Teacher	(3)	What do we say when words sound the same?
Children	(4)	Hog, bog, rog, log . . . [said at same time as teacher's question].
Teacher	(5)	You say 'rhyme' don't you?
Child A	(6)	'Hedgehog' begins with 'h'.
Teacher	(7)	Well done, and 'h' and 'og' together spell 'hog'.
Child B	(8)	. . . [indistinct] rarren, gallen . . .
Teacher	(9)	That's right, they rhyme with my name [which is Allen].
Child B	(10)	. . . randy, gandy . . .
	(11)	Patrick, ratrick [Child B is called Patrick].
Child C	(12)	Ratrick, rucksack.
Teacher	(13)	Words are fun aren't they? You can do all sorts of things with them.

In this short extract the teacher manages to make several important teaching points particularly in her efforts to raise the children's phonemic awareness. For instance, in the exchange about 'rhyme' (3–5) she is giving the children a piece of metalanguage

(language about language) that they need for talking about reading. She draws their attention to the way letters combine to make words in this case dividing the word 'hog' into its onset ('h-') and rime ('-og') (7). She responds to the children's enjoyment of the sounds and rhymes and, importantly, links their word play with names (9). Her final comment (13) is one of the many messages she gives the children about the enjoyment to be had from reading.

After this sort of session, if you have left the book on the stand, you will see young children using it and pointing at key features just as you have done. They may lie on the classroom floor, turning over the large pages and recreating the good reading experiences which they have had with you and the Big Book. The children are not just playing; they are reworking and internalising the lessons that you have recently taught them. An EAL child from the class above was observed during a quiet reading session. She chose *To Town To Town* ('Story Chest') from the box of Big Books and lay on the floor with a friend. When they reached the words 'boing, boing, boing' she pointed at them with her finger. This was the first time she had given evidence of one-to-one matching. Her teacher's focusing on it in a class session made this possible.

At the other end of the school a Year 6 class are looking at an enlarged version of an extract from Alfred Lord Tennyson's 'Morte d'Arthur'. The teacher is able to show the children that lines such as

He heard the deep behind him, and a cry
Before.

depend upon different conventions for layout from prose and even from some of the modern poems that they are used to. The children find other examples of run-on lines and capitalisation at the start of lines when they are reading from poetry anthologies in groups.

Shared writing

Shared writing is used primarily to demonstrate aspects of the writing process but there are clear links with reading because it is through writing that we create the texts that we go on to read. Where children are involved in the creation of a text from the outset they will come to read it for themselves with more certainty, ownership and understanding. This routine can be used very effectively to draw the attention of less experienced readers to print; the following snippet of a group of Year 1 children composing a text based on *Rosie's Walk* (Hutchins 1969) about a fish going for a swim shows how easily these points can be made:

Teacher   What shall I put to end it?
Child   Full stop . . . you forgot to put 'and got home . . . and got to her friend's house in time for tea'.
Teacher   That finishes in the same way as *Rosie's Walk*. I'll cross that full stop out and put [writes with children joining in] 'just in time for tea'.
Child   Just put a 'T'.
Teacher   I could just put a 'T' couldn't I? Though that would make it just a letter 'T'. For the word 'tea' you need to put those letters 'e' and 'a' on the end.

In addition to working on aspects of the reading process that relate to decoding, shared writing can also be used to support other important aspects of the reading process such as knowing how to read different kinds of texts. We have already discussed some of the difficulties children may encounter with non-fiction texts and one way of learning how these are organised is by being involved in making information books. In this example, Year 5 children are writing an information book about boats. They have already brainstormed with their teacher possible areas for research and done some reading. They come together for a whole-class session where they decide on two major sections for their book: 'early boats' and 'boats today'. Then they compile a list (which the teacher writes up on an easel) of all the boats they will include in the first section and go away to find out about them. At the next session the teacher uses shared writing to model how to structure the information about each boat. She chooses the example of a raft and, using the children's ideas, she writes under four headings: 'What was it made from?', 'How was it powered?', 'Who used it?' and 'What was it used for?'. What remained on the easel was a coherent and logical model of information writing that the children could refer to as they wrote their own sections.

Further reading

CLPE (1990) *Shared Reading Shared Writing.* London: CLPE.

Laycock, L. (1999) 'Shared Reading and Shared Writing at Key Stage 1', in Goodwin, P. (ed.) *The Literate Classroom.* London: David Fulton Publishers.

Washtell, A. (1998) 'Routines and Resources', in Graham, J. and Kelly, A. (eds) *Writing Under Control, Teaching Writing in the Primary School.* London: David Fulton Publishers.

THE CLASS READER

A class reader is a children's novel which you select for reading with the whole class. Typically you will read it aloud to them. There is not space for such sustained reading aloud within the Literacy Hour but the framework recommends that you find time for this practice outside the hour, perhaps in the traditional story time slot. Although it is possible and even desirable that books are read aloud to children unaccompanied by written and other activities, in this section we are assuming that the class reader will have been chosen by you because of qualities and depths which can profitably be explored through related activities, some of which may take place in the Literacy Hour.

Why?

We have already talked about the importance of literature in children's lives and we know that it develops and extends their imaginative faculties. It allows them to enter 'secondary worlds' (Tolkien 1964) where they will encounter other situations, places and times and where they can empathise with other characters. A class reader can be a powerful medium for developing children's experiences of, and responses to, literature. It provides a point of shared culture in the class through the communal experience of listening, discussing and responding to the same text.

One criticism of the Literacy Hour is that it can offer children only fragments of text and deny them the experience of the whole book. Working with a class reader can go some way to restoring the balance.

This is another routine that ensures children of all abilities and languages have access to books which provide appropriate challenge. As we said in 'Reading Aloud to Children', you can read books to children that they may not be able to tackle for themselves; for struggling readers this access to books with rich language and plots that meet their interest level is crucial. The class reader is also another context for developing children's reading repertoires and their competence in choosing books for themselves. For example, you might decide to read Dick King-Smith's *The Sheep Pig* which is about a pig who believes he is a sheepdog. You could then lead the class to other books by the same author such as *The Fox Busters* or to other anthropomorphic stories such as *Charlotte's Web* (White). The book could also be an incentive to read information books about sheepdogs and pigs. Reading a short novel such as *Clockwork or All Wound Up* (Pullman) may act as a launch pad for some children to start reading his more demanding *Northern Lights* (the first part of his *Dark Materials* Trilogy). In the same way, shorter novels by Anne Fine such as *The Angel of Nitshill Road* could inspire individuals to move on to *Goggle Eyes*. In addition, this routine provides a further opportunity for the teacher to model reading aloud (see 'Reading Aloud to Children').

How?

First choose your book. You will need to try reading some of it out loud to see how well written it is. Look for a good balance of dialogue and narrative, rhythmic language, varied sentence length, recognisable characters who are credible and consistent and a well-paced plot that will sustain the children's interest. Your own commitment to the book also matters; your enthusiasm will help to motivate the children but will also motivate you in terms of the effort you put into presenting and mediating it to the class. There are different ways of organising how the book is read with the class. The most usual model is of the teacher reading aloud to the children. If resources allow, the children can read from their own copies at the same time (although this practice is more often found in secondary schools). Sometimes children and teacher share the reading aloud in reading round the class. This is a long-standing practice but the pressure of reading aloud for struggling readers can be detrimental to their self-esteem and progress. The tension for these children of waiting for their turn, often trying to anticipate their passage in order to practise it, can completely detract from the benefits that are claimed for this routine. One student told us of a memory she has from school of a rather more benign version where the class all sat together on the carpet with their readers and chose whether or not to read aloud.

In a very crowded curriculum teachers, realising that they may not be able to read the whole novel out loud, might think that the solution is to choose only short novels. This would be a mistake as it would preclude the selection of many books that children want to hear. One way round this is to use multiple copies and taped versions which can be rotated among groups who are asked to read prescribed sections for homework. For those children who could manage it, the book could also be read in group sessions while those who cannot read it for themselves could listen to the same section on tape. When teachers plan activities to accompany class readers they are guided by a wish to enhance children's responses to literature, to provide opportunities for contextualised

English work and sometimes to draw out cross-curricular links. These also provide the teacher with opportunities to assess children's literary development in speaking and listening, reading and writing. Here is a worked-through example from a Year 5 class who read Michael Morpurgo's *The Dancing Bear*, a short but complex novel. The teacher's planning was governed by the *NC* requirements for reading at Key Stage 2 but speaking and listening and writing requirements were met too, reminding us how interrelated the programmes of study are. He also found that he was able to incorporate many of the activities into the formal hour he gave to literacy every morning.

Before reading the book

Before embarking on reading the book the teacher planned two separate activities. Firstly, he set up a display about the author including some of his many other books, which a number of the children knew already. Secondly, because the film crew in the novel arrive to make a film of *The Pied Piper of Hamelin*, the teacher read the class extracts from Browning's poem in a version illustrated by Andre Amstutz.

Introducing the book

The teacher then introduced the class to the book by focusing on the front and back covers. The children were asked in pairs to speculate about the front cover and the relationship between the girl and the bear who appear together in the foreground. They then turned to the back cover where the blurb confirmed some of their speculations and added new detail which made them want to read the book (e.g. 'arrival of glamorous film crew'!).

Reading the book

When he was ready to begin reading the teacher alerted the children to the fact that this book is written in the first person narrative voice of a middle-aged schoolmaster. The reading of the book was carried out to the whole class over three sessions, with the sections to be read chosen as follows: the first was about the main character, Roxanne, and her early life in the village with the bear; the second was the arrival of, and early rehearsals with, the film crew which included a young and handsome pop star; the last section was where Roxanne is seduced away from the village by the pop star and the bear dies.

First section: activity

The teacher's aim for the activity connected to the first section was to emphasise the peaceful, rural simplicity of the mountain community and how the novel sets up the lull before the storm. In a whole-class session the children talked about and then listed individually what was different in Roxanne's life from their own lives, for example the making of cheese, being cut off by the snow, making honey and having a bear in their midst. They then formed groups and made two predictions about what they thought would happen next. When they reported back to the whole class the most popular predictions were: that the bear would have to die soon and that Roxanne would be heartbroken; and secondly, that as a young woman Roxanne would lose interest in the bear.

Second section: activity

In the second activity the teacher's purpose was to explore the extent of the disruption to the community as experienced by the characters. The class as a whole with the teacher as scribe listed the differences between the community and the visitors, such as the high-tech equipment, their outrageously gaudy clothes and, particularly, the presence in their midst of the glamorous Niki. Role play in fours where each child was a character in the story talking about the day's filming led to individuals writing an entry in a diary which their character might have kept during the filming. Then they made two more predictions: most popular was that Roxanne does not agree to appear with her bear in the video in the major role envisaged for her; and second was that she does and that the bear wrecks the whole film.

Third section: activity

By this stage the children's involvement in the story was so great that they could hardly wait to see which of their predictions would come true. The teacher's aim for the third activity was to ensure that the children could see that the ending was appropriate even though sudden and tragic. Immediately after the reading the whole class talked about Roxanne's departure and the bear's death and how it made them feel. The teacher hoped that through this discussion the children might appreciate that the bear's death was the price the village, personified by Roxanne, had to pay because it had sold out to the commercial world. If this sounds a tall order, remember that the activities for sections one and two were leading up to this. The final written activity required the children to write individual letters to Niki in the role of Roxanne on her return to the village many years later.

There are two important caveats about activities: firstly, do not kill the book with a surplus of activities; secondly, do not try to make every book connect with ongoing work in other curriculum areas. Literature can teach many lessons on its own without constant curriculum connections and extending activities. Make sure you have literature there for literature's sake.

However you choose to organise the reading, you need to ensure that the children have access to the reader at other times, so a special place in the book corner is needed. This can be enhanced by an associated display (see 'Managing and Organising the Resources' in Chapter 2), maybe including other books by the author, related books (e.g. *The Boy and his Bear* by Harriet Graham), poems (e.g. 'My Mother saw a Dancing Bear' by Charles Causley in Patten, ed.) etc. You will find children eager to reread sections (or to read ahead!) but this is also a way of giving the children a chance to look at the small black and white line illustrations that are a feature of so many longer novels for children and that cannot easily be seen by the whole class.

What should you do if the children do not like the book? You can use the opportunity to demonstrate that readers can make choices, that they do not have to read everything! You can discuss with the children why it is not working and use the opportunity to develop their critical awareness, maybe getting the children to write reviews saying why they would not recommend it. However, you may have planned a unit of work around the novel which means it is not practical to abandon it. If this is the case you could still discuss the difficulties with the class, bearing in mind it would be most unusual for everyone to dislike it; critical reviews could still ensue as could a class search for other books with similar themes. But you could also inspect the way in which you are working with the book and ask yourself some questions. Are you reading for too long or too short a time? Are you leaving too long a gap between the readings? Are you ending the reading at sufficiently interesting points that will encourage the children to want to know more? How enthusiastic is your reading aloud? Are you killing the book through overuse of related activities? Would some judicious editing (see 'Reading Aloud to Children') move things on a bit?

The teaching of reading deserves the same attention as you would give to any other area of the curriculum so remember why you are using a class reader and, as with any planning, keep reviewing its success and adjusting it appropriately.

Further reading

Graham, J. (1997) *Cracking Good Books*. Sheffield: NATE.

Marriott, S. (1995) *Read On: Using Fiction in the Primary School*. London: Paul Chapman Publishing.

Millard, E. (1994) *Developing Readers in the Middle Years*. Buckingham: Open University Press.

Thomas, H. (1998) *Reading and Responding to Fiction: Classroom Strategies for Developing Literacy*. Leamington Spa: Scholastic.

TELLING STORIES

The emphasis in this section is on story-telling, not on reading a story from a book. Your initial response may be rather guarded. You may feel that story-telling cannot have much contribution to make to children's literacy; don't they need to have their eyes on print to become readers? In addition, you may feel that it is an activity for those with time to learn stories off by heart and confidence to leave behind the safety of the printed page; that it is fun and even quite mesmerising but has little place in the day-to-day work in school.

We would like you to keep an open mind about story-telling and we are encouraged to press our points here because we have so frequently seen its benefits in the class-room. Indeed, of all the activities that student teachers rejoice in, story-telling comes highest. Students and teachers may be filled with doubt and anxiety beforehand but their eyes brighten when later recounting the total absorption in the story shown by the class and the obvious value of the activity, not least in terms of class bonding. The value in terms of literacy is not so instantly visible but we argue our case in the section below.

Why?

Story-telling and story-reading of course share many aspects: children have from both a model of complete, patterned narrative, with beginnings, middles and ends; both typically have a major character (or two) who faces challenges and ultimately over-comes them. Both stories read and stories told inform, entertain, create new worlds, make sense of experience, develop empathy and even morals. Both give us the same opportunities to contemplate, store images and rework feelings.

So why are we persuading you to go off and learn stories to tell your class with all the extra work that it appears to involve? You probably need to experience being told a story yourself before you will accept that something akin to magic occurs when a story-teller has drawn a class into the world of the story. With luck, you have felt this anyway, but descriptions of the experience usually refer to:

- the excitement of 'seeing' the story in your mind's eye, created through the power of language (with perhaps a few gestures, facial expressions, voice modulations, and even props for younger or bilingual pupils);
- the extra tension in the air because the story-teller has no text;
- the delight in hearing the perfect word or phrase, including refrains, selected from memory rather than read from the page;
- the warm feeling of receiving the gift of a story. You feel very valued if you know someone has worked hard to learn a story for you;
- the feeling that your eyes and everybody else's are on the story-teller and yet you are not really seeing the story-teller. You are looking through her to the story itself. But the communality of the experience feels very bonding;
- the feeling that this is an ancient process, a natural activity, that has roots in each of us, as well as in our cultures.

Laura Simms, a professional story-teller from the USA, on a visit to this country in 1987, spoke of the extra quality of story-telling rather than story-reading in these terms:

> The meaning of the story occurs because it's a reciprocal art-form. An extra dimension occurs between the story-teller and the told. Something is co-created which wasn't there before and though it is ephemeral, it is vivid and changes one for ever. The meaning is beyond words.
> (Laura Simms, in performance at the University of Greenwich)

It really does seem that the impact of hearing a story can change children for ever. Certainly, they remember images and even whole stretches of language and can summon these up years later if the story's title is mentioned or if they see the story-teller again. If the story language and the story characteristics as outlined above are also laid down in this permanent, imprinted way, then it can be seen that the benefits of story-telling are of great significance to literacy, as we know that this story knowledge is an essential component of becoming literate. Of course, children also need to have full and varied exposure to print but we cannot ignore the 'bigger shapes' of literacy learning to which story-telling contributes. In addition, very young children and EAL learners learn language quickly through the repetition and the accumulating text that are so often features of told stories.

We associate story-telling with other lands and cultures, and certainly it does appear that the recent growth of interest in story-telling owes something to the arrival in Britain of children from cultures that are rich in the oral tradition. A British oral tradition survives in nursery rhymes, in jokes, riddles, proverbs and superstitions, as well as in many traditional tales that are still handed down, at least in some parts of the country. It is important that, while celebrating British culture, we are aware of and honour a wide range of stories and notice the recurring cross-cultural themes. Many traditional stories are at the base of such popular books as 'The Jolly Postman' series (Allan and Janet Ahlberg) and other 'intertextual' stories. When readers know these stories, it is evident that there is an incentive and a rewarding bonus to the reading.

How?

If you are going to tell stories in the classroom, you will need more than the pointers we list below. However, they will serve as a start and we list books which will provide further help.

Preparation

Browse at length among books of traditional stories and choose a story you know or that instantly attracts you. A story with plenty of continuous action, lots of direct speech and humour will help in the first instance. Do not learn the story off by heart but visualise it and hear the voices. Tell the story to yourself lots of times making sure you have the sequence of events clear in your head. Decide if you want any audience participation.

Telling

Bring the class on to the carpet or into a circle around you. Give an introduction to and a little information about the story so as to reduce interruptions and questions. Do not have the written version anywhere near you. Keep eye contact with all the children. Do not explain things and especially do not tell the children the moral. Do not ask the children questions in the middle of the story and do not say you have made a mistake; rather, say, 'Did I tell you that. . . ?' Use props and dramatisation sparingly except per-haps with very young children and those new to English. Do not rush. Keep the magic in your voice but keep your voice natural.

After the telling

Having said 'and that is the end of the story' or something similar, let the next words come from the children. Do not quiz or question them but receive their comments with interest. Do not be persuaded to extend the story-telling beyond 20 minutes with classes unused to it.

Retelling

Give children the opportunity to retell your story, a little bit each perhaps. Move, when children are confident, towards children telling their own stories, including personal ones. Be very positive in your reaction to stories from children; aim to give them confi-dence, responsibility and a sense of achievement. Make time for your class story-telling and invite other classes and visitors to join your community of story-tellers.

A final point

Told stories are a little more trouble for you initially but soon you get quicker and quicker at learning them and better and better at telling them. So does your class. If, however, it all seems too daunting, make sure you still read well and frequently to your class. Narrative is 'a primary act of mind' (Barbara Hardy's expression in Meek *et al.* 1977), and it seems that we all need and like stories, not least because we are amazed that such order can be put on life, such coherence, such completeness, such meaning.

Proper beginnings, middles and ends – especially ends – are not easily identifiable in real life with its continuous stream of events. Seeing art imposed on life is a magic that we should share early and often with children.

We end with the words of our colleague Fiona Y. Collins:

> By including the telling and retelling of traditional tales in the range of language activities offered to children, we can enable and encourage their growing confidence as competent language users. In moving from the oral to the literary forms of language, the child, in his/her individual progress, is mirroring the development seen in different civilisations, a pattern of moving from using purely oral to using both oral and literate forms of communication. Hearing and retelling oral stories, and recognising them retold in book form, helps to bridge what can sometimes seem to the child to be an impassable abyss between orality and literacy. As teachers, we are doing more than encouraging a love of stories when we tell and retell traditional stories with children. We are inducting children into an understanding of oral and literate forms of language which will underpin all their knowledge about language, in the nursery and primary school, and beyond.
>
> (Unpublished Ph.D. thesis)

Further reading

Barton, B. and Booth, D. (1990) *Stories in the Classroom, Storytelling, Reading Aloud and Role Playing with Children*. Portsmouth, NH: Heinemann Educational Books.

Grainger, T. (1997) *Traditional Storytelling in the Primary Classroom*. Leamington Spa: Scholastic.

Grugeon, E. and Gardner, P. (2000) *The Art of Storytelling for Teachers and Pupils*. London: David Fulton Publishers.

Howe, A. and Johnson, J. (1992) *Common Bonds: Storytelling in the Classroom*. Sevenoaks: Hodder & Stoughton.

DRAMA AND PLAYING IN ROLE

So much spontaneous play and re-enactment goes on around the books and reading experiences we encounter that it is easy to take them for granted, undervalue them or fail to capitalise on them. Add to this the common response from teachers (terror at worst, apprehension at best) to the idea of classroom drama and you can see why it does not always become a classroom routine. It is helpful to appreciate how much drama there is in the average classroom, to value it more and to extend its use.

Dramatising a text is something many teachers do spontaneously. They know that the book they have chosen is rather challenging or they see that some children are perhaps not involved or are becoming restless. They want to give more help with 'lifting the voice off the page'. Watch a teacher reading the opening of *The Iron Man* (Hughes). She will use her voice, her eyebrows, her hands and her arms to emphasise the size, the mystery and the movements of the Iron Man. You may think this is instinctive and not particularly thought through or conscious, but over the years teachers have realised the need to add this dramatic support to their readings and have seen, from listening, for instance, to children's retellings, how powerfully such enactments have contributed to children's understandings and recall. Another example of this might be when a teacher stops her reading (of, say, Shirley Hughes' *Dogger*) and asks, 'And what do you think Dave's parents said to him when he kept waking up in the middle of the night because he was missing Dogger?' The children then move into a mini-drama in answer to the teacher's invitation to deepen response. In this section, we want to encourage you to see how much potential there is in classrooms for extending children's spontaneous play towards texts of all sorts. With careful planning, you can employ drama and role play systematically, before, during and after reading or story-telling.

Why?

As you start to read a story, images – of a forest, perhaps, a ramshackle cottage, two waif-like children – are supplied by the brain. Certain expectations are aroused and these depend not only upon our reading of other stories but also on our personal life experiences. The reader is active in recreating the story and moving into a secondary world. Many students and teachers are quite taken aback to realise that this process, so effortless and unquestioned for them, is actually not easy for everybody. Some children, and they may be those who lacked enough experience of playing in their early years, do not seem to have this easy access to the meanings implied by the print. The words remain black marks on the page and imagined characters, settings, move-ments, emotions, dialogue, tension and anticipated endings are not part of reading for them. These children are the ones for whom reading may remain difficult. Drama, whether spontaneous or planned, has a valuable role in enabling children to reach the deeper levels of meaning in literature. It is also a way in which you can breathe life into non-fiction texts. Behind sentences such as 'This seventeenth-century map of Barbados shows a sugar mill worked by slaves. Sugar plantations in the West Indies made vast fortunes for their owners' lie many peoples' stories, many points of tension, many issues to do with having and not having power, all of which would lend themselves to drama. Given what we know about boys' generally expressed preferences for non-fiction and their enthusiastic response to active reading practices (with fiction as well), there is all the more reason to build drama into our teaching routines.

How?

The ways into dramatic exploration of text with a class can be brief and controlled and need not place any of the participants, including the teacher, at risk. Although there are some problems in working from a known text (children want to stick to the story-line), you can persuade them that the book is only ever part of the story and that they can amplify it through their drama. If you develop drama from a picture book text, the point can be made that many other scenes could have been illustrated and that it is the unseen parts the class will be working on.

The following points can help you think about using drama in the classroom to help children develop a closer relationship with texts:

- Think about situations in the story where the characters have a problem to solve and thus where there is dramatic tension.
- Get the children to see parallels with their own lives. Even the simplest picture book such as Pat Hutchins' *Titch* has themes (sibling rivalry, growth) of great significance to all children.

- Extend the story backwards, before the story began, or forwards, after it is finished.
- Develop a scene only glossed over in the original story.
- Develop a minor character from the story and his or her reactions to events. You can add characters not in the original story.
- Present the class with new problems which could have arisen in the story.
- Think of ways in which the class can be divided to form separate groups with different roles.
- Think about how a character from the text could be 'hot-seated', i.e. asked questions by the rest of the class about their actions, feelings, thoughts. Children can 'be' the character and answer in role.
- Use other specific drama strategies such as freeze-framing or thought-tracking to help understand fictional relationships and motivations.
- Think of how your role in the drama can be minor but facilitating. Often if you take a questioning, worried or sceptical line, you will find the class providing you with information and opening the situation out.

Some of the above underpin the accounts of the two drama activities that follow. A teacher working in a school for physically handicapped children had been reading John Burningham's *Would You Rather?* The book poses a series of impossible options and in response to the question 'Would you rather your house was surrounded by water, covered with snow or surrounded by jungle?' the children opted for living in a house surrounded by snow. The reading area became the house and everyone was drawn into a collective drama that constructed a secondary world. The teacher started complaining about the cold. The children joined in. Soon the issue of escape arose. They proposed and searched for various tools to help dig them out, including a broom and an egg whisk. Hypotheses were made and tested. Implications of escape from the house were raised – where could they go once out? The drama developed but it was governed by the original text; the snow was not going to melt. This rule of 'playing constrained by the text' did not have to be introduced by the teacher. Children know these rules from their long experience of make-believe play. For the majority of the children, the original text became richer and more multi-layered when they returned to it and the bonding with and return to the book more significant.

A Year 2 class was studying the theme of houses and was working on the story of Goldilocks. The story was not re-enacted but the class entered the world of Goldilocks and the Bears. In role as children who disobey, they entered a forest and created havoc as Goldilocks had done in the cottage. When moral irresponsibility had done its worst, the teacher changed their roles completely and they tried alternative viewpoints as bears who wanted to teach the children a lesson. Eventually they concocted a 'cordial of leaves and berries' to 'bring the sweetness back to their hearts'. Once again, even though the children were new to this way of working, they did not need training for they were engaging in the rule-bound nature of play. Empathy with, and an examination of, the implications of the text was deepened here and they were prepared for further journeys as readers.

You will see from these accounts that the drama we are talking about is not to do with acting out the story or with keeping faithfully to the plot or with performance. It is to do with human behaviour, with concepts, with the ideas that lurk below the surface.

It need not be a long drawn-out process and you can even employ it – as teachers frequently do – to illuminate non-fiction texts. A classroom exploration of desert life, for instance, can as usefully proceed through a Bedouin family reporting at an oasis police station the theft of their goat-skin tent and other possessions as through other activities. The teacher is principally a provider of situations within which she and the class ponder. Children bring what they know and what they are learning about life and living to these situations and surprise themselves and us with their depth of involvement. Books and stories are not the beginning and end but for many teachers they provide the holding framework.

Further reading

Clipson-Boyles, S. (1999) 'The role of drama in the literate classroom', in Goodwin, P. (ed.) *The Literate Classroom*. London: David Fulton Publishers.
Hendy, L. (1994) 'From Drama into Story: Strategies for Investigating Text', in Styles, M. *et al.* (eds) *The Prose and the Passion*. London: Cassell.
Hendy, L. (1996) 'With the Wind Behind You: Language Development Through Drama Activities at Key Stage 1', in Styles, M. *et al.* (eds) *Voices Off Texts, Contexts and Readers*. London: Cassell.
Toye, N. and Prendiville, F. (2000) *Drama and Traditional Story for the Early Years*. London: Routledge.
Language Matters, 'Drama and Play' Spring 1999

TEACHING PHONIC AND GRAPHIC KNOWLEDGE

Grapho-phonics is one of the cue-systems that we looked at in Chapter 1. We indicated that more recent models of the reading process have separated out the graphic and phonic strands. Phonics, of course, is about working with sounds while graphic work focuses on recognition of words and letter strings. We also gave the background to traditional, synthetic approaches to phonics teaching and the more recent analytic approach. You will remember that synthetic approaches begin at the level of the phoneme and were based on a common-sense view that saw the reading process to be a simple matter of decoding. Analytic approaches work with bigger chunks of words and encourage pattern detection across words.

In the section below we will be considering the teaching of phonics using both methods and we will also discuss ways of teaching children graphic knowledge.

Why?

The *NLS* points out that 'All teachers know that pupils become successful readers by learning to use a range of strategies to get at the meaning of a text' (DfEE 1998a p. 3). The searchlights model, based on the cue-systems, reminds us that effective readers draw upon as many of these strategies as possible. We have stressed throughout this book that no single approach to reading is likely to benefit the child and, in Chapter 1, we talked about the American research into learning styles (Bussis *et al.* 1985) that indicated that many children need direct teaching about the smaller units in reading.

Clearly, using phonic and graphic strategies to decode unfamiliar words is a crucial part of reading proficiency. Fluent readers are only aware of how their phonic and graphic skills are operating when they come to a new, long or difficult word. Take a word such as 'diphenhydramine' (on a bottle of cough medicine), read it out loud and you will notice that, unless you are a pharmacist, you use phonic and graphic skills to decode it. Early readers of necessity use decoding skills, among the other cue-systems, more often and more consciously, simply because they are less experienced with print. Some of these young readers will swing more toward guessing, making insufficient use of decoding strategies that they do need to be taught.

What teachers need to know

Giving yourself lessons

If you are to feel in control of this area, the first requirement is to give yourself some lessons about the grapho-phonic system. Of course you operate it successfully yourself but now you must make these implicit understandings explicit to yourself. To help with this, we have included, at the end of this section, a glossary of terms you need to be familiar with.

The first thing we need to understand is that there are four principles underlying the phonemic system (DfEE 1999b).

- Sounds/phonemes are represented by letters
- Phonemes are represented by one or more letters

You will remember from Chapter 1 that a word such as 'man' is represented by three letters, one for each phoneme. A word like 'planet' is no different in this respect; six phonemes are represented by six letters. (Note that 'p' and 'l' are separate sounds but are run together and known as a cluster – see glossary on pp. 91–3). However, take a word like 'thick' and count its phonemes. You should have noticed that it has three phonemes despite its five letters: 'th' and 'ck' are each only one sound. They are called consonant digraphs. Now take a word like 'thief'; five letters, three phonemes again, but this time the 'i' and the 'e' make one phoneme and are called a vowel digraph.

- The same phoneme can be represented in more than one way

Look at these four words: 'pain', 'flake', 'sleigh' and 'day' and notice that they all share the same vowel phoneme but it is represented differently in each case ('p<u>ai</u>n', 'fl<u>a</u>k<u>e</u>', 'sl<u>eigh</u>', and 'd<u>ay</u>'). You will have noticed that 'ay' comes at the end of its word while 'ai' precedes a consonant. Test this out on other words and see if this generates a rule. You may also have noticed that the word 'flake' has what used to be described as a 'magic' or 'silent' 'e' at the end where it has the power to make the previous vowel 'say its name'. Check out other words with this pattern and see if this rule holds. Words that end in 'silent e' are described as 'split digraphs' (DfEE 1999b).

In the *NLS Progression in Phonics* materials (DfEE 1999b; see below) carefully chosen words are used to teach children about split digraphs. For example the children listen to the words 'tie', 'toe' and 'cue' and identify two phonemes in each. Then three children, carrying cards with 't', 'i' and 'e' on them, will be asked to stand up and represent the word 'tie' with 'i' and 'e' holding hands. Now the children are asked to turn 'tie' into 'time'. Child 'm' joins the word and splits the vowel digraph 'ie' apart. However, despite this disruption the 'ie' digraph retains its sound. This is represented by the 'i' and 'e' children continuing to hold hands behind the back of child 'm'. This is then repeated with 'toe' and 'tone', 'cue' and 'cube'.

Work that focuses on different ways of representing phonemes develops children's graphic skills which they will need if they are to move on from early phonetic spellings where they tend to write things like 'sed' (said) and 'woz' ('was) and 'lovelee' (lovely').

● The same spelling may represent more than one sound

This principle can be illustrated by reading the following passage:

> *The man who boarded the train to Reading was reading the newspaper. He read that the Queen had flown to America on a state visit and forgotten to take her crown. He imagined himself bowing to the Queen and noticing that she had a pretty bow in her hair instead.*

Words that look the same ('bow' and 'bow', 'Reading' and 'reading') but sound different and have different meanings are called homographs. As long as children do not lose sight of the fact that reading is about understanding the text, mispronunciations of such words are likely to be recognised as not making sense and will be reread and self-corrected.

If you look back to the definition of phonics from David Crystal that we used on page 11, you will notice that he has used the word 'regular' and not without reason. Most early phonic reading schemes avoided irregularities so that the rules they offered did seem to work. The 'magic e' rule that we discussed above falls down with some very common words such as 'come' and 'have'. We think that if you look objectively and with curiosity and interest at our written language system, you will be able to demonstrate this curiosity with children and explore the language in ways that make them comfortable with the complexities of English. If children know that they are dealing with a system that frequently privileges other things, such as meaning and the origin of words, rather than one-to-one letter/sound correlation, they are far less likely to feel anxious when the system appears not to work than if they are led to believe it is all susceptible to logical working out.

Phonic progression

Traditional approaches to teaching phonics have sequenced the teaching into a structured progressive order. Within this order, minor variations can be seen across approaches and schemes. Many teachers focused first on the identification of initial and final sounds in consonant–vowel–consonant (CVC) words and then shifted attention to the medial vowel sounds ('a' in 'cat'). They might have then moved on to initial consonant clusters ('sp̲it', 's̲t̲one') followed by final consonant clusters ('la̲s̲t', 'co̲r̲n', 'ha̲r̲d'). Then they may have taught consonant digraphs ('c̲hurch', 's̲hip', 'so̲c̲k'). On the whole, silent letters, prefixes and suffixes and work on polysyllabic words tended to be taught at a later stage.

The *NLS* provides a detailed breakdown of the phonic and spelling work children should cover from Reception to Year 2 (DfEE 1999b p. 64, List 3). As a progression it provides a useful structure. However, be prepared to use it flexibly if you discover that your Year 1 children are curious about the vowel phoneme 'air' ('fair') before they have reached the prescribed moment for teaching it (Year 2, Term 2).

Questions of terminology

As in all curriculum areas, there is an issue regarding when and whether it is appropriate to introduce children to specialist terminology such as 'digraph' or 'phoneme'. The danger lies in assuming that because you have taught the label you have taught the concept; this is not always the case. Nevertheless, it is generally agreed that children need some metalanguage so that they can discuss and reflect upon their own language use, and teachers have to make considered decisions about when and how to introduce this. You will also find that children positively enjoy having the labels. If they can relish labelling the parts of a flower or mini-beast, why not the parts of language too? In addition, as teachers, we need to be equipped with precise terminology in order to talk about the teaching of reading.

The *NLS* provides a useful glossary of terminology and lists 'Technical Vocabulary' for use with each year group. It states that 'most of these terms should form part of pupils' developing vocabulary for talking about language' (DfEE 1999b p. 69). As with any such list, there has been discussion among teachers about why some terms are deemed suitable to be introduced in one year group and not in another. This in itself has proved a healthy debate as, at its heart, it challenges preconceptions about notions of 'readiness' and brings into sharper focus our thinking about conceptual development. Perhaps the liveliest debate has centred around the use of the term 'phoneme' which enters the *NLS* list in the Reception year. To explore the thinking about this, it helps to consider the possible alternative word(s) that could have been used. The most obvious choice is the word 'sound'. 'Sound', of course, is a word that has been used by teachers of reading for many years. However, consider what the word 'sound' is likely to mean to young children. It has many everyday applications in their lives in addition to the 'sounds' in words. On the other hand, 'phoneme' precisely describes the concept of the smallest unit of sound that can be spoken or heard. Working with the phoneme is of course fundamental to phonics teaching in the *NLS*. Additional *NLS* materials (*PIPs* and *ALS* – see below) have games that work with phonemes involving the children in 'phoneme counts' and using 'phoneme frames'. It would appear that many teachers start off by using the term 'phoneme' interchangeably with the word 'sound' but try gradually to shift frequency of use towards the technical term.

Your observations and assessments of children will help you decide when it is appropriate to use terminology. Our advice here is to make absolutely sure you understand the terms you use; then you will be able to use them with children, if the need arises, with clarity, confidence, exemplification and conviction. The sections below exemplify the most important thing about phonic teaching which is that all terminology and the concepts to which it refers should be sited in enjoyable and meaningful contexts.

How?

We have discussed both analytic and synthetic approaches to the teaching of reading and know that there are elements of both in the *NC* and *NLS*. You will need to draw from both approaches in order to make decisions about the best way to help a child tackle an unfamiliar word. Where it is a regular word such as 'animal', then phoneme-by-phoneme blending may well be the best approach. However, if it is an irregular word that chunks easily into onset and rime, such as 'France', then you might start by asking the child to read the initial cluster (onset) – 'Fr-'. At this point many children will go on to predict the rest of the word. If they do not, it might be useful to encourage the child to make an analogy with another word that shares the same rime ('d-ance' or 'ch-ance'). The advantage of this way of analysing words is that the child has a far less variable set of letters in '-ance' than she has in any of these letters separately. Similarly, the cluster 'fr' is a safer set to learn than either of the letters on their own. What we have to do is realise that differing approaches do not have to be pitched against each other; rather we should see them as enriching our understanding of the different strategies we can offer children for 'getting at' words.

What we must remember is that learning of the letters and sounds becomes very hard because much of the teaching is abstract in nature, so we do need to ensure that the child does not lose sight of the whole picture of what reading is: the making of meaning. Phonic and graphic knowledge must be taught within a balanced programme of reading. The balance means keeping an eye on the big shapes and this is why it is so important that you carry out teaching in contexts that are meaningful for children. There are many sources of ideas for teaching phonic and graphic knowledge available in a variety of forms e.g. books, games, and CD-ROMs. At the time of writing, the *NLS* has produced extensive support materials to which we have already referred, known as *PIPs* (*Progression in Phonics*, DfEE 1999b). These materials take the form of games through which the children practise four key skills: identifying sounds in spoken words; recognising common representations in writing for each phoneme; blending phonemes into words and segmenting words for spelling.

The early years

In the early years your focus will be on developing children's phonological and early graphic awareness. By making a special feature of the ideas below we can begin to sensitise children so that they listen out for sounds generally and begin to isolate phonemes. Here are some suggestions, some of which draw on the *PIPs* material mentioned above:

- Sound walks: take the children for a walk where they are asked to focus on the different sounds they hear in the environment. These may vary from bird song to gurgling radiator pipes. This can be done in the classroom as well with the children closing their eyes.
- Spot the instrument: put well-known classroom instruments (e.g. tambourine, drum, triangle) in a bag and ask the children to guess which one you are playing. Be ingenious, add your own (the spoons maybe?). Use cassette tapes of different sound effects.
- Voice play: play with sounds that are part of our repertoire for expressing astonishment (oooooooh!) or the need for quiet (ssshhhh!) or being hurt (ow!). Note that these are all sounds that children will later learn more formally as phonemes.
- Rhythm and rhyme: let the children hear, sing, recite, and learn as many rhymes as possible – daily! Try oral activities such as changing the rhyming words in nursery rhymes ('hickory, dickory, dock/The mouse ran up the watch') or leaving a gap in familiar rhymes so children are encouraged to predict a possible rhyme. Let the

children use good quality CD-ROMs such as *Nursery Rhyme Time* and *Ridiculous Rhymes* (Sherston).

- Odd-one-out games: say (or sing) words that rhyme but throw in one that doesn't (clock, sock, lock, mock, tock, watch). The children should clap each time they hear the odd one out.
- Big Books: use enlarged versions of rhymes so that children have the opportunities to look at rhyming words and begin to see their differences and to observe onsets and rimes.
- Syllable sensitivity: plan clapping activities (e.g. to the syllables of their names, place names, dinosaur names etc.).
- Alliteration activities: read, recite and teach the children tongue twisters ('Peter Piper'). Use enlarged versions of these so children can spot the recurring phoneme. Compose class alliterative nonsense sentences such as 'Brave Betty bought beautiful bright blue bananas'.
- Games: play 'I Spy' using a set of familiar objects such as 'Things we use in the bathroom', 'Things we put in our lunch boxes'. Cards naming the items, with the opening phoneme highlighted, could be used later and put alongside the objects.
- Alphabetic knowledge: play with alphabet letters (in playdough, sand and on a magnetic board); sing the alphabet and share many different alphabet books e.g. *An Alphabet of Animals* (Wormell); *Charlotte's Voake's Alphabet Adventure* (Voake). Without a thorough knowledge of the alphabet, children will find it very difficult to develop phonic knowledge and indeed to read and write. They need to know that there are 26 letters in the alphabet and how to name them. Children and teachers need to be able to talk about letters and in order to do this we should provide them with the relevant metalanguage. We need to teach them the letter names of the alphabet so that they are equipped with a way of referring to any letter in any situation.
- Names: make special books for each child e.g. 'David's All About "D" Book'. The child's name is a common starting point for developing alphabetic knowledge. From a very early age children begin to notice names in their environment and quickly start to identify letters that are significant to their lives. The first word that most children learn to spell is their own name and after that they rapidly learn how to write the names of their family and friends. When they start school, they are surrounded by names in print, for example the label by their coat peg, on their tidy trays, paintings and books. They readily notice similarities and differences in their names, making comments such as 'Christopher's name starts the same way as Christine's', or 'There are three children whose names start with a "T"'. You can use this interest deliberately to introduce children to aspects of grapho-phonic knowledge. You could make a set of name dominoes based on the children in your class and play games that draw attention to initial and final sounds and letters.

The preceding ideas have emphasised the place of structured games and play-based contexts as opportunities to develop children's growing phonological and grapho-phonic awareness. As well as this, you will also need to plan for whole-class and group sessions which use texts as a context for your teaching.

Direct teaching: groups and the whole class

You will also need to plan for group and whole-class sessions. In the following
example a reception teacher had been sharing nursery rhymes with her class, using Big
Books and her own poem cards so that children could see the print as they chanted the
words. One of the poems was 'Monkeys on the Bed' (traditional):

> Three little monkeys
> Jumping on the bed.
> One fell off
> And bumped his head.
> Mother called the doctor,
> The doctor said,
> 'No more jumping on the bed.'

The children were delighted with this poem which they learned off by heart very
quickly. The teacher decided that it could be the basis of some shared writing to
consolidate their current understandings. She planned that they would compose a
verse. She began by asking the children if they thought the monkeys would jump on
the bed again and when they said 'yes' she invited the children to help her list, on a flip
chart, other parts of the body which could be at risk. They suggested: 'neck', 'arm',
'leg', 'back', 'knee', 'hand', 'foot', 'chin' and 'nose'. They also suggested two-syllable
words ('bottom', 'shoulder') which the teacher listed in a separate column, saying that
those would be used another day. Then they had to think of places where the monkeys
could be playing and get hurt. She listed these, again in single-syllable and multiple-
syllable columns. In the single-syllable column they had: 'ground', 'chair', 'mat',
'sand(pit)', 'bath', 'tree', 'stairs', 'road', 'street' and 'wood'. She then said that their poem
would be very easy to write now if they could see a word in the first list that rhymed
with one in the second. The two rhymes that they spotted were 'hand/sand' (if they left
out the 'pit') and 'knee/tree'. As the teacher promised, the poem wrote itself and gave
us the following verses:

> Two little monkeys
> Playing in the sand.
> One fell down
> And hurt his hand
>
> One little monkey
> Playing in a tree
> She fell down
> And broke her knee.

In the process of this enjoyable session, the children had been encouraged to look at
how phonemes are represented and at features of print in the most pleasurable way.
All were attentive and several children did not want to stop trying to add more rhymes.
The activity was purposeful, was set within a meaningful context and linked to the *NLS*
requirements for word level work. The teacher's aims were clear, her planning was
staged thoughtfully and she kept the teaching in context throughout. Although the
lessons learned were made explicit by the teacher, she was well aware that her class
was learning similar phonic lessons all the time from the routines she regularly

undertook. She also believed that rhyme, word play and games (the rationale for which she put firmly in the area of enjoyment) had a part to play.

Direct teaching: the individual child

Focusing direct phonics teaching when working with an individual child needs very careful planning. Your prior observations, your running records or miscue analysis (see Chapter 4) or your scrutiny of the child's writing will lead you to decide on a teaching point. Depending on the age of the child, you may have more than one teaching point to make.

Here is a teacher working with five-year-old Patrick. He is very fond of *Titch* (Hutchins 1972) and knows it off by heart, but he always says that Titch holds a 'windmill' in his hand, rather than the 'pinwheel' of the text. The teacher has decided to focus on this miscue and is going to make use of Patrick's interest in his own name. She lets Patrick read the story to her and they talk about it briefly. Then she produces a card on which she has written, 'Patrick paints a picture of a purple pinwheel'. They enjoy the alliteration and Patrick reads each word, pointing as he goes. 'Can I really paint a picture of a pinwheel?' asks Patrick. 'Of course,' says his teacher, 'Do you know what a pinwheel is?' A discussion ensues which includes the illustration in the book. The teacher then asks, 'On the card, where does it say pinwheel?' Patrick finds it. 'Where does it say it in the book?' Patrick reads the whole sentence and finds it again. 'Oh!' he says, 'I always say "windmill" but it says "pinwheel" doesn't it?' Further discussion, stressing the initial letters of both words, consolidates the learning and the teacher leaves Patrick to paint a picture of a pinwheel on the card.

To describe this teaching takes rather longer than the actual exchanges and it is worth pointing out that focused teaching like this need not be drawn out. The prior observation, the clear aim, the prepared material and the maintained focus accomplish the teaching effectively.

Key Stage 1

Whole-class word level teaching

In Key Stage 1, in the majority of schools, phonics is now taught through the *NLS* framework using the 15-minute, whole-class, word level slot in the Literacy Hour. This might be followed up in ensuing group work (guided or independent). In the whole-class slot, you may decide to take your teaching points from a text the class knows well. Bear in mind that the text you choose should be one that lends itself, possibly because it indulges in word play anyway, to close inspection of its words. It should go without saying that a serious, emotionally charged story such as John Burningham's *Granpa* should not be used for this sort of work. An ideal text would be Quentin Blake's *Fantastic Daisy Artichoke*. Lots of work could be done on how the long vowel phoneme 'o-e' and 'oa' (Year 1, Term 3) can represent the same sound as in 'Her three fat cats we like to stroke/Her raven with its awful croak'.

Whole-class word level teaching may also take the form of games. *PIPs* provide a range of these which fall into three types:

- Demonstration: here the teacher models a particular phonic skill to the class maybe using a flip chart and pens, small stretches of text or magnetic letters. For example, you could put up an enlarged fragment of a well-known text with some final phonemes removed. As you read the children supply the phonemes. For example: 'Pat-a-cake, pat-a-cake baker's ma—/Bake me a cake as fast as you ca—'.

- Show me: here the children are asked to respond to a request from the teacher e.g. 'How many phonemes in 'man'? Using small whiteboards (the modern equivalent of the slate) divided into three columns, the children record their phoneme count in pairs. You may also use customised letter fans for these games. For instance, the teacher asks the children to identify the vowel in the middle of 'man'; they show on fans which have all the vowels written on them. The advantage of this type of game is that it enables the teacher to make a rapid assessment of the responses and use errors and misconceptions as a basis for the speedy re-teaching of the objective.
- Get up and go: here the children are physically active in their response to the teacher's commands. For instance, in 'Full Circle', each child has a phoneme card to hold. The teacher calls out the first word which might be 'toad'. 't' , 'oa' and 'd' stand up and make the word. Then the teacher calls out 'toast'. Child 'd' sits down and is replaced by 's' and 't'. 'Boast' is next, so initial phoneme 't' sits down with 'b' taking her place. So the game goes until 'toad' is reached again at which all the children shout 'Full circle!' Note how well a text such as *Fantastic Daisy Artichoke* or Blake's earlier well-loved rhyming text, *Mr Magnolia*, would lend itself to such a game.

All these games require thoughtful preparation on your part but, if you are using *PIPs*, then the manual does much of this for you but you will still have to prepare the materials.

Group word level teaching

It is when children read in groups that we can be sure our whole-class phonics teaching has been effective. We need to know that the children can apply knowledge learned from the kind of work described above to their strategies when working on continuous stretches of text. It is here also that we help children to bring back together all their reading skills by integrating phonic and graphic strategies with the other cue-systems (or searchlights). As well as warming the content of the book to be read, remind the children of some of the recent phonic work you have done that you hope they will remember when they read. An example would be that if you had been looking together at the 'o-e' split digraph, you would find one example in the text e.g. 'bone' and reassure them that they will be able to read similar words without problem.

Independent group work could be used as a time when children do a 'word hunt' for examples of whatever your focus has been. They could also use a CD-ROM such as *Oxford Reading Tree Rhyme and Analogy* (Sherston) to reinforce earlier teaching points.

Key Stage 2

By the time children reach Key Stage 2 their phonic knowledge should be reasonably secure. Of course, there will be children who are still struggling and they may still need the kind of phonic teaching described above. The *NLS* has published materials (*Additional Literacy Support (ALS)* DfEE 1999d) that are designed to support such children and make use of the sort of games already mentioned. In Key Stage 2 children must move on from early phonic and graphic knowledge to more complex areas of spelling.

The *NLS* provides a useful set of spelling materials in the form of a *Spelling Bank* (DfEE 1999e). Drawing from the *NLS* objectives, this provides many ideas for working with older children and places strong emphasis on investigative and interactive approaches. The strength of the materials is that sets of relevant words are ready-made, the children are encouraged to form hypotheses, try these out and then to explain the underlying rule.

Other routes

There are, of course, other ways of sustaining children's phonological awareness at Key Stage 2. More sophisticated alphabet books, such as Oxfam's *W is for World* (Cave), provide a useful means of reinforcing alphabetic knowledge through material that is appropriately pitched. It is also important to sustain children's interest in rhyme in Key Stage 2; children with weak phonological skills will benefit from regularly hearing, reading and writing rhyming poetry. In addition, they will enjoy nonsense poetry and tongue twisters. Working with homophones (words that sound the same but are spelled differently such as 'their' and 'there', 'through' and 'threw') can also help children develop their phonic knowledge and increase their spelling power. With older children, you could try compiling a class list of homophones and then ask the children to select pairs of homophones which they think could be used to form pairs of rhymes in a nonsense poem or in a joke. First demonstrate the technique by sharing and then composing a whole-class homophone poem; then ask the children to select some more homophones from the class list in order to write their own poems.

Games such as Hangman, Boggle, Shannon's Game and Scrabble can be used to develop phonic knowledge as well as to increase children's confidence in spelling. They encourage children to inspect likely patterns and letter sequences and to make their implicit knowledge explicit in their efforts to play the game. A seven-year-old playing Hangman was heard to say 'You need a vowel in there' and a nine-year-old said that you could not have anything except a vowel after the three consonants 'scr' and so quickly got the word 'scream'. For further guidance on these games see the suggestions for further reading on p. 93.

Glossary of Terms

ALLITERATION: words in a phrase or sentence which begin with the same sound, e.g. 'Peter Piper picked a peck of pickled peppers'.

ANALYTIC PHONICS: an approach to the teaching of phonics which works by analysing chunks of words and encouraging pattern detection across words.

BLEND (verb): the process of merging phonemes together to decode a word. *Blend* (noun) is sometimes used to refer to a 'cluster' of sounds which run together e.g. 'br' ('bread') or 'spl' ('split').

CLUSTER: sounds which run together (see examples under *Blend* (noun)).

CONSONANT(S): a sound which is produced when the speaker interrupts the air flow with lips, tongue or throat; the letters that usually occur at the beginnings and ends of syllables (all letters of the alphabet except for vowels; the letter 'y' can also function as a vowel as in 'ay', 'ey', 'oy').

CONSONANT DIGRAPH: two consonants which represent one phoneme, e.g. 'ch', 'gh', 'ph', 'sh', 'wh', 'gn'.

DIGRAPHS: two letters representing one phoneme, e.g. 'ch', 'ai' (see *Consonant digraph* and *Vowel digraph*).

DIPHTHONG: two vowel sounds which combine together to make a new sound within a syllable. The mouth changes position during the sounding process, e.g. 'cow', 'oil', 'they', 'toy', 'out', 'few' ('w' functions as a vowel).

DOUBLED CONSONANTS: two identical consonants which make the sound of one consonant, e.g. 'bb', 'dd'.

GRAPHEME: the smallest unit of sound represented as a written symbol. The 26 letters of the alphabet are graphemes and so are groups of letters which emerge as one sound, e.g. 'ow' as in 'hollow'.

GRAPHIC KNOWLEDGE: knowledge which draws from visual cues; relates to recognising whole words, common letter patterns and parts of words such as prefixes and suffixes.

LONG VOWEL SOUNDS: vowel sounds in the English language that are also the names of the alphabet letters, 'A', 'E', 'I', 'O', 'U'. While there are other long vowel sounds, for instance the 'oo' in 'hoot', this definition is useful because it distinguishes them from short vowel sounds. (NB vowel length can be influenced by dialect and stress within a word.)

MONOSYLLABIC: a word consisting of one syllable, e.g. 'bun'.

ONSET AND RIME: 'onset' is the consonant or cluster of consonants at the beginning of a word or syllable which precede the vowel, e.g. str(-ing). 'Rime' is the rest of the word or syllable, including the vowel, which enables the word to rhyme with other words, e.g.(str-)ing.

PHONEME: the smallest unit of sound that can be spoken or heard such as 'b' in 'bat'. Meaning changes with the replacement of the phoneme, e.g. 'cat' or 'bag'. Over 44 vowel and consonant phonemes have been identified in English. *Phonemic awareness* is the ability to detect such phoneme distinctions.

PHONETICS: the study of speech sounds, e.g. how they are produced in the mouth and how they are heard by the ear.

PHONIC KNOWLEDGE: 'the skills of segmentation and blending, knowledge of the alphabetic code and understanding of the principles which underpin how the code is used in reading and spelling' (DfEE/1999b).

PHONOLOGICAL AWARENESS: the ability to hear and detect difference in sounds; may operate at the level of syllables, onset and rime or phoneme.

POLYSYLLABIC: a word that has more than one syllable, e.g. 'caterpillar'.

PREFIX: an affix at the beginning of a word, e.g. '*dis*appear' or '*un*pleasant'.

SEGMENT: hearing and isolating the individual phonemes in a word. When a child spells a word she has to select the appropriate grapheme for each phoneme she detects. Note that when a child BLENDS she has the word in front of her and decodes it phoneme by phoneme whereas when she SEGMENTS, it is in her head and she represents it phoneme by phoneme.

SHORT VOWEL: sounds the sound qualities of the vowels in such words as 'bag', 'beg', 'big', 'bog', bug'. If a word has a short vowel the final consonant needs to be doubled when you add suffixes such as '-ing,' '-er' and '-ed' as in the words 'begging', 'bigger' and 'bugged'. (NB vowel length can be influenced by dialect and stress within a word.)

SILENT LETTERS: letters used in the spelling of a word which do not have a sound in the word; these can occur at the beginning, middle or end of words, e.g. 'thought', 'knock', 'thumb' and 'psalm'; 'e' is frequently silent at the end of words, e.g. 'rose', 'made', where it often signals a long vowel sound for the preceding vowel.

SPLIT DIGRAPH: a vowel digraph (e.g. 'ie', 'oe') when it is separated by a consonant and retains its sound ('ie' – 'ti_e_'/'ti_me_'; 'pi_e_'/'pi_le_'; 'oe' – 'to_e_'/'to_ne_'; 'ho_e_'/'ho_me_'). (This convention used to be described as the 'magic e' rule when children were told that the vowel at the end of the word made the preceding vowel 'say' its name.)

SUFFIX: an affix at the end of a word, e.g. 'count*ed*' and 'help*ful*'.

SYLLABLE: a rhythmic segment of a word, spoken or written, which is composed of a combination of vowel(s) plus consonant(s) or consonant(s) plus vowel(s).

SYNTHETIC PHONICS: an approach to the teaching of phonics which works by isolating the phonemes in a word. The phonemes are then blended together to decode the word.

VOWEL DIGRAPH: a combination of two vowels that represent a single sound. Examples of vowel digraphs include: 'ai', 'ay', 'ee', 'ie', 'oa', 'au'.

VOWELS: sounds which are produced with no, or relatively little, interruption to the air flow from lips, tongue or throat movement; letters that usually occur in the middle of syllables ('a', 'e', 'i', 'o', 'u'. The letter 'y' can also function as a vowel as in 'ay', 'ey', 'oy').

Further reading

Dombey, H. and Moustafa, M. (1998) *Whole to Part Phonics: How Children Learn to Read and Spell.* London: CLPE.

Kelly, A. (1998) 'Spelling', in Graham, J. and Kelly, A. (eds) *Writing Under Control: Teaching Writing in the Primary School.* London: David Fulton Publishers.

Laycock, L. and Washtell, A. (1996) *Curriculum Bank: Spelling and Phonics Key Stage 2.* Leamington Spa: Scholastic.

Layton, L. *et al.* (1997) *Sound Practice, Phonological Awareness in the Classroom.* London: David Fulton Publishers.

Palmer, S. (2000) *A Little Alphabet Book.* Oxford: OUP.

Thompson, G. B. and Nicholson, T. (eds) (1999) *Learning to Read Beyond Phonics and Whole Language.* Newark: International Reading Association.

Washtell, A. and Laycock, L. (1996) *Curriculum Bank: Spelling and Phonics Key Stage 1.* Leamington Spa: Scholastic.

NLS materials

DfEE (1999b) *The National Literacy Strategy, Phonics: Progression in Phonics.* London: DfEE.

DfEE (1999d) *The National Literacy Strategy, Additional Literacy Support Module.* London: DfEE.

DfEE (1999e) *The National Literacy Strategy Spelling Bank.* London: DfEE.

GROUP READING/GUIDED READING

For many years some teachers have chosen to organise children so that they read together in groups. The *NLS* has, to some extent, formalised this with the inclusion of 'Guided Reading' into the structure of the Literacy Hour. Guided reading is distinguished by the presence of the teacher and the organisation of the children into differentiated groups. Group reading has never been so sharply defined and covers a multitude of different practices. What we offer in this section is an open framework for organising group reading as well as an account of what guided reading looks like in practice.

Why?

Group reading activities are an ideal way of developing greater understanding than might be achieved individually. Children will not only be reading; they will be talking about their reading with each other and with you. This is a forum where children can develop a critical perspective. Asked to reflect on the opening chapter of *Fire, Bed and Bone* (Branford), Year 6 children shared with each other the point at which they realised the narrator was a dog. They analysed what it was that gave them the clue and what they found themselves doing then (i.e. reading back and forth to search for further confirmation).

Children also develop particular reading abilities (such as predicting plot development, discussing characterisation, sharing different views or extracting key points from an information text) in a teacher economical way! Reading in a group can support both the struggling and the more competent reader. A child who is ready for a challenge can join a group of slightly more able readers. Such a group can be given a more difficult book than individuals could handle on their own and readers will be able to persevere given group support. In a group reading of *Mrs Wobble the Waitress* (Ahlberg) a Year 1 child was overheard telling a less experienced reader that 'You can read on and then you get it'. It was the group context that enabled a child to make explicit a particular strategy.

Guided reading has been developed in order to make the most efficient use of teacher time. OFSTED's (1996) findings that teachers spent too much time trying to listen to each child led to the formulation of 'Guided Reading'. With the children organised in 'ability groups', working from sets of the same book, the teacher is in a position to focus on points that are relevant and appropriate for the whole group. One further point about reading in groups: it does seem that boys respond more positively to the active and interactive nature of such readings so incorporating the reading of plays, and encouraging expressive reading aloud of well-chosen passages could all contribute to their involvement in reading.

How?

You will need multiple copies of a range of texts (stories, plays, poems, information books). Before you start you will need to spend some time planning the session. As with any kind of work with texts, the more intimate you are with their contents, the more focused the activity you provide will be. Read your chosen book through and decide on: suitable stopping points, vocabulary you want to 'gloss' with the children and any particular conceptual difficulties you anticipate the children might have. Initially, all this takes time, but it is time well spent as you can keep activity cards with this planning recorded for future use. These could be stored centrally in wallets together with activity cards or sheets (e.g. questions to encourage prediction in a story, activities involving use of the index in an information book).

In the Literacy Hour, guided reading slots are timetabled for 20 minutes and this is a useful length of time for group reading too. Actual sessions can be organised in many different ways: some teachers have established 'Literature Circles' in which children who have been reading the same book in their own time come together with their reading logs to talk about their responses (which might include additional research carried out on the internet or with a CD-ROM). What follows are just a few suggestions of ways you might structure group work. For convenience we have grouped them according to three genres of texts – fiction, non-fiction and poetry – but you will see that many of the activities could be used with different genres.

For those of you who are implementing guided reading rather than group reading, you will need to appreciate that it is the children in the group who are reading rather than you reading to them. It is the chance for the children to respond to the modelling that you have offered them in Shared Reading (see above). With younger children the session starts with a joint warm-up in which the teacher introduces the book and shares potential areas of interest and difficulty; this is followed by the children reading their books independently and at their own pace. The teacher then 'tunes in' to each child in turn allowing her to focus on individual needs. Points in common can be discussed at the end, as can more general reflections on the book. More fluent readers may read allocated passages silently but the session will be 'topped and tailed' in the same way. You will find more detail in the guided reading examples which follow the group reading examples below.

Group reading: Fiction (a picture book), Reception/Key Stage 1

This is an activity for young, inexperienced readers that will develop their response to literature and understandings of features of texts.

1. Before reading

Look at some or all of the following with the children:

(a) the picture on the front cover;
(b) the title of the book;
(c) the pictures.

Depending on the age of the children and their experience of working in a group you might decide to leave them to look at one particular aspect, such as the front cover. They could brainstorm their ideas about it ready to report back to you. You would probably only leave them for a few minutes.

2. The reading

Read the book aloud to the group, perhaps more than once.

3. After reading

Give the children their own copies to browse through with a specific task in mind (e.g. finding a particular character in the illustrations, spotting letters from their name).

Group reading: Fiction (a novel), Key Stage 1/2

This is an activity for more experienced readers but one that could be adapted for use with less experienced children. It is intended to develop children's imaginative response to literature.

1. Before reading

Give the children a short time to consider what can be found out about the book by looking at some of the following:

(a) the front cover;
(b) the title;
(c) the blurb;
(d) the first few pages.

Join the children to get their feedback and to find out what they know about the author and any other books s/he may have written.

2. The reading

Decide how much you want the children to read in the session (perhaps up to a key event which you have identified). There are different ways of organising how they go about the reading:

(a) you could read aloud to them from the opening chapter;
(b) they could take it in turns to read a page each;
(c) they could read silently;
(d) they could listen to a prepared tape.

Before they start reading, you will need to let them know what particular aspects of the text you will be asking them to focus on next (use *NLS* objectives to guide you).

3. After reading

After reading a chapter or more (but not the whole book) give the children some way of structuring and drawing together their discussion. You might ask them to:

(a) list ways in which the *setting* of the book is established in the opening chapter; draw annotated pictures or maps of the setting as they envisage it so far, with the annotations referring to relevant passages from the text;
(b) make posters about the main *characters*, adding some key words, based on their reading so far;
(c) list their *predictions* of what might happen.

Group reading: Poetry, Key Stage 1/2

This group activity helps develop children's active response to literature. It can also be organised as a whole-class lesson. Because you choose an appropriate poem it can be adapted for children in Key Stage 1 and used throughout Key Stage 2. You can also easily differentiate the activities. You need to choose a suitable poem, one with a clear pattern and rhythm and one that you think will engage the children.

1. Before reading

Divide the class into four groups. Give each group a version of the poem prepared in one of the following ways:

a) without the title;
b) with the last two lines missing;
c) with words/phrases blanked out (this procedure is known as 'cloze' – short for 'closure' – and the words you choose to remove will add to or lessen the difficulty of this version);
d) cut up for re-assembling. This 'sequencing' activity is based on the coherence and logical ordering that is found in all texts (large chunks will be easier to work with than lines or half lines so prepare according to the competence of the group).

2. The reading

The children work in groups with their version. You will need to emphasise that the activity is not about guessing what was in the poet's head but about the ideas that the children have. It is best to take feedback in this order: title, cloze, last two lines, cut-up sections. Use the children's ideas as a springboard for discussing issues such as what makes a good title, or why the poet made particular vocabulary choices.

3. After reading

An extension of this activity is to ask the children to make a couple of statements about the poem (e.g. 'It is sad', 'I like the description of the old man's house'). Then help the children to turn these into questions ('Why is it sad?', 'What is good about the description?'). They can either answer these themselves or pass them on to another group. This version of 'traditional' comprehension-type questions has the advantage of starting with the children's reading and understanding of the poem. The whole activity invites close scrutiny of the text itself and you will find children referring closely and confidently to it.

4. Rereading

A final activity is to ask each group to prepare a group reading of the poem. By this time they know it well and will have explored aspects such as voice, audience and hidden meanings. Close knowledge of this kind informs and gives resonance to such group readings.

Group reading: Non-fiction, Key Stage 2

Note that these activities can be adjusted for work with children throughout the key stages. They are particularly important because, as we stated in the introduction to this chapter, many children find reading non-fiction texts difficult.

1. Before reading

There are three things to consider and to plan activities around as necessary:

(i) Check that the text is as reader friendly as possible. Talking about the content or providing a chart or diagram can help but it is also important that children know about and can locate the features that are typical of non-fiction texts: contents page, index, glossary, sub-headings.

(ii) Make sure that the children are clear about the purpose of their reading. Initial activities that will help with this include brainstorming what they already know about a topic and identifying what they would like to find out about.

(iii) Give children practice in close reading, combining this with a search for key points. Any one of these activities will help:

  (a) Cloze procedure: filling in key terms can inform you as to the extent of children's preliminary knowledge. It can foster interest and close reading and can help you decide whether or not a text is suitable for the children. It is best used with short passages.

  (b) Sequencing is another invaluable technique whether it is with words, sentences, paragraphs or pictures; again this demands close reading and can be used to draw the children's attention to words such as 'moreover' and 'nevertheless' which can be easily overlooked but may be fundamental in creating an argument.

  (c) Adding irrelevant words or sentences that children have to *delete* is an entertaining way of helping children to pay close attention to the text. Bobbie Neate (1992 p. 149) provides the following example of this: 'Stone Age people found out how to make a fire. They did not like central heating. They twisted or rubbed a stick in a groove of another piece of wood, while watching television'. *Errata* (Wood and Allen) is a book where children have to detect the historical errors in the pictures.

2. The reading

All the above activities may seem lengthy (and you would want to use them selectively across a number of sessions), but they should give children some idea of the kind of approach to reading they will need to adopt. They should help children decide whether they need to *skim* the whole of a passage or book, or *scan* to look for specific words or ideas.

As children read they could do any of the following:

(a) *highlight* key points (words or sentences);
(b) *note* answers to questions they have posed (see 1. (ii) above);
(c) *list* information under headings previously determined by or decided with you.

3. After reading

The children could re-present the information for another audience as:

(a) an information book or glossary about the topic for a younger class;
(b) a poster, chart, flow diagram for the rest of the class or for an assembly;
(c) a talk for the class, another class, the school, etc.

The children could use a CD-ROM that covers the same content. Set a challenge to find out three facts about dinosaurs (using the excellent *Look! Hear! Talking Topics* [Sherston] for example) and then to check these against at least two information books.

Guided reading: Picture book – Jasper's Beanstalk (Inkpen and Butterworth) – with Reception

1. Before reading

Look at:

(a) the front cover: 'What are all the things he's carrying?' 'What do you think he's going to do?'
(b) turn the pages with the children and stop where you think there might be a conceptual difficulty e.g. when Jasper inserts a bamboo cane to mark the spot where his bean is planted; when Jasper protects his bean from night-time slugs and snails;
(c) find a suitable stopping point, e.g. where Jasper throws his slow-growing bean away in despair, and ask the children to predict what will happen;
(d) focus on particular words such as the days of the week which structure the story or the word 'hoed' which the children may not know. All the tools in the pictures provide their verbs in the written text (e.g. 'hoe'/'hoed'; 'rake'/'raked') except for 'spade'/'dig' so you may need to tell the children that you dig with a spade.

2. The reading

The children read aloud, each at their own pace (which may mean they are not reading in unison). The teacher tunes in to each child in turn and makes notes on significant reading behaviour.

3. After reading

Ask the children to find the best bit in the story and to give their reasons for their choice. You may find they make those all important links with their own experience. For instance Matthew (5 and a half) said, 'I like the slugs and snails page best because I like night time. The moon faces my bedroom and I like the moon. When my brother wakes me up I look at the moon and it makes me fall asleep again'. Another child said, 'I know another story about night time when a little bear goes to the moon' (the reference is to Jill Murphy's *Whatever Next?*).

Guided reading: Short story – 'George and the Dragon' (in McCaughrean) – with Year 5

1. Before reading

Ask the children what they already know of the story of George and the Dragon. If necessary, tell them that dragons often feature as mythical beasts and that the character of George is probably based on a real life Christian martyr. If you plan to focus on something like the figurative language, which is a distinctive feature of this retelling, then briefly recap previous work on this.

2. The reading

With older children, you will need to decide on the mode of reading for the session. If all the children are reading fluently then you may want them to read to themselves. However, if there are some who still need support with decoding, then you may decide on a mixture of silent reading and reading aloud which is the model we offer below. In the *NLS* model there is no place for the teacher reading aloud; however, you may decide that an important part of warming the text is that you read the opening paragraph or two for them.

(a) Ask the children to read the first two paragraphs to themselves. Stop to discuss challenging words (e.g. 'balefully' and 'palisades'), encouraging the children to predict using the context. Use this as an opportunity to remind the children about strategies for difficult words.

(b) Then the children silently read up to a dramatic point, for instance where Princess Sabra is chosen in the town lottery as the next victim for the rapacious dragon. Ask the children for their predictions of what will happen next.

(c) To vary the reading, the next section could be read out loud by the children. They could take it in turns or read independently (as above) with you tuning in. This is where you might pick up on examples of figurative language such as the onomatopoeic effect of the 'chank chank chank' of the city bell.

(d) The children read to the end.

3. After reading

Children often go on thinking about what happens after the story has ended on the page. With this story, you could ask the children to speculate about the celebrations in the town after the dragon's defeat.

Independent group work

In all of the examples above, the teacher, or another adult, is working with the children which means that several groups will need to work independently. Among all the other things that children could be doing in this time – such as writing their predictions as to how the story they met in Shared Reading will develop, planning a fable based on their reading of other fables, researching the author of a book they are currently reading (on the internet perhaps) – this period of group work may well be a good time to set up some children with a CD-ROM with a specific task to do. For instance, a pair of children from a Year 2 or 3 class would benefit from working with Dorling Kindersley's *My First*

Incredible Amazing Dictionary. If you have familiarised yourself with this CD-ROM and you know the particular interests of your children, you will be able to ask them to find and record definitions of, for instance, wild animals and different sports. This will require them to scan the dictionary for each letter, selecting animals etc. as appropriate and collecting definitions. As the CD also offers a range of games and spelling activities the children could go on to these if they finish their task. Story-based CD-ROMs, such as *Spot's Busy Day* (Europress) suitable for very young children, could also be used at this time.

Further reading

Mallett, M. (1999) *Young Researchers, Informational Reading and Writing in the Early and Primary Years*. London: Routledge.
Smith, V. (1999) 'Everyone's a Criminal? Reflections on Critical Reading in the Primary School', *English in Education* **33**(3).
Wray, D. and Lewis, M. (1998) *Practical Ways to Teach Reading for Information*. Reading: Reading and Language Information Centre, University of Reading.

READING PARTNERS

In this section we look at the routine of pairing younger and older classes so that a child reads regularly with a reading partner from another class. This is also sometimes known as 'paired reading', a term coined to describe a technique used when an adult reads with a child (see 'Working with Parents' at the end of this chapter). In order to avoid confusion we will use the term 'reading partners'.

Why?

For the younger child this is an enjoyable routine and the one-to-one attention from an older peer can be highly motivating as well as flattering. It is another valuable opportunity for extra reading practice and, if the routine is carefully structured (see below), it can also be an opportunity for the children to talk about their reading in a non-threatening context.

There is much potential for the older partner too. As you yourself are probably discovering, being placed in the role of teacher means you have to think hard about the learning processes involved; it means standing back from the learning and trying to make it clear for a less experienced learner. For instance, the older children have to think about the books they will share with the younger partner; this means thinking about the content, illustrations and language that make a book appropriate for a younger reader. They will realise that choosing a book for someone else also means that they need to know a bit about the reader's interests. This routine offers a meaningful context for children to consider these different aspects of the reading process.

Where schools operate reading partnerships successfully, the benefits for boys are especially noticeable. When younger boys see older role models enthusiastically involved in reading their own views of reading are likely to be positively affected.

When it comes to the actual reading session itself, this metacognition (thinking about thinking) is pushed further. When children read with less experienced readers than themselves, they are forced to make explicit things that readers do. They may not have needed to think about or articulate these things before. In the earlier section 'Reading Aloud to Children', we talked about Vygotsky's idea of a 'zone of proximal development' and this is another instance of its relevance. For the younger child the partnership allows for development within the 'zpd', while for the older child the routine itself is empowering as it pushes their thinking on.

All this makes reading partnerships a particularly powerful routine for struggling older readers. Confidence and motivation are typically very low for these children and the opportunity to work with easier texts in a setting that genuinely requires them is a valuable one. And, of course, the opportunity to stand back from the reading process in the way described above is equally as important for this group of readers.

How?

Reading partnerships work best as part of a whole-school policy in which classes are systematically paired and there are regular timetabled slots for the routine. However, it can be organised between two classes (e.g. with a mentor, or another student in the school). In some schools it runs across the whole academic year; others prefer to use it across just one term. Whatever the pattern, you and your colleague will need to plan both the partnerships and the sessions with care. Decide on partners first, bearing in mind reading experience, personality, interests and also gender considerations. This is a routine that needs careful preparation if it is to be effective; in particular, give the children a clear structure for the session.

The older class

1. Introduction

This could be done as a whole class and would need to include:

- introducing the routine;
- looking at a range of picture books for younger children and using these as the basis for a discussion about the kinds of books younger children enjoy. This list could be brainstormed in groups of two or three and then fed back to the whole class who could come up with an initial shortlist of books they might take to the first session;
- shaping a 'mini-conference' that the older child could carry out with the younger one. Again children could think about questions they might ask the younger child (favourite books, authors, topics, etc.) which could be collated to construct a shared prompt sheet;
- deciding on a structure for the session. Obviously this will vary but a typical structure might be:

5 minutes	Older child reads to younger child
5 minutes	Mini-conference
5 minutes	Younger child reads
2/3 minutes	Praise, review, and looking forward to the next session.

2. Pairing up

You will need to plan the actual session itself with the other teacher and decide how you will physically organise the children (for instance, half going to each class). In one school two classes met in the hall. It is probably best to keep early sessions quite short and build up towards the kind of structure described above. You might decide on an initial introductory session during which you talk to the two classes and then put the partners together for a few minutes in which the older child shares a pre-chosen book with the younger one. The next week's slot could be a little longer to include the conference. As with other routines, you may feel that you have to spend a lot of time at the outset establishing ground rules and clear expectations about behaviour; this is time well spent as once these are all in place you can get on with the important job of teaching.

What is your role in these sessions? Firstly, it is an invaluable opportunity for observing the children (see Chapter 4). Secondly, you may well find you need to intervene from time to time to keep the children focused or to make suggestions. For instance, we recently overheard a teacher's suggestion to a Year 6 child that he encourage his younger partner to use initial sounds. To another Year 6 child the advice was to be less punitive when the child made miscues. To yet another child from this class the teacher suggested that the younger child could tell the story from the pictures rather than be made to pick her way through a written text that she was not yet ready to read. The way you introduce and conclude these sessions is important too; it is yet another opportunity to talk about books and reading with children. You might, for example, ask two children each week to provide a very brief account of what they have read and learned. Or you might comment on particular book choices the children have made, saying why you think they were so appropriate. A teacher commented on a child's choice of *Handa's Surprise* (Browne), saying 'I liked your choice of this book; it's a wonderful story and it's got lots of the different fruits that we are learning about in our food project'.

Some teachers have found it helpful to construct a brief sheet that the children jointly fill in at the end of the session; one such example included the titles of the books the children had shared and was signed by both children. It is a very simple idea but one that gives the children ownership of the routine and gives the teacher a record.

3. Following up

Some time needs to be spent after the session asking the children how it went (what went well? any difficulties?), what they learned, what they might do differently next time, what book they are going to choose, etc. Again, a whole-class lesson would be appropriate here with the children forming pairs to discuss specific questions before reporting back to the class. You can use this time for more forward planning too; collecting books around a theme that the younger class will be working on (e.g. 'Toys', 'Food', 'Light') or making some books (see 'Books Made by Children' in Chapter 2).

The younger class

There will be many points in common with those made above. In particular, the section on 'Pairing up' applies to both classes.

1. Introduction

Again, a brief whole-class introduction to the routine would be appropriate. After telling the children that they will be reading regularly with an older partner you might propose that they think about choosing a favourite book ready to show their partner. You could collect the suggestions they make and write them up on a large sheet of paper in the book area. Later you and/or the children could collect the books and put them in a specially labelled box ready for the first session.

2. Following up

A focused follow-up session with the younger children might include asking them what they enjoyed about the session, what books their partners brought for them, and what they would like to take next week.

Further reading

Maybin, J. and Mercer, N. (1992) '"Scaffolding" Literacies: Supporting Readers in YTS and Primary School', in Dombey, H. and Robinson, M. (eds) *Literacy for the Twenty-first Century.* Brighton: The Literacy Centre, Brighton Polytechnic.
SCAA video *Gathering Evidence of Children's Understanding In Reading* (Albert and Junior reading together *Oscar Got the Blame* by Tony Ross).

READING TO THE TEACHER

Why?

For many years the one-to-one reading session between teacher and child was the only reading routine that really 'counted'. Confined almost entirely to the early years, it typically consisted of children reading a short extract from their current teacher-chosen 'reading book', with the teacher recording the pages read and words to be learned. The 'ideal' teacher heard her children read every day. Such practice was based on a partial view of what comprises reading; it is one where decoding is privileged above aspects such as understanding, response, personal involvement and strategies for choosing books.

In 1981, Southgate and Arnold's research cast a different light on this practice. They revealed that short spurts of reading practice were not as productive as fewer, but longer sessions. From their work came the idea of developing the session into one which included some discussion with the children about their reading. Through such discussion the child's response to literature was developed as well as their decoding skills. Terminology changed too; with Liz Waterland's (1985) discussion of the 'apprenticeship approach' to reading came the idea of reading 'with' children. More recently the term 'reading conference' has gained in popularity. The Centre for Language in Primary Education (CLPE) makes extensive use of the term and practice in its publications. What all these shifts denote is a broadening of the view of what might go on when teacher and child meet on a one-to-one basis. There is no doubt that in this wider sense, reading to the teacher is still a tremendously important routine. It provides the context for noting and teaching to a child's individual reading needs (see Chapter 4 for information on informal sampling, running records and miscue analysis, all of which can be carried out during a reading conference).

As mentioned earlier, OFSTED criticised this routine as ineffective and time consuming and 'Guided Reading' was developed as an alternative. However, many teachers still feel that one-to-one reading is an important part of their work with children, particularly for those children who are struggling.

How?

(NB For convenience in this section we will refer to the child as 'he'.)

Organising the session

There are some steps that need to be included in any reading session with one child, whatever the child's age. These are:

1. 'warming up' the text;
2. reading:
   (a) together (for inexperienced readers)
   (b) alone (for more experienced readers);
3. reviewing the book;
4. concluding the session.

Before you start, make sure the child feels relaxed and comfortable. If possible, try to sit next to him at the same height level. The important thing is to establish a positive atmosphere so that he feels at ease.

Reading with beginners (Nursery and Reception/Key Stage 1)

Step 1 'Warming up' the text

Start by talking about the book together: look at the pictures; encourage the child to predict the story; make links with the child's own experience where appropriate. Encourage the child to handle the book and turn the pages. You may also decide to read the book to the child.

Step 2a Reading together

Read the book again but this time ask the child to join in with you. He may do this intermittently or may 'echo' you as you read. As you read, point to the print and ask the child to turn the pages. From time to time make sure that you ask him to show you where to start reading. Talk about the story and pictures with him.

Step 2b Child reads alone

Ask the child if he would like to try on his own. At this stage some of the things you would look out for are:

- 'reading-like behaviour' (the child's retelling of the story in his own words as well as the words of the story);

- any predictions he makes about the story;
- any comments he makes as he reads;
- how he turns the pages;
- whether he is 'reading the pictures';
- whether he is trying to track the print (using a finger maybe);
- evidence of:
  - one-to-one correspondence (the spoken word matches the written word)
  - phonic knowledge
  - graphic knowledge
  - alphabetic knowledge.

If the book is a rhyming one (like Allan and Janet Ahlberg's *Each Peach Pear Plum*), see if he can hear and/or find some of the rhyming words.

Step 3 Reviewing the book

We have argued that developing children's confidence in responding to books is important and it is essential to build in this reflective strand from as early as possible. As well as asking the child what he thought of the book and which characters, illustrations and sections he liked, you can also raise more general issues about the child's reading. This might include what he reads at home, where he likes to read, what kinds of books he enjoys.

Step 4 Concluding the session

Commend the child for his achievements and discuss what book he might read next, helping him choose if appropriate.

Reading with moderately fluent readers (Key Stage 1/2)

Step 1 'Warming up' the text

As with beginner readers it is still important to 'warm up' the text (see above).

Step 2a Reading together

As above, but the child should be more responsible for taking the lead in the reading, joining in with confidence (e.g. trying to decode the words), tracking the print (which will tell you how well his one-to-one correspondence is developing), turning the pages, predicting the text and offering his own responses.

Step 2b Child reads alone

You can monitor the early concepts of print as described above. In addition you will be helping the child to develop a wider range of strategies for decoding words. For example, you should give him the time and opportunity to tackle unknown words. If he gets stuck, encourage him to predict what the word might be, using some or all of the following:

- phonic knowledge, e.g. initial and final sounds;
- graphic knowledge, e.g. sight vocabulary;
- grammatical knowledge, e.g. reading ahead and going back to try to insert the problem word;

- contextual understanding, e.g. drawing on existing knowledge of the story to help work out a word, knowing what makes sense;
- picture cues.

You have the difficult job of judging when to supply words for the child and when to ask him to have a go. If he is getting stuck on most of the words then the text is either too hard or he needs reminding to draw on reading strategies (e.g. using initial sounds or prediction). If all else fails, finish the story for him.

You also have to decide what to do if the child makes a mistake. Look at the mistake (or 'miscue') and see if it makes sense or not. For instance, if he reads, 'The duck dived into the *pool'* instead of 'The duck dived into the *pond'* you know he is still making sense of the text. However, if he reads 'The duck dived into the *post'* you know that he has lost the meaning and will find it hard to continue the reading making use of all the cue-systems. This is where you need to stop him and say 'Does that make sense?' and to check that he can see what the graphic and phonic differences are between the two words. Listen hard and note the child's responses to his miscues; they too can be very revealing, as this example from a six-year-old shows. Tom was reading from *Mr Gumpy's Outing* (Burningham) and misread 'cow' for 'children'. He self-corrected straightaway, saying 'No, not "cow", cow's got three letters'. 'Well done!' said his teacher. It is this kind of evidence that can be noted in your records and allows you to target very specific support for the child.

Step 3 Reviewing the book

As above, discuss the child's response to the story, favourite characters, parts of the story, etc. You may want to do this as you go along and it is certainly worth watching out for the child's responses as he reads. As a six-year-old was reading *Winnie the Witch* (Paul and Thomas 1987) he looked at the picture of her house and said, with feeling, 'She's got a high house. I wouldn't like to live there. This gives me the spooks'. He continued the reading with great gusto!

Step 4 Concluding the session

Discuss and commend the child's achievements (e.g. 'I really liked the way you read the page about . . .') and select one or two areas for him to work on (e.g. 'When you're reading on your own and get stuck on a word what can you do to help yourself?'). Choose a suitable book for the child to read independently.

Reading with fluent readers (Key Stage 2)

As children move into and through Key Stage 2 they should be reading an ever greater range of texts and should also be reading silently. Routines such as whole-class quiet reading are therefore very important in providing opportunities for this. Some children will still be experiencing reading difficulties and will need the kind of direct support with decoding strategies suggested above, but for the fluent reader the one-to-one reading session with the teacher will focus less on hearing the child reading aloud and more on encouraging the child's response to his reading and to developing the choices he is making as a reader. What follows is one way of structuring a session with such a fluent reader.

Before you start, try to let the child know that you will be reading with him later that week. He should choose a favourite passage from the book he is currently reading and prepare it to read aloud to you. He should also plan how he will set it in context for you.

Step 1 Previewing

First of all discuss the child's book. Points for discussion could include: why he chose it; the cover; plot; themes; characters; other books he knows by the same author; other books of the same genre (e.g. adventure story, ghost story, information book); the language of the text itself (e.g. use of dialogue, sentence length, imagery).

Step 2 Child reads alone

The child talks about his chosen extract and reads it aloud to you. Things that you will be looking for include: overall understanding and fluency; expression, intonation and response to punctuation; miscues; self-correction strategies.

Step 3 Reviewing

Concentrate on the extract itself. You can pick up on anything you observed in Step 2 but also develop discussion about particular characters (e.g. 'Tell me what you think Roxanne might be going to do now'), significant plot developments, or the language of the text (e.g. 'Can you find an example of dialogue which shows us that the visitors speak differently from the mountain community?').

Step 4 Concluding the session and looking ahead

You can discuss the child's reading more generally, perhaps finding out what he is reading at home or whether he has used information books that week. Finally you can decide on an action plan with the child. This could include activities to be done when he finishes the book (e.g. review card or recommendation for other children); keeping a reading log of all his reading in one week; specific strategies arising from the reading session; a particular book recommendation.

Conclusion

Finding time in a busy teaching day for one-to-one reading sessions has always been a challenge for teachers. If, when working within the Literacy Hour, you have been able to establish well-structured and monitored guided reading times, there may be less pressure on you to have one-to-one sessions with all children every week. Decide which children you feel will benefit from such attention and timetable this in each week. Some teachers have support from parents and helpers but you do need to be extremely rigorous in liaising with, sharing ideas with and supporting such helpers. They complement but do not replace you.

Further reading

Arnold, H. (1982) *Listening to Children Reading.* Sevenoaks: Hodder & Stoughton.
Campbell, R. (1988) *Hearing Children Read.* London: Routledge.

WORKING WITH PARENTS

PACT is the acronym commonly used to describe arrangements made between Parents and Children and Teachers, all working together to promote literacy. The term is used to describe schemes, set up by the school, in which parents are involved in helping their own child at home with reading. Typically the child takes a book home, the parent is encouraged to read to the child and to listen to the child reading, and then to enter comments on a reading record card or in a booklet.

Parents have not always been regarded as a resource. Many schools in the past kept them at arm's length and certainly believed that parental attempts to help with reading were likely to do more harm than good. *Children and their Primary Schools* (The Plowden Report, DES 1967), *A Language for Life* (The Bullock Report, DES 1975) and numerous research projects set up in the 1970s and 1980s (details below) changed our perceptions of the role of parents, showing that children made more literacy progress where parents were involved and encouraged their children's reading. In fact, parents have always cared about their children's literacy and there are few schools nowadays which do not realise how important it is to work in cooperation with parents. Many schools now have PACT schemes and the evidence is that they improve attitudes and attainment.

Why?

Parents are their children's first teachers and many would say that they are their children's most natural teachers. They know more about their children than teachers will ever know and their investment in their children is greater and more personal. They spend more time with their children than teachers do, and the time they give can frequently be one-to-one.

In school, the individual attention and ample time which are critical in the process of becoming literate are harder to reproduce. Parents give their children 'differentiated' reading lessons; they respond to the child's comments and questions as they arise; they tolerate interruptions; they sense when the child is tired; they judge when to allow the child to take over the reading; they allow the child to have his/her own choice of text; they encourage and understand the personal or private connections that the child makes. Parents are potentially in the very best position to make reading a personally rich and rewarding experience. However, not every parent will model and encourage reading in exactly the way described above. Literacy practices vary tremendously in different communities as Shirley Brice Heath (1983), Hilary Minns (1990) and Eve Gregory (1996) have shown. In some families there may be more story-telling or there may be more recounting of happenings or TV stories. However, there will, in nearly all families, be models of reading and writing in situations where the purposes become clear for children. Checking TV programmes or recipes, writing a note for the milkman or a shopping list are examples of meaningful literacy events. In addition, most parents will respond to children's interest in the environmental print around them and in turn will draw children's attention to print, sharing speculations and observations.

But even if there were to be little of this shared family literacy (and we should be very careful in the assumptions we make that some homes are not literate places), the evidence is very clear that school/home liaison is of great benefit to children's literacy. In the first place, if we find out about how much children have already learned about literacy practices before they come to school and build on this, we need not imagine that we are starting from scratch with totally ignorant children. (This has never been the case though it is only relatively recently that serious attention has been paid to the learning that has gone on before school.) Secondly, if adult males can be encouraged to take a full role in the partnership, school/home liaison can provide an important context for developing boys' views of themselves as readers. Finally, if children feel that their parents and their teachers are talking to each other about them, keeping tabs on their progress and seeing eye to eye about their needs, they will feel far more secure and positive about their learning than if parents and teachers are not exchanging information. In the worst scenario, sometimes fuelled by media comment, parents can mistrust and openly criticise teachers. Children's learning is then adversely affected.

How?

We cannot give here a full recipe for setting up successful PACT schemes though we list below some key points. What must be discussed with parents is the need for reading encounters at home to be enjoyable. This is not as easy to put into practice as it is to state, and it would be a mistake to believe that there is never any conflict in the parent/child reading encounters. Reading raises anxiety levels in parents and often this worry cannot be hidden from children. Parents often want progress to be faster and are alarmed that the child wants the same book again and again, that the child appears to be reciting by heart rather than reading, that the child does not appear able to 'sound out' the words, that the child loses interest quickly. In addition, parents may believe that their own literacy levels are inadequate (and the comments card may present terrors in this respect) and that they cannot keep up with the school's high expectations of them to spend time with their child. For those parents for whom English is a second language the problems may be to do with feeling that they cannot make judgements on their children's reading in English. In this respect, it is important that schools encourage reading in the home languages too. So, the encounter may not always be easy but enjoyment and pleasure must be the result or the activity will be counter-productive.

We do know that where schools have taken trouble to guide parents and to sustain the scheme, parents learn to trust the school's approach. They see that reading to the child is as important as listening to the child read; they learn to reflect on the content of what is being read; they appreciate that looking at the pictures is not cheating; they learn that the 'pause, prompt, praise' routine is more helpful than criticism; they learn that it is better to keep the sessions short and frequent. They may learn from the school some of the features of the 'paired reading' technique which was developed by Topping and Wolfendale (1985) from a procedure devised by Roger Morgan (1976). In this procedure an experienced and a less experienced reader work together. The idea is that both read in unison with the aim of keeping up the momentum of the reading and avoiding an overemphasis on mistakes. If the child wants to read alone or pass the reading entirely over to the adult, s/he indicates this and there is no price to pay either way. It is helpful if parents can spend time in the classroom to see the teacher's approach in practice; equally, the teacher should learn from parents of their successful practices and approaches.

The following points may be useful to consider when setting up formal PACT schemes once the children are in school:

- PACT schemes need to be set up with the full support and shared understanding of the school staff. Without the preparation and agreement of everybody, they are difficult to start or to operate successfully and even harder to sustain.
- The PACT scheme needs to be introduced in detail to the parents, probably at parents' evenings. Reading jargon needs to be avoided. Schools have successfully used videos or demonstrated the process of reading with a child. Many schools pro- duce a booklet for parents, attractively illustrated and translated into other languages where necessary. Interactive sessions, with perhaps small groups working together, are useful.
- All efforts have to be sustained. Subsequent meetings are needed to keep the issues and the parents' interest alive.
- The books that are taken home from school need to be quality books so that the child and the parent can remain interested in the text. The child should always be involved in choosing; the books may sometimes be chosen from the public library or the child's home.
- Reading sessions at home should be kept short; no more than ten minutes unless the child requests longer.
- Ensure that parents use 'pause, prompt, praise' when listening to the child.
- Parents should be encouraged to make comments on a reading card or in a little booklet, noting what has been done and adding comments. As the record of books read grows, so does the child's confidence and competence.
- The teacher should respond and enter her own comments, often guiding the parent towards a deeper understanding of the reading process. (This situation may some- times be reversed: a colleague, who is a literacy tutor, gently educated her child's teacher towards a more balanced view of her child's efforts!)
- Continued renewing of efforts and of contacts must be part of the scheme; otherwise the benefits may start to subside.
- Where the link with the home is successful, there may be opportunities to extend the scheme into other curriculum areas. Maths (IMPACT) and science PACT schemes have been introduced with success in some schools.

As a student teacher you are unlikely to be in the position of setting up such a scheme, but where one is in operation you will want to find out about the following:

- how many times books are taken home each week;
- whether there is a timetabled slot for choosing books to take home;
- how the books are sent home (in book bags, folders . . .);
- what additional documentation goes with the books (e.g. book/card for parent and teacher to write on; different coloured bookmarks, perhaps labelled 'Please read this book to your child' or 'Your child can read this book to you').

Further reading

Branston, P. and Provis, M. (1999) *Children and Parents Enjoying Reading – Parents and the Literacy Hour: A Teacher's Guide.* London: David Fulton Publishers.

Hannon, P. (1995) *Literacy, Home and School.* London: Falmer Press.

Sanger, J. *et al.* (1997) *Young Children, Videos and Computers: Issues for Teachers and Parents.* London: Falmer Press.

Chapter 4

Monitoring and Assessing Reading

INTRODUCTION

Children's progress in reading has always been a matter of great concern – to parents, to teachers, to local education authorities and to governments, as well as to the children themselves. Children's reading attainment is certainly one of the major yardsticks by which schools are measured, by which parents judge the effectiveness of a school and by which children judge themselves and their success as learners. Teachers have the enormous responsibility, not only of teaching reading, but also of monitoring children's progress and of maintaining careful records of their development.

Because reading is seen as so important, it is the area where most control is exerted by those outside the classroom. Sometimes the means of assessment which are imposed are not those which teachers feel are the most revealing or effective. It is vital that you take the responsibility and control into your own hands and that you are able to provide evidence of children's progress and attainment. The record of this evidence will not only demonstrate achievement to those to whom schools are accountable, but, more importantly, it will be the basis for your planning of further reading experiences and specific teaching. If you understand, monitor and record each child's reading knowledge, strategies, strengths, difficulties, confidence and skill, you will be able to ensure, through planning appropriate teaching, that progress is maintained.

Assessing children's knowledge, skills and understanding, as well as their confidence, independence and learning approaches, is not something which can be tacked on at the end of the learning. The *Report of the Task Group on Assessment and Testing* (DES 1987), which was set up to consider the assessment and testing of the *National Curriculum*, stated

> The assessment process itself . . . should not simply be a bolt-on addition at the end. Rather, it should be an integral part of the educational process, continually providing both 'feedback' and 'feedforward'. It therefore needs to be incorporated systematically into teaching practices and strategies at all levels. (DES 1987: para. 4)

It is important that children be involved in their own assessment as it has a role in helping them understand what they are learning. Opportunities to review their own work and progress, to reflect on their understanding and needs, in discussion with teachers, enable children to set realistic goals for themselves and to see their learning and achievement in a positive light.

As we have shown throughout this book, reading is a complex and multi-faceted skill. On a day-to-day basis, teachers can observe what children have learned about letters and sounds but there are other aspects of reading which are just as important, such as what children have read, the cueing strategies they use, their approach, enthusiasm, confidence and attitudes, and their strengths and weaknesses (which are areas for development). Systems for monitoring and assessing progress need to enable teachers to assess the basic skills as well as these more complex aspects of reading, especially if the information gained is to be made use of in developing teaching strategies.

In each of the sections below we examine the contexts in which you can make full assessments of children's reading. These are:

- informal observation;
- conversations with children;
- structured semi-formal assessment;
- formal assessments which include tests and assessment tasks. You will need to combine all of these areas to obtain a full picture of attainment and progress.

INFORMAL OBSERVATION

A great deal of information about children's interest in, and commitment to, reading can be gleaned from day-to-day observation of children in the classroom. Some observations can be made during ongoing activities such as play in the home corner. Even unexpected events in the classroom like a note coming round about the school photographer, which a child finds she can read, can be entered in your notebook.

Interactions with books

Some children will choose to read whenever there is an opportunity; others will rarely opt for reading when there are other alternatives. You will need to note and record observations of how children go about selecting a book, whether they explore a range of reading material, whether they choose carefully and seem to know what they are looking for, or whether they pick up a book without much thought. Such observations might indicate that some specific teaching is needed about how to use the information presented about the book: how to interpret the cover; how the publisher's blurb describes the book; how to use chapter headings; how to sample; and how to use knowledge about authors and illustrators to inform choices. It might also be apparent that some children read a very narrow range of books, either from choice or because there is little alternative. You might also note whether children turn to books confidently when they are seeking information relating to other curriculum areas.

Behaviour at quiet reading times ('Everyone Reading in Class')

This routine is not carried out as often as it used to be, but, even when opportunities for quiet, sustained reading are less frequent, much information can be gleaned about individuals when they do have the chance to read quietly. The teacher will note whether children are able to concentrate on, and persist with, their reading. Such observations might raise questions about the range and suitability of the books available to the children, as well as about the planning, timing and duration of such sessions.

Reading across the curriculum

As we have already said, the ability to read is necessary in every area of the curriculum and not all texts have to be read in the same way. You will need to know, for example, whether a child's inability to cope with mathematical or science tasks, presented in text books, is related to reading problems or to a lack of understanding of the mathematical or scientific concepts. This might be a matter of vocabulary which has a subject specific meaning (for example, 'mean', 'table', 'current', 'desert') or it might be a matter of diagrams, charts, graphs, tables used in many subject areas which are not 'read' in the same way as continuous text.

The *NC* and the *NLS* identify the range of genres children should encounter including computer texts and CD-ROMs. Children are also asked to acquire the specific skills of 'skimming', 'scanning' and 'detailed reading'. You need to observe and record competence in these skills not only in English but in other curriculum areas. Opportunities to read information texts are, of course, present in the Literacy Hour and these texts are increasingly being linked to other areas of the curriculum (e.g. science, history, geography, RE).

CONVERSATIONS WITH CHILDREN

Children's informal comments

When children talk about their preferences, enthusiasms, likes and dislikes, perhaps as a part of discussions following a teacher reading aloud session, much can be learned which will inform your records of individual children and the choices you make about book provision.

Reading conferences

Surprising insights into children's reading can emerge in the one-to-one conversations which you have with them. Children will talk about a range of interests – such as football and other sports, animals, computers or music – all of which may involve reading in the family context. There may be a wealth of reading material at home, from newspapers, magazines and manuals to CD-ROMs and information books about their interests. If children do not appear to be enthusiastic readers of what is available in school, this may not mean that they are doing no reading. Particularly by Key Stage 2, many children will have discovered, and be reading at home, books which they fear may not be approved of at school. You need to acknowledge this and be prepared to enter into discussion so that you can help readers develop a critical approach to all published material. The teacher has a role in moving a reader beyond what is currently the favourite genre.

Many children who are using English as an additional language talk about the reading they do in other languages and the classes they attend after school. Hilary Minns (1990) and Eve Gregory (1996) have documented the wide range of literacy in which children from minority communities are engaged. It is important for you to record that the children are willing and able to share with you their understanding of different scripts and languages. You will be also be strengthening all children's understanding when you demonstrate your interest in this wider reading.

Reading aloud to the teacher or other adults

Although opportunities for teachers to read with individual children are probably fewer since the implementation of the *NLS*, there is still much to be gained from such occasions. In many schools classroom assistants and/or parents have received some training in reading with children. Where this is the case and these adults have learned both about supporting readers and about recording their reading strategies, they could become an invaluable support for teachers. You do, however, need to monitor the records made by others; it is the class teacher's responsibility to know and plan for the learning needs of all the children in the class. You must remain in control of monitoring progress. Informal assessments carried out when a child reads to the adult are useful for all age groups and you will remember that the section on 'Reading to the Teacher' in Chapter 3 gave you a structure for doing this. For a nursery child you may find yourself recording that she has made a coherent story using the pictures and she can identify where the character's name comes up on each page. For an older fluent reader you may record the child's comments on the sad ending of *The Dancing Bear* (Morpurgo) and how they had not expected it. You might also record that they found the first person narrative difficult and that you gave them *The Turbulent Term of Tyke Tiler* (Kemp) to read as the first person narrative in this book is more accessible.

Bilingual children may feel confident enough to read aloud in their first language. Although it is obviously useful if children can read aloud to someone who shares their language, so that the reading can be more accurately monitored, it is still possible for you to glean useful information about a child's reading confidence and competence, without understanding a word. You could, for instance, record that the child explained the story to you and read with apparent expression and perseverance.

As you will see below, these sessions are occasionally used to make more formal assessments of the children through the use of 'running records' or 'miscue analysis'. At this point it might be useful for you to scan the glossary at the end of the chapter (pp. 134–5) in order to appreciate some of the definitions and distinctions that we make below.

STRUCTURED SEMI-FORMAL ASSESSMENTS

Early concepts of print

Marie Clay (1979c) devised a procedure for checking whether beginner readers are familiar with the way in which books and print work. The intention is to identify what a young child knows by asking questions as the child and teacher share a book. This will allow you to observe and record the following things:

- whether the child can identify the front of the book;
- whether the child realises that it is the print (rather than the picture) which tells the reader what to say;
- where one starts to read and which direction to go in (directionality);
- where one goes at the end of a line (return sweep to left in English);
- whether the child understands 'first' and 'last' (words and letters);
- whether the child notices when the line order is altered;

- whether the child notices incorrect word order (1:1 correspondence);
- whether the child is aware that one reads the left-hand page before the right-hand page (in English);
- whether the child understands the meaning of full stops, commas, question marks, and speech marks (inverted commas);
- whether the child can identify upper-case (capital) and lower-case letters;
- whether the child knows the difference between 'word' and 'letter';
- whether the child notices words which have been reversed ('was'/'saw'; 'no'/'on').

Two commercially published booklets, *Sand* and *Stones* (Clay 1979, a and b) were written so that teachers could survey children's book and print knowledge in a systematic way on a score sheet. Some teachers feel that the booklets, with their deliberate printing errors, are confusing for young children, as well as being rather dull and dated. They prefer, therefore, to draw up their own checklist of the concepts and to use a more appealing ordinary book. Goodman (1987 p. 27) reports on a 'Bookhandling Knowledge Task' which has some helpful suggestions as to how you might choose such a book:

- Take a picture storybook that is suitable for reading to a pre-school child.
- Make sure the book has a title page which includes the title of the book and the author's name.
- Make sure that the pages have clear, bold print and that there are many pictures in the book. If possible, there should be a page with print on one side and a picture on the other.
- Try not to give too much information or direction.

This is followed by a list of questions that focus on the same concepts as Marie Clay's (above).

The principles embodied in these observations are now evident in many of the 'Baseline Assessment' frameworks (see p. 127).

Running record

(NB For convenience, we refer to the child as 'he'.)

Many teachers are now familiar with carrying out running records because the SATs for Key Stage 1 have made use of a version of the procedure, although in this context, the errors are scored (right or wrong) rather than being analysed as described below. As with the 'early concepts of print' assessment, this was also devised by Marie Clay. It is really a simplified version of 'miscue analysis', which is described below, and it is intended for use with children who have moved beyond the very earliest stages of reading and who are just beginning to read known texts independently. Making a running record is a way of looking in a focused manner at what a child is doing as he reads aloud; you can analyse the child's miscues (errors) to inform further planning for that child. A child may comment extensively on what is in the book or ask questions. These should also be noted as they frequently provide insights into the child's thinking. The following procedure will help you implement a running record.

Procedure for carrying out a running record

1. Choose a book which is known to the child, but not so well known that he can recite it from memory.
2. Decide how the reading will be recorded (see below). You may also want to consider tape recording the session especially as you are familiarising yourself with the procedure.
3. Ensure that the child is at ease and is happy about the book to be read.
4. Ask the child to read aloud from the book.
5. Do not intervene/give words too quickly; allow time for the child to think or work it out.
6. Do intervene if the child becomes distressed or cannot read the book: if this happens, simply take over the reading yourself and read to the end, without criticism or negative comment.
7. Allow the child time to comment, look at pictures, ask questions, if that is what he wants to do.

Recording the miscues

The miscues can be recorded in two ways. Either make a copy of the text or the part of the text on which you wish to concentrate (photocopy or write it out) and mark this as the child reads or mark the reading on a blank sheet of paper, keeping to the same line arrangement as the text (as in the example below). Mark the reading, using the following symbols:

(i) A stroke (/) for each word read correctly;
(ii) Write 'T' for every word TOLD to the child;
(iii) Write a substituted word above the actual word of the text e.g.
    said (substitute)
    shouted (text);
(iv) Circle a word missed out;
(v) Write 'SC' alongside any error which the child self-corrects.

Leave a column alongside the recording of the reading (or write on the text, if using a copy) to note any comments or questions. Marie Clay offers detailed guidance for interpreting the miscues in the reading. You will need to look back to Chapter 1 (p. 5) to remind yourself of the cueing systems used in reading and use these to decide which cues the child is utilising or ignoring. The child who substitutes 'said' for 'shouted' is using meaning and syntax though he fails to fine-tune the reading with attention to graphic and phonic cues. It is worth quoting Clay's advice to look at every error recorded in the running record:

> To work out whether the child is responding to the different kinds of cues that could be used, you need to look at every error that the child makes and ask yourself 'Now what made him say that?' 'Did he miss out on the visual cues?' 'Was he ignoring meaning?'. It is misleading if you do this selectively; you must analyse every error and count those that show this or that kind of cue. You want to be able to conclude, on sound evidence, that 'he pays more attention to visual cues than meaning' or 'he is guided by structure and meaning but does not search for visual cues'. It is only when you go to the trouble of analysing all the errors that you really get any indication of what his strategies are on reading. (1985 p. 56)

In the example of a running record and the analysis shown below, the child's reading strategies are revealed clearly in the miscues. The teacher observes the child's positive strategies but can also see where further support and teaching is needed.

Example of a running record

Child: E (girl)
Age: 5 years 2 months
Text: *Titch* (Pat Hutchins)
(Numbers in brackets indicate child's comments which are given below.)

Titch was little.	/ / /	
	T T	
His sister Mary was a bit bigger.	/ / *marry* / / / *digger* Mary bigger	
	T	
And his brother Pete was a lot bigger.	/ / / *Pet* / / / / Pete	
	SC	
Pete had a great big bike.	/ / / *greet* / / great	
Mary had a big bike.	/ / / / /	
And Titch had a little tricycle.	/ / / / / /	
	SC	
Pete had a kite that flew high above the trees.	/ / / / / / *over* / / above	(1)
Mary had a kite that flew high above the houses.	/ / / / / / / / / /	
And Titch had a pin-wheel that he held in his hand.	/ / / / / / / / / / /	(2)
Pete had a big drum.	/ / / / /	
Mary had a trumpet.	/ / / /	
	SC	
And Titch had a little wooden whistle.	/ / / / / *wo-oo-den* / wooden	
Pete had a big saw.	/ / / / /	
Mary had a big hammer.	/ / / / /	
	SC	
And Titch held the nails.	/ / *had* / / held	
Pete had a big spade.	/ / / / /	
Mary had a fat flowerpot.	/ / / / /	
	T	
But Titch had the tiny seed.	/ / / / *teeny* / tiny	
And Titch's seed grew	/ / / /	
and grew	/ /	
and grew.	/ /	(3)

Child's comments:

(1) 'We had a kite last Christmas, made of plastic. It didn't work.'
(2) 'At the end he gets the good thing.'
(3) 'He did – see!'

Teacher's analysis:

1. marry/Mary: error arose from E sounding out the word, using phonic knowledge.
   TOLD the correct word;
2. digger/bigger: error perhaps arose from confusion of 'b' and 'd' written symbols.
   TOLD the correct word;
3. pet/Pete: error arose from use of phonic knowledge to sound out word; final 'e' not
   noticed/taken into account? TOLD the correct word;
4. greet/great: error arose from use of phonic knowledge to sound out word. SELF-
   CORRECTION because first reading did not make sense;
5. over/above: error arose from prediction of word which made sense; further look at word
   printed, using phonic knowledge to check, and at the pictures led to SELF-CORRECTION;
6. wo-oo-den/wooden: error arose from use of phonic knowledge to sound out word,
   resulting in three syllables. SELF-CORRECTION when this did not result in a word
   which made sense;
7. had/held: error arose from prediction of next word, based on previous use of 'had'.
   A further look at the word led to SELF-CORRECTION;
8. teeny/tiny: error arose from prediction of a word which made sense and partial use
   of grapho-phonic cues. TOLD the correct word.

Teacher's comments:

The text was read confidently. She was not afraid to attempt words that were new to
her. She was involved in the text, as her comments show. Some expression in her
voice, especially when words appeared to be known or easily read.

She was definitely using her previous knowledge and memory of the text. It was
remembered well. She used the pictures to help with words such as 'kite' and also drew
on her real experience of kites. In many cases misread words still made sense (5, 7, 8),
so she was drawing on semantic cues. She was using grapho-phonic knowledge (1, 4,
6, 8) to work out unknown words, with some success. She has a strong reliance on
phonic knowledge, though she also uses other cues.

She seemed to enjoy reading the text. When asked, at the end, who the 'titch' was in
her house, she replied, 'me in the people, the stick insects in the pets'. This shows she
understood the concept behind the story.

Future support: E. is confident and should be guided into tackling a wider range of
more demanding texts. Her use of phonic knowledge should not be discouraged in any
way but she needs to have additional strategies suggested e.g. using similar, familiar
words as a guide. Encourage her to continue to focus on the meaning and check
whether a word makes sense. Group reading opportunities, where she could read with
others and observe others' strategies, would be useful.

(Mary Thompsett, student at University of Surrey Roehampton)

Miscue analysis

(NB For convenience we will refer to the child as 'he'.)

As we described in Chapter 1, Kenneth Goodman (1973) devised a procedure which he called 'miscue analysis' as a way of opening a 'window onto the reading process'. It is a procedure which differs from running records in that it is generally used with older children whose reading is giving you some cause for concern. You do not need to use the procedure with readers who are reading independently, fluently and with good understanding. It is also different from running records in that you work from a book that is unknown to the child. Traditionally, the way of recording miscues looks different from the running records but both share the purpose of diagnosing and analysing error and both inform your subsequent teaching. Miscue analysis looks at what a reader does when reading aloud and it is worth remembering that this is a different kind of activity from reading silently, because the reader has to be aware of his or her 'performance'.

Several variations of Goodman's original procedure have been developed over the years, some of which simplify it so that it can be used more regularly and is more manageable in the classroom (e.g. Moon 1984; Arnold 1982; Campbell 1993). The version described in the *Primary Language Record* (Barrs *et al.* 1988) incorporates an element of silent reading preceding the reading aloud. A version used in Western Australia (Sheridan 1982) records the miscues in a way which allows percentages for different kinds of miscue to be worked out very easily. The version given here draws on all of these.

If miscue analysis is new to you, it can be very helpful, the first few times, to use a recording sheet so that the patterns of the miscues can be seen clearly. Once the procedure is familiar, the miscue patterns will become clearer and you may not need to make a detailed breakdown in order to identify a reader's strengths and areas of difficulty. It is certainly true that, once a few careful analyses have been carried out, your ear becomes attuned and you will notice aspects of a child's reading of which you have not been aware before.

Carrying out a miscue analysis

Selecting the text(s)

An analysis of miscues can be carried out on a reading of a text which is unknown to the child and slightly more demanding than his or her current reading material. It could be an extract from a longer narrative or a complete short story. Non-fiction texts do not lend themselves as well to this procedure because of the amount of new vocabulary, proper names and the complexity of the sentence structure. It is important to choose a text which is interesting, flows well and which takes account of the child's literacy, linguistic and cultural experiences. It is a good idea to have several texts to hand so that, if one is too easy and the child makes very few miscues an alternative can be used. If the child has great difficulty (as a guide more than one miscue in every ten words) it is likely that he will lose the sense of what is being read, so a different text should be used.

Preparation

From the text, select the passage which you intend to analyse and make a copy of this. The passage should be long enough to provide scope for a substantial number of miscues (about 300 words), though the analysis should not begin until after the first few paragraphs, so that the reader has time to get into the text. A photocopy can be used if there is room to write in the miscues, but it may be necessary to rewrite the text onto an 'analysis script' if there is not much space between lines. This copy is for the teacher; the child should read from the original book.

Ideally, have a tape recorder to hand so that the reading can be tape recorded and analysed later. It is easy to miss things if marking is done during the reading, especially at first when the coding symbols are unfamiliar to you. Listening to the tape more than once allows all the detail to be noted.

Procedure

Ensure that the child is comfortable and fairly relaxed. Explain that, while he reads this book you are going to listen very hard and that you want him to try to work out any difficulties and unknown words without your help. You also need to say that this is not a test and that it is going to help you, the teacher, to help the child. Explain the tape recorder if the child is not used to seeing it used to record reading. Explain that, when the reading aloud is finished, you will be asking him to tell you what it was about.

Ask the child to begin reading. He should read the whole text or extract, even though only part may be analysed. If the child tires or appears very worried by the activity, you should take over the reading and finish the story, rather than allowing the child to struggle on. If the child gets completely stuck, particularly if there are unfamiliar names in the text, you should give the word but let him have a go before you intervene – the intention is to see what strategies are being used to deal with difficulties, so thinking time should be allowed. It is surprising how often a child can solve the problem alone when given the chance.

After the reading has been completed, ask the child to tell you about what has been read. It is better not to ask testing or closed questions. You could ask whether he enjoyed it, make links with the child's experience and ask for opinions about the characters or events. Make a note of the child's comments, responses, questions and ideas.

Marking the miscues

If a recording has been made, listen to the tape as soon as possible and mark the 'analysis script' using the following symbols. These are the standard symbols and the advantage of using them is that the script can be interpreted by others. This is important if the marked script is to be included in the child's records.

- Substitution: word substituted written over the text
                down
  e.g. She looked through the low branches of her tree.

- Omission: phrase, word or part of word omitted is circled in the text
  e.g. She saw (only) the empty garden.

- Insertion: word inserted written above omission mark
                                        by
  e.g. . . . said Mr McFarlane as he passed λ .

- Reversal: words reversed marked with a continuous line

    e.g. . . . . Mr Fandango, when he\was at home, lived in the house . . .

- Self-Correction: the miscue is written above the word in the text, then marked 'SC'

    SC *remind*

    e.g. She remembered an arrow she had lost . . .

- Repetition: words repeated are underlined. Double underlining indicates repeated twice; triple underlining, repeated three times, etc.

    e.g. There was no one about.

- Block, or Teacher gives help: word(s) given written above, marked by capital 'T'

    McFarlane T

    e.g. In the lane she met Mr McFarlane.

- Pause of over 2 seconds: oblique stroke before the word paused at

    e.g. The lane was cool and shady and very/agreeable after the hot bright streets.

- Punctuation ignored: parallel lines above and below punctuation

    e.g. He's started hunting Joe thought. He was right.

Analysing the miscues

In general terms, if children's miscues do not change the meaning of the text, they are probably using positive strategies and making sense of the text. Positive strategies include:

- reading ahead in order to help work out a word;
- going back and repeating a previously read phrase or sentence, in order to establish or check the context;
- stopping if what is read does not make sense and self-correcting;
- using the grapho-phonic features of words to confirm predictions.

If children's miscues do change the meaning then they are probably using negative strategies and not reading for meaning. Negative strategies might include:

- reading word by word and not using the context to help work out the meaning;
- sounding out words and settling on a word which may be graphically or phonically similar, but which does not make sense, or is a non-word;
- leaving miscues uncorrected when the sense is disrupted.

NB If a miscue is uncorrected, but the sense of the text stays intact, it is not a miscue of the same serious order as the other negative strategies mentioned above as it is probable that the reader is attending to the meaning. However, it is not accurate and it is something that needs noting.

The miscue analysis which follows begins with a piece of text on which the miscues have been marked by the teacher. If these are entered on a chart, as shown in Table 4.1, it is easy to see, at a glance, the pattern of the reader's errors and thus the areas which need intervention and further support and teaching.

Example of a miscue analysis

Child: N (girl)
Age: 8 years 10 months
Text: Short story *Lew, the fabulous detective* by Catherine Storr

Caroline and Jane said, 'You are silly! There's nothing boys can do that girls can't. Why not

just be a girl?'

But Lucy said, 'All the same, I want to be a boy.'

Her mother said, 'Girls are just as nice as boys. Nobody else wants you to be a boy. We like

you just as you are.'

But Lucy said, 'Well, I still wish I was a boy.'

'Why?' her mother asked.

'Boys are stronger. They have bicycles and real fights. Boys have adventures.'

'So do girls,' her mother said.

'Not such exciting ones. Mother, if I wished very hard on a wishbone, couldn't I turn into a boy,

even now?'

'No, I'm afraid not. At least, it's never happened.'

'All the same, I shall wish,' said Lucy.

On Wednesdays Lucy came home from school at lunchtime and had a free afternoon. But the

lane behind her house was deserted: there were no boys playing there, because the boys were

at school. So were Caroline and Jane.

'I shall be a detective,' Lucy said. 'I shall walk around and find some terrible crime going on. I

am Lew, the fabulous detective.'

In the lane she met Mr McFarlane going home for his half day off. Mr McFarlane looked after

Mr Fandango's garden, and Mr Fandango, when he was at home, lived in the house behind the

high wall that ran the length of the lane. Mr McFarlane's position made him, he thought, a very

important person indeed. He was helped in the job by Willie Prouty, who lived in Mr Fandango's

house with Mrs Willie Prouty and their baby son, the Stinker. But Mr McFarlane never spoke of

'Mr Fandango's garden'. He said, 'My garrden. My roses. My mixed borrderrs.'

'Grrand day, Miss Lucy,' said Mr McFarlane as he passed.

'Fine,' Lucy agreed, though just then she felt far too hot.

Just behind Mr McFarlane, but not walking with him because he was only the under-gardener,

was Willie Prouty. He was also off for his half-day. He wore his best dark suit, and a hard hat

instead of a cap. Behind Willie were Mrs Willie Prouty and the Stinker, very grand in their best

clothes too; she very pretty and pink and frilly, and the Stinker, who was fat and two years old,

in gleaming white.

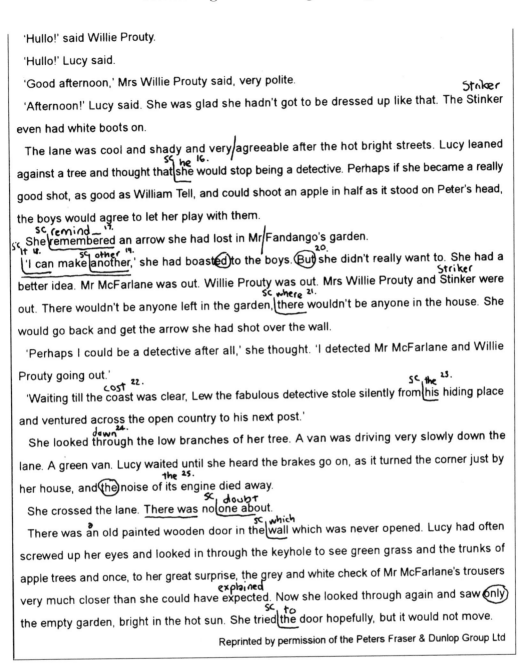

'Hullo!' said Willie Prouty.

'Hullo!' Lucy said.

'Good afternoon,' Mrs Willie Prouty said, very polite.

'Afternoon!' Lucy said. She was glad she hadn't got to be dressed up like that. The Stinker even had white boots on.

The lane was cool and shady and very agreeable after the hot bright streets. Lucy leaned against a tree and thought that she would stop being a detective. Perhaps if she became a really good shot, as good as William Tell, and could shoot an apple in half as it stood on Peter's head, the boys would agree to let her play with them.

She remembered an arrow she had lost in Mr Fandango's garden. 'I can make another,' she had boasted to the boys. But she didn't really want to. She had a better idea. Mr McFarlane was out. Willie Prouty was out. Mrs Willie Prouty and Stinker were out. There wouldn't be anyone left in the garden, there wouldn't be anyone in the house. She would go back and get the arrow she had shot over the wall.

'Perhaps I could be a detective after all,' she thought. 'I detected Mr McFarlane and Willie Prouty going out.'

'Waiting till the coast was clear, Lew the fabulous detective stole silently from his hiding place and ventured across the open country to his next post.'

She looked through the low branches of her tree. A van was driving very slowly down the lane. A green van. Lucy waited until she heard the brakes go on, as it turned the corner just by her house, and the noise of its engine died away.

She crossed the lane. There was no one about.

There was an old painted wooden door in the wall which was never opened. Lucy had often screwed up her eyes and looked in through the keyhole to see green grass and the trunks of apple trees and once, to her great surprise, the grey and white check of Mr McFarlane's trousers very much closer than she could have expected. Now she looked through again and saw only the empty garden, bright in the hot sun. She tried the door hopefully, but it would not move.

Reprinted by permission of the Peters Fraser & Dunlop Group Ltd

Teacher's analysis:

This analysis indicates effective reading strategies. There were 10 self-corrections and 12 of the 15 miscues which were not corrected did not disrupt the meaning.

There is a slight over concentration on grapho-phonic cues (15 of the 25 miscues were graphically similar). Despite this, when the sentence did not make sense, she usually corrected or attempted to correct the miscue. The use of grapho-phonic cues was balanced by the use of syntactic cues. Syntactic miscues were generally corrected. All cue systems appear to be being used and the level of correction, when the meaning is disrupted, showed good prediction and confirming strategies.

CHILD'S NAME N   AGE 8.10   TITLE OF STORY 'Lew, the fabulous detective'

Miscue no.	Word(s) in text	Word(s) read	Does the miscue look like the text? (Graphic similarity) Yes / No	Does the miscue sound like the text? (Phonic similarity) Yes / No	Does the word make sense in this context? (Semantic) Yes / No	Is the sentence grammatically acceptable? (Syntax) Yes / No	Was the miscue corrected? (Self-correction) Yes / No	Is a dialect variation involved in the miscue? Yes / No	Comments
1	home	___	No		Yes	Yes	No		
2	were	was	Yes	partly	Yes	Yes	No	Yes	Caused by her speech; always uses 'was' for singular and plural
3	terrible	trouble	Yes	No	No	No	No	No	
4	he was	was he	Yes	No	No	partly	Yes	No	
5	position	position	Yes	No	partly	partly	No	No	Graphic similarity but word not recognised. Consistently said 'Protty' throughout (also 'Striker' for 'Stinker')
6	Prouty	Protty	Yes	No	No	Yes	No	No	
7	their baby	where his	partly	No	No	No	No	No	
8	said 'My …	was Mr	partly	No	No	No	partly (Mr/My)	No	Did not notice the extra letters in 'Scottish' accent in the text!
9									
10	then	by	No	No	Yes	Yes	No	No	
11	under-gardener	underground gardener	Yes	Yes	Yes	Yes	Yes	No	Corrected although the miscue made sense. Unfamiliar phrase; substitutes known word to try to make sense
12	was	while	Yes	No	No	No	No	No	
13	wore	were	Yes	No	No	No	No	No	
14	a hard	had a	Yes	No	No	No	No	No	
15	very	___			Yes	Yes	No	No	Omission of word still makes sense
16	she	he	Yes	Yes	Yes	Yes	No	No	This is surely caused by shift from 'Lew' to 'Lucy'; the same person
17	remember	remind –	Yes	partly	No	No	Yes	No	
18	I	it	Yes		No	No	Yes	No	
19	another	other	Yes	partly	No	No	Yes	No	
20	But	___	Yes		No	No		No	
21	there	where	Yes	partly	No	No	Yes	No	
22	coast	cost	Yes	Yes	No	Yes	No	No	Idiom unknown to her
23	his	the	Yes		No	Yes	No	No	
24	through	down	No		No	Yes	No	No	
25	the noise of / its	noise / of the	Yes	Yes	Yes	Yes	No	No	Two linked miscues; 'the' perceived earlier and inserted to make sense?

Fewer than half miscues corrected, but most of those uncorrected did not disrupt meaning.

Table 4.1

Prediction

The story has an open ending so I left the prediction until the end and then asked N to tell me what happened to Lucy after she had been driven off in the robbers' van. She said she thought they would catch her but, because she was only a little girl, they would let her go; then she could go to the police and tell them the van number. I asked if she would do anything like Lucy did, if she saw burglars, and she said, 'No – I'd run and tell somebody what was happening'.

Retelling

In the retelling she explained the events in sequence, giving some details about the garden and the trees and what the robbers looked like. She was rather confused about who Mr McFarlane, Mr Prouty and Mr Fandango were, perhaps because of the very unfamiliar names, and also about their relationship with each other. She did not recognise the written representation of a Scots accent, nor recognise McFarlane as a Scottish name. She thought Lucy was very brave and very clever. I think she missed the subtlety of 'Lucy' becoming 'Lew' in the narrative, and the change from 'she' to 'he' when Lucy was pretending to be a detective.

I think she needs more opportunities to talk about her reading, both with me and with a group of friends (in group reading sessions), to help her look below the surface of a story and appreciate the more subtle meanings, such as the game Lucy was playing in this story.

FORMAL ASSESSMENTS

Baseline assessment

Under the 1997 Education Act, assessment of four- or five-year-old children beginning statutory education is now compulsory. This assessment takes place a few weeks after they start school in Reception classes. Literacy knowledge is, of course, only one strand of the baseline assessments, but you need to be familiar with both the *Early Learning Goals* DfEE/QCA (1999c) and the outcomes expected at the end of the foundation stage (i.e. when the children join Year 1). The exact content of the assessment activities is slightly different in different LEAs, but all must be accredited assessment schemes and conform to National (QCA) Baseline Assessment scales. In relation to reading, most schemes require assessment of early reading behaviour (very similar to the concepts identified by Marie Clay), letter knowledge (including the child's own name) and phonological knowledge (ability to recite rhymes, recognition of initial sounds). Many assessments can be made from teachers' existing knowledge of the children, though specifically planned activities can be used. Teachers are advised to carry out assessment activities within the normal classroom contexts (e.g. as part of a relaxed one-to-one reading session, playing with plastic letters, singing rhymes) so there should be no undue pressure on children, even though this is a statutory assessment.

A word about 'reading age'

As soon as we move into the area of formal assessments and reading tests the concept of 'reading age' rears its head. 'Reading age' was described as long ago as 1975 as a 'misleading concept, obscuring more than it reveals' (*The Bullock Report*, DES 1975: 33).

More recently Barry Stierer has questioned its continued acceptance:

> It is worth asking why a normative, linear and age-related concept should persist in relation to reading, when it would not be acceptable in other areas of the curriculum. Is it because reading, unlike anything else taught at school, is still widely seen as skill and not knowledge, and therefore instrumental to the curriculum rather than an element of it? There is also reason to believe that 'reading age' persists merely to ensure some continuity of comparability with the past: because 'reading age' was the unit of currency used in the past, we still need it in order to compare 'standards over time', despite the many coherent and persuasive criticisms which have been made of the concept of 'reading age'. (Stierer and Bloom 1994 p. 74)

The *NC* levels attempt to define the characteristics of readers at different stages, rather than ages, though we feel that the assumption that 'all 7-year-olds should have reached Level 2' implies that this is the description of a '7-year-old reader', something which *The Bullock Report* defines as 'only a statistical abstraction'. The report goes on to say that 'it simply cannot be assumed that children having the same reading age read in the same way, require identical teaching, and will profit from similar books and materials' (DES 1975 p. 33).

Few of the most frequently used tests claim to have a diagnostic function, and this is perhaps their greatest weakness, because a teacher needs to know not only whether readers are progressing as well as their peers, but also where any difficulties might lie. Then the teacher is able to provide appropriate support.

Standardised reading tests

This is perhaps the area where we see the greatest external control of reading progress. There have always been objective tests for reading; teachers' subjective judgements about their children's reading have not had the same validity or status as these standardised tests. The debate about objectivity/subjectivity is one which continues and lies at the heart of many of the points we make below. All standardised tests of reading set out to identify/test discrete reading skills (e.g. phonic knowledge, decoding skill, word recognition, accuracy, fluency and comprehension) and to provide activities which measure the pupil's ability to use the skills. There is no test which can probe every aspect of reading and each one reflects its compiler's view of what is important.

Many of the tests focus on the reader's ability to decode separate words (e.g. *Schonell Graded Word Reading Test* 1942; restandardised 1972); others offer progressively more difficult sentences to read (e.g. the *Holborn Reading Scale*, Watts 1948) and the *Salford Sentence Reading Test*, Bookbinder 1976). In an attempt to assess a reader's understanding of what is read, later tests include sentences (e.g. Young's *Group Reading Test* 1980) which the reader has to complete with one of several given alternatives. In others there are paragraphs with gaps (*GAP Test*, McLeod and Unwin 1970) for which readers have to provide an appropriate word (cloze procedure). Some tests, which take considerable time to administer, attempt to assess the child's 'reading behaviour' and skills of comprehension, reading accuracy, use of syntax, ability to sequence as well as decoding, in order to produce a 'profile' of the reader (e.g. *Edinburgh Reading Test*, Godfrey Thomson Unit 1977–1981).

More recently, the *Effective Reading Tests* (*ERT*) (Vincent and De La Mare 1986) have attempted to reflect a wider view of reading, especially of reading for information. They use glossy, illustrated booklets with sections of text which the children have to read and then answer questions about. Despite the glossiness there are still many aspects which cannot be assessed in this test.

The revised (1988) *Neale Analysis*, for which children have to read aloud a short narrative, makes use of an approach based on 'miscue analysis', but the errors are marked right or wrong to provide a 'summative measure of reading accuracy, comprehension and rate'. Accuracy is important as far as the scoring is concerned, though the information available from the child's errors can be analysed to show the pattern of the reader's strategies. The manuals for both the *ERT* and the revised Neale do warn users that test results should be seen as only *part* of a picture of a child's reading: '. . . reading is a complex skill and no test can hope to sample all the various components of the reading process . . . The results of any reading test should not be considered as the definitive statement about a child's ability in this area, but rather as samples of the child's reading behaviour' (Neale p. 34) and 'The progress tests . . . should be treated as no more than a component of a cumulative education record' (Vincent and De La Mare 1986 p. 13).

Whatever their focus, such tests are marked in a way which provides a numerical 'reading age', a 'reading quotient' or a 'standardised score' (with all the questions about reading ages, raised above). Statistically, they enable comparison of one child with another and with national norms. Many schools still give great weight to standardised test scores, using them to supplement SAT scores in order to secure extra support for pupils with reading difficulties.

Standardised reading tests, if they are used, must be regarded as providing only a part of the information about a particular reader. Teachers need to be very clear about their purposes in deciding to use such a test and to look carefully at the test manuals to find out the date of the test and the beliefs about reading current at that time, the compilers' views of what reading involves and what they believe their test will assess. Many of the tests are culturally and linguistically biased so that their content will disadvantage children from Britain's many minority groups who may be unfamiliar with the material and language used. In deciding whether to use a standardised test of reading, the following questions could provide a starting point for reflection on assessment procedures and the use of tests.

- Why do I want to use this test?
- What is being tested?
- Will I know more about the child's reading ability when I have used it?
- Will it tell me what support or help the child needs?
- What aspects of reading are not covered by the test?
- Is there a better way of finding out what I need to know?

(Laycock 1989 p. 29)

FREQUENTLY USED READING TESTS

TEST	DATE	TYPE OF TEST	PUBLISHER

Edinburgh Reading Tests	1977	Diagnostic. Group. Written. Timed. Age-range
		    Stage 1 7.00–9.00
		    Stage 2 8.6–10.6
		    Stage 3 10.6–12.00
		Sentences and paragraphs
			Hodder & Stoughton

Effective Reading Tests	1986	Attainment/Diagnostic (Progress/Skills). Separate tests. Group. Written. Untimed.
		Age-range Level 1 7.3–9.8
		    Level 2 8.3–10.8
		    Level 3 9.3–11.8
		    Level 4 10.3–12.8
		Reading booklets and answer sheets
			Macmillan

GAP Reading Comprehension	1970	Attainment. Group. Written. Timed. Age-range 7.08–12.06 Paragraphs; cloze procedure	Heinemann
Group Reading Test (Young)	1968	Attainment. Group. Written. Timed. Age-range 6.05–12.10 Words and Sentences	Hodder & Stoughton
London Reading Test	1981	Attainment. Group. Written. Untimed. Designed for Y6. Score range equivalent of 6.0–12.0. Paragraphs; Cloze procedure and comprehension questions.	NFER (ILEA)
Holborn Reading Scale	1948	Attainment. Individual. Oral. Untimed. Age-range 5.09–13.09 Sentences	Harrap
Neale Analysis of Reading Ability	1988 (revised)	Attainment/Diagnostic. Individual. Oral. Untimed. Age-range 6.0–12.0 (separate forms) Scores for Accuracy, Comprehension, and Rate of reading Paragraphs	NFER/Nelson
Schonell Graded Word Reading	1942 (restandard-ised 1972)	Attainment. Individual. Oral. Untimed. Age-range 6.06–12.06 Words	Oliver & Boyd
Salford Sentence Reading	1976	Attainment. Individual. Oral. Untimed. Age-range 6.10–11.9 Sentences	Hodder & Stoughton

Table 4.2

National Curriculum Standard Assessment Tasks/Tests (SATs)

Although there have been slight variations in the content of the SATs over the years since they were first introduced, the general form they take now seems to be fairly well established. In the beginning, they were defined as 'Standard Assessment *Tasks*' which were to be undertaken as part of normal classroom activity, especially at Key Stage 1. But there has been a shift of meaning so that they are now referred to as 'Tests' and are thus perceived as being outside the teacher's control, more formal, and different from the assessments a teacher might carry out on an informal basis.

Key Stage 1

The SATs for reading at the end of Key Stage 1 are a mixture of individual reading to the teacher, for the least independent readers, and pencil and paper tests for the more competent readers.

Reading to the teacher

Instructions for 1999 indicate that the teacher must choose 'three or four books from the list for the level (she is) assessing' . . . 'but the text must not be familiar to (the child)'. Teachers are 'to take all appropriate measures to ensure that the books used for assessment are not familiar to the children, for example by excluding them from class book collections'. The requirement for the texts to be 'unfamiliar' to the child does raise issues about equality of opportunity and fairness. Since publishers and booksellers make public the list of SAT books, there are certainly many children who will not only be familiar with the books, but who will have practised reading them at home, before the SAT is carried out at school.

The child whom the teacher expects to be at Level 1, is asked to choose one book from the selection offered, and to read with the teacher, who will help if necessary. The reading is preceded by talk about the book to enable the teacher to establish the extent of the child's knowledge about books and print. For children judged to be reading at Level 2, different lists of children's books are designated as 'SAT books' from which passages are identified for the assessment activity. The child may decide which of the three or four books to read but the actual assessment must be carried out using the identified passage. The procedure is based on the 'running record' (see p. 131) and the child's eventual score depends on how much of the text is read accurately. There are three levels of accuracy, allowing the child to be graded 2A, 2B, or 2C. The child must also be able to retell the story and 'express opinions about the main events or ideas in the text' and be able to 'talk about the meaning and significance of what he or she has read'. While completing the running record, the teacher is asked to classify the strategies the child uses when attempting to read unfamiliar words, as either 'graphic', 'phonic', 'syntactic' or 'contextual' and to use this information to judge whether the child's strategies are 'appropriate'.

These SATs, in line with the level descriptions, demand a degree of understanding from teachers about the range of strategies a young reader might employ to make sense of a text, and the ability to judge the appropriateness with which they are used. Teachers who are familiar with running record and/or miscue analysis procedures will certainly be better prepared to undertake these assessments.

Reading comprehension tests

It is now a statutory requirement for all children who attain Level 2A, 2B or 2C on the reading task to take the Level 2 reading comprehension test. This is contained in a booklet (entitled *Pot of Gold* in 1999) and consists of a short story (*Skyfire* by Frank Asch) and an information text (about honey). The test is taken in two parts with a break in between; this can be short (break or lunch-time) or long (completion the following day). Although the test is not strictly timed, teachers are advised that 'most children demonstrate what they can do in about 45 minutes'. It is carried out in formal test conditions in May. Teachers are told to 'ensure that children can work undisturbed, individually and without access to materials that could give them an unfair advantage. Changes to the usual classroom layout may be necessary'. The teacher introduces the test by explaining the different sections of the booklet and working through two examples of questions with the children in the test booklet. After that, the children must work alone; they cannot be helped to read anything in the reading booklet. Precise detailed instructions for both administration and marking are given in the Teacher's Guide. For many seven-year-olds, even if they are quite confident readers, this unusual situation is likely to prove challenging.

Children who perform well in both the reading aloud tasks, as described above, and the Level 2 reading comprehension test, achieving Level 2A, must be moved on to further assessment at Level 3 using a different reading comprehension test. In 1999 this took the form of a booklet, similar to those of many of the Standardised Tests of Reading. It contained a story in two parts and two poems which the children had to read and then answer questions about in an answer booklet. Most of the questions required factual recall of the text though some of them required both inference and reflection. Detailed marking instructions are given and the score determines whether the child achieves Level 3.

Key Stage 2

As for Key Stage 1, teachers must make an initial judgement about the level at which the child is operating. If children are at the earliest stages of reading (Level 1 or 2) they will read with the teacher. Although the selection of books offered will be different, the procedure is the same as that for Levels 1 and 2 of the Key Stage 1 SATs.

Most children, judged to have reached Level 3 or above by Year 6, will have to do the full range of SAT tests. These are administered as examinations in one week (May) and all are unseen and strictly timed. Reading is one of these tests. For Levels 3–5 the test takes one hour: this is made up of 15 minutes' initial time to read the reading booklet, and 45 minutes for completing the reading answer booklet. The reading booklet consists of a set of readings linked to a theme (which, in 1999, was spiders) and two are extracts from published books. They consist of two information texts and a poem.

The questions which children must answer mostly require direct identification of specific information, rather in the manner of traditional comprehension exercises, except that the answers do not have to be full sentences. Some questions ask the children about the structure, layout and genre of the information texts and others ask questions about the way the poet has chosen to write.

For many children the test procedure can be demanding and sometimes confusing as they have to move back and forth between the two booklets. The number of marks it is possible to get for each answer is printed below each question, and this is also pointed out to them in the instructions, which puts additional pressure on the most conscientious children. Anxiety can be created if they feel they cannot answer a particular question and have to miss it out. After 45 minutes they must stop even if they have not finished.

Although these test compilers have made an effort to present the reading booklets in an appealing way, with colour illustrations, the test remains a very tough reading experience as the children must switch from one kind of reading to another in a short space of time and must read accurately and rapidly to complete the tasks. Children who are believed to be working at Level 6 are given an Extension Paper which contains two factual texts and a poem on the same theme (which was called *Chinese Characters* in 1999) and answers must be written in an answer booklet, in the same way as the main test, though the final item requires an extended piece of writing and the test takes 60 minutes.

The completed answer booklets have to be marked externally rather than by the children's own teachers, though the teacher information booklets explain the mark scheme and show what kinds of answers will earn marks. After the tests have been completed, schools are sent information on how the scores will be converted to *NC* levels.

These tests take the assessment procedures out of the control of teachers. The teacher's only contribution is in the initial assessment of the level at which each child is working; if the test result is different, then the teacher must indicate the two different marks. As with all tests of reading which assess a child's competence on the basis of a single reading activity, the outcome may not reflect the child's true achievement. This means that teachers' ongoing assessments, even if they have to be modified, still have an important role in providing a fuller picture of a child's reading as well as evidence of what has been accomplished and information on which to base planning for the child's future needs.

FRAMEWORKS FOR ASSESSMENT AND RECORD KEEPING

Assessments of children's progress need to be recorded carefully and in ways which make the information accessible to all who may be involved with a child. Records of the 'tick-box' kind (e.g. lists of books read or of the letters/sounds a child can recognise) give little information about a child's needs, strategies, attitudes or strengths. Neither do they allow children themselves to be aware of or reflect on their progress. In a climate where target-setting is assuming greater importance for schools, teachers and children, records which reflect what learners have achieved become essential. In many schools a number of key learning outcomes are identified for each term or half term; these are shared with the children who then decide, at the end of that time, how far the targets have been achieved, before moving on to set new targets.

Within the *NLS* you will need to identify opportunities for different kinds of assessment. These might include:

• targeted questions in whole-class or plenary sessions to check individuals' understanding or thinking;

- criterion-referenced tasks set during independent activities (e.g. ability to use dictionaries effectively, ability to scan and locate specific information in an information text);
- group reading records (which could include comment on a member's reading strategies, involvement in a text, ability to infer meanings, as well as specific skills observed);
- planned opportunities for discussion between teacher and individual pupils, at least twice in a year, to review progress and set individual targets (e.g. reading conferences);
- skills checklists/observation grids related to specific learning intentions or contexts you have provided to allow children to demonstrate this knowledge.

It is important that records are made of these assessments. Sometimes these can be kept in group folders but often your observations will need to be recorded in the individual child's record.

The purpose of all assessment and record keeping is to guide teachers in moving the children's learning forward, so the findings from assessments must be used to inform future teaching. Various record-keeping formats which are already in existence help the teacher organise and structure her observations. Many of these have been developed by LEAs and by individual schools and most draw heavily on the *Primary Language Record* which was developed in 1987/8 and was published in *The Primary Language Record Handbook for Teachers* (Barrs *et al.* 1988), before the *NC* came into being. This was the framework for teacher observation and assessment which was recommended by the first version of the *NC* as the starting point for the development of such records.

The purpose of these frameworks is to enable teachers to observe and sample a child's work in English, not only to record achievement but also to identify a child's strengths and areas for development in all modes of language (Speaking and Listening, Reading and Writing).

The framework for reading in the *Primary Language Record* collates evidence from discussions with parents, informal observations of the child, conferences with a child about his or her reading and regular sampling of individual reading sessions. The *Primary Language Record* has also been very helpful in raising awareness about the role of bilingual helpers in recording EAL children's progress. Other frameworks show reading competence statements on a chart or circle or as a jigsaw, and these are highlighted or ticked off as the child demonstrates them. Such records do not generally include evidence of reading strategies or of independence, attitudes, enthusiasm or interest in reading. You may feel that, to provide a full and detailed profile, the widest possible range of information should be gathered and that frameworks such as *The Primary Language Record*, and records derived from it, can support you in doing this.

GLOSSARY OF ASSESSMENT TERMINOLOGY

The terminology which is used to talk about different kinds of assessment can be rather confusing, so some definitions and distinctions are offered below.

ASSESSMENT is a general term which incorporates all the means generally used to appraise, judge or evaluate performance. It can encompass individuals or groups and refers to both broad appraisal of many sources of evidence and many aspects of learners' knowledge, understanding, skills or attitudes, as well as to one particular occasion or means of assessment. Assessments may be formal with a precise focus on one activity or informal and based on cumulative records of a range of activities.

CRITERION REFERENCING takes place when a pupil's performance is set alongside certain defined criteria. Descriptions are provided relating to different aspects of performance and the pupils are judged according to how well they met those criteria. *NC* assessments are criterion-referenced because they are made by comparing a child's performance with the descriptions for each level of attainment.

DIAGNOSTIC ASSESSMENT can be both formal or informal. Its purpose is to identify where a child's difficulties lie, in learning to read, for example. Results are scrutinised in order that appropriate help, guidance and teaching can be identified and implemented. Formal diagnostic tests are often used by educational psychologists when a child is identified as having Special Educational Needs. More informal diagnostic procedures, such as miscue analysis, are commonly used by classroom teachers, for the same reasons.

FORMATIVE ASSESSMENT is an ongoing part of classroom activity. It is cumulative and provides information on which teachers base further planning. Formative assessments will be recorded as part of a teacher's profile of an individual child. They will record development in progress, rather than completed development.

MEASUREMENT: many tests claim to measure children's reading ability and the results are expressed quantitively. The reader's score is related to a scale or norm and the result is given as a 'reading age' or 'reading quotient'. Scores from such tests are generally used in debates about reading standards, as they are used to measure a rise (or more often, a fall!) in reading standards.

NORM REFERENCING is based on the notion that, in a given sample of people, results of tests will be distributed according to a 'normal curve of distribution'. In other words, there will be a proportion of the sample who will fail and a proportion who will do exceptionally well, while the majority will fall in the middle. Pupils' scores are placed in rank order and the individual's performance is compared to the performance of the others. The grade or score given is not based on the quality of the individual's performance, but on how she or he compares with others in the predetermined proportions of the normal curve.

SUMMATIVE ASSESSMENT is, as the term suggests, a summary of completed development or learning. Such assessments are generally made at the end of a period of teaching or time, such as end of year or end of Key Stage. Summative statements will form part of records for future teachers and/or parents and they will often be compiled using information recorded from formative assessments.

TESTING is a particular category of assessment which is carried out formally, with set contents and specific procedures. It often consists of externally prescribed questions which are marked according to rigid rules, so that comparability of results can be ensured between different test administrators and between different test occasions (for example, *NC* SATs). Test results are perceived as being more objective than teachers' judgements. Standardised tests of reading are pilot-tested with a representative national sample and are published with marking instructions and data on the levels of response established for a national sample at specified ages.

Further reading

Gipps, C. (1995) *Intuition or Evidence? Teachers and National Assessment of Seven-Year-Olds.* Milton Keynes: Open University Press.

Guppy, P. and Hughes, M. (1999) *The Development of Independent Reading.* Buckingham: Open University Press.

QCA (1998) *The Baseline Assessment Information Pack, Preparation for Statutory Baseline Assessment.* London: QCA.

Nutbrown, C. (1999) 'Purpose and Authenticity in Early Literacy Assessment', *Reading* April.

Chapter 5

Meeting Individual Needs

INTRODUCTION

You will know, if you have been in schools for any length of time, that the child who finds reading difficult is the child whom teachers constantly talk and worry about. Of all the curriculum areas, reading is seen as the start of sophisticated thinking and the gateway to all future academic learning. Recognition of this lies behind the concern of all teachers.

Reasons for failure to read

The reasons for underachievement in literacy are never straightforward to identify and it is unlikely that there is only one cause behind a child's failure to learn to read. Interrelated reasons, such as a home where the child is not read to, illness and absence at the start of schooling and a teacher whose classroom is not well organised, might be responsible for a child's failure to make progress; but for every child who fails in such a set of circumstances there are several others who become successful readers. Many children with poor eyesight and poor auditory discrimination become good readers while children with no problems in those areas do not. Some children arrive at school having learned to read from watching advertisements on TV; others, with whole shelves of their own books, seem interested in anything rather than reading. So, while we can broadly say that some circumstances are more likely than others to result in reading difficulties, we can never be categorical nor forget that children continually surprise us. All this needs to be borne in mind while we discuss children with reading difficulties under the headings below.

Characteristics of struggling readers

While reasons for underachievement may be multiple and varied, the characteristics of children who are becoming aware that they cannot read are easier to pin down. These children do not seek opportunities to read, they employ delaying tactics when asked to read, they claim that they do not need to read in their lives, they are afraid of being seen to fail, they blame the book ('it's boring Miss', 'that book's for babies Miss') or their previous teacher ('she never taught me the sounds the letters make Miss'). They tend to over-use one single strategy: some children sound out and believe that accurate decoding is what reading is about and all they need to get better at; some guess at words wildly and appear unable to bring grapho-phonic abilities into play. None seem to have access to the pleasure that reading provides and their views of reading are almost always utilitarian: 'It helps you get a job'.

Characteristics of successful readers

These children, even in the first years of school, have much less fear of failure. They know books off by heart, reread favourite books, 'play' at reading texts which others have read to them, talk about books, make cross-connections to other books read, see relevance in books to their own lives, draw on first-hand experience to aid compre-hension, enjoy writing and are curious about written language. They self-correct when reading aloud, selecting from a full range of strategies as appropriate. Older children are confident enough to read the author's name on a book, to scan the blurb on the back or to assess the contents, using chapter headings or lists of contents, and to use such information in making decisions about whether or not to read. Indeed, knowing that you can choose and that you do not have to read everything is one of the freedoms that successful readers enjoy.

What inexperienced readers need

What inexperienced and struggling readers need is what all readers need – but in every case they need more of it. They need much more of someone reading aloud to them and the accompanying opportunity to have their eyes on print. As teachers can never read enough to them, we have to use cassette tapes and helpers, older children and parents, TV and radio programmes to keep up the modelling and exposure to the pleasures and benefits of reading.

As well as listening to much more reading, these pupils need:

- to be given extra time to browse, revisit old texts, make their own choices and to come at reading through purposeful activities;
- to experience the power of dramatising a text or of extending a text into make-believe play;
- to be asked their opinion of texts;
- to have responses to their volunteered remarks;
- to have their efforts to create texts of their own taken seriously and to have them put into class or individually published books;
- to have an organised classroom, with the full range of routines employed and easy access to a range of books and other resources;
- to have a teacher who is sensitive to their learning styles, monitors progress and keeps – maybe with the child – an accumulating record of all books read;
- to have a teacher who praises appropriately and never loses her optimism, enthusiasm and high expectations;
- to know that teacher and carers at home are in agreement over literacy and the activities which support it.

All this sensitive scaffolding contributes towards an improvement in the child's self-esteem and attitude towards reading that is all-important if we are to meet that child's needs.

As the children read aloud, the listener should be ready to take over the reading when they are clearly struggling (errors of more than one word in ten is a handy guide); paired reading (see Chapter 3) has shown itself to be most effective in terms of the extent to which it both challenges and supports. They need to be reassured that approximations which sustain meaning and 'guesses' are not sinful, though both will need to be fine-tuned against the print on the page; for example, to read 'scared' when the text says 'frightened' preserves meaning but the teacher will need to go back after the reading to talk about the miscue with the child. Similarly, they need to be reassured that decoding is commendable but that meaning will help the fine-tuning; for example, to read 'shepherd' as 'sheferd' shows the child trying to use phonic skills but the context should be used to supply thus the meaning and thus the accurate pronunciation. (The fine judgements that the teacher makes with these miscues are described in Chapter 4.)

Almost certainly, struggling readers require early intervention (see pp. 123–4 on Reading Recovery programmes). It used to be thought that the dangers of labelling a child early on as having literacy difficulties were greater than the task of remedying the problems later. The evidence is clear that early help is not only more humane and productive but that it is also more cost-effective.

What inexperienced readers do not need

A narrowing of focus on to the 'bits and pieces' of reading, the teaching of sub-skills in a decontextualised form without a rich reading environment, results in, at best, only a temporary improvement in these sub-skills and no noticeable gain in fluent reading (see Wasik and Slavin 1993). A programme that is mostly exercises, rote-learning and non-reading-related games is not likely to make much of a difference. On the other hand, a programme where the child hesitantly reads from books which are too difficult or where reading is always of new texts which remain 'cold' because they have not been introduced or discussed, is not helpful either. We can only emphasise again how important it is that you help children choose books with care and skill, that you introduce them in a way that 'warms up' the text and that you leave them with a feeling that the book has been a worthwhile event in their lives.

The children who continue to underachieve in school are often those whom teachers and parents pressurise. In their anxiety, adults forget to commend what the child does well, tending only to see the repeated errors and forgetfulness. A tension can be generated about reading failure that is hugely destructive to progress. Children need praise; they need to know exactly what it is they have done well, whether it is self-correction or a wise prediction or an interesting reflection when the book is finished. They do not need blanket or unmerited praise, any more than they need collusion with their wish to avoid reading.

The support the teacher can expect

The *National Curriculum* is an *inclusive* curriculum: one to which all pupils, irrespective of ability and achievement, are entitled and in which they have the right to participate. Children's additional needs come in all shapes and sizes and this notion of inclusivity can be a challenging one for a new teacher. *The Warnock Report* (DES 1978) established the principle that some pupils should have a statement of 'special need'. The 1993 Education Act tightened up arrangements and set out a *Code of Practice* (DfE 1994) which stressed the need for early identification of difficulties, affirmed that children with Special Educational Needs should be educated in the classrooms of mainstream schools and stated that their assessment should be school-based. It also established the notion of an Individual Education Plan (IEP) to be drawn up as part of the school-based assessment. Your greatest support and source of information in all these matters will be the school's Special Educational Needs Coordinator (SENCO). You will liaise with her over any worries you have about an individual's reading and, if it comes to it, you will construct an IEP with her guidance.

What procedures should you follow if you are concerned about the progress of an individual child? You may, for instance, be concerned that your child is exhibiting signs of dyslexia (see our note on this below). What follows is a checklist for you to use whatever your concerns:

• Look out for early warning signs.

As well as difficulties specifically associated with tackling texts, accompanying early warning signs may take the form of a range of difficulties such as: negative attitudes and poor self-esteem; difficulties in sequencing, remembering, coordinating; discrepancy between language skills and other abilities.

• Carry out appropriate diagnostic procedures.

As well as your ongoing formative assessment (and ensure that this includes phonological awareness), carry out either a running record or miscue analysis (depending on the age and experience of the child).

• Implement an initial action plan.

Use evidence from the above to plan some very specific teaching for the child with well-focused targets.

• Liaise with SENCO and parents.

Discuss your findings with the SENCO and then with the child's parents and share your plan with them. The greater the partnership between you and the parents the better it will be for the child.

• If the child makes progress – good! Continue with carefully targeted steps.

• If the child does not make progress – keep liaising with the SENCO. You may decide that the child needs additional support and that an IEP should be drawn up.

A note about dyslexia

Dyslexia received its first official recognition in the Code of Practice (DfE 1994). For most of the twentieth century, dyslexia (often called 'word blindness'), as a particular difficulty with reading, was not fully acknowledged nor accepted by the teaching profession. As new teachers you need to know how dyslexia is currently defined and how you go about seeking the extra help your pupil will need. The references at the end of the chapter will enable you to expand your understanding of this specialist area.

The literal meaning of dyslexia is difficulty with words but the area has been complicated by the inclusion of many other 'symptoms' such as clumsiness, disorganisation, poor short-term memory and bad behaviour. More relevant to the teacher of reading is the understanding that children who are diagnosed as dyslexic may have problems not only with word blindness but with all-important phonological processing as well. We do know that children whose reading is developing with great difficulty will develop other behaviours (such as truculence in the face of books) but it is not those behaviours that define dyslexia. Because dyslexia is such a broad term, you will find that the term 'Specific Learning Difficulties' is used to pinpoint more precisely the nature of a child's problems. You may however also hear the terms used interchangeably; in either case you will know that you are facing a child with serious literacy difficulties who will need additional specialist support. We offer you Gavin Reid's useful definition:

> patterns of difficulties relating to the processing of information within a continuum from very mild to extremely severe which result in restrictions in literacy development and discrepancies in performances within the curriculum.
>
> (1998 p. 2)

There are specific diagnostic assessments that can be carried out for dyslexia (e.g. *COPS*, Singleton 1996) but you will not have to administer these yourself; the important thing for you to do is be sure that you have taught, monitored and assessed the children as well as you possibly can so that you can hand on full and well-focused information to specialist teachers with whom you liaise.

In the rest of this chapter we look at ways in which you can support the particular reading needs of the children in your class. We start with assessment, where you identify those needs and then we look at ways of responding to them through out-of-class support (from Reading Recovery programmes) and through your own in-class teaching strategies.

ASSESSMENT

As we have said above, when planning to meet the needs of children who are struggling with reading you should start from your observations and assessments of the children. For a full discussion of assessment issues, you need to look back at Chapter 4. Here we want to make some general points as far as they relate to pupils who are finding reading difficult. First of all, you need to ensure that your records contain evidence of the child's achievements as well as his or her difficulties. The parent and child conferences, on the lines of *The Primary Language Record* discussed on p. 134, are a useful contribution to your overall view of the child. We have also talked about observing and recording the child's strategies as you read with them.

For most children these records and observations will provide you with sufficient information; however, for the children who are giving you concern, the additional information to be gained from methodically employing a running record or miscue analysis and analysing your findings is essential. It is at this point that you should be able to decide to what extent you can meet the child's needs in your classroom as these assessment tools will allow you to plan for tailored teaching that is responsive to the child's needs. If you think that you cannot, then you will need to discuss the child with other staff (e.g. the teacher with responsibility for English, the Reading Recovery teacher and/or the SENCO) in order to establish what additional support is available to you and whether an IEP is needed (see checklist above). Whatever the outcome of your discussions, the running record and miscue analysis will still provide you with sufficiently focused information to allow you to meet the *NC*'s 'principles for inclusion':

- the provision of suitable learning challenges;
- response to pupil's diverse needs;
- overcoming potential barriers to learning and assessment for individuals and groups.

(DfEE 1999a p. 30–3)

At the heart of these principles lie your secure understanding of the reading process and of appropriate assessment procedures.

In Chapter 4 we emphasised the need to reduce pressure on the child when carrying out a test. This is even true in a miscue analysis or running record which some under-achieving children construe as a test. Do tell the child that the analysis will help and that you will share all the findings with him or her. As a rule, you should only use other kinds of tests when there is no other way of obtaining information and when you know that you can use the results to focus teaching. Unfortunately, some testing is officially required of us and you will expect to see your poor readers suffering at these times!

Everything that we have included in the chapters on resources and routines is relevant here. What is good practice for your class in general is good practice for your struggling readers. But, because they are struggling, because they lack experience, uppermost in your planning must be the question 'How am I going to engineer more exposure to print?' Everything we have said about Big Books is particularly important for poor readers; you must ensure that your poor readers can see the text and that they remain focused. Print everywhere in the classroom, access to computers, TV pro-grammes, the school bookshop (owning a book makes a big difference), the active promotion of books, books chosen with care, time to read, free choice, shared reading and writing, responsibilities given and purposes for reading made obvious – all these should guide your planning and management of the classroom and should support all your readers. You should also consider the pairing of your poor (older) reader with a younger child. As we show in 'Reading Partners' (Chapter 3) and on pp. 147–8 below, the benefits are two-way.

MEETING INDIVIDUAL NEEDS IN AND OUT OF THE CLASSROOM

Since *The Warnock Report* (DES 1978), the withdrawal of children from class to receive extra individual support has become less common and in-class support is probably now the norm. There are advantages and disadvantages to both systems. It could be said that mature, competent readers read privately and that retirement to a small, quiet, comfortable room without distractions symbolises the act of reading. It is perhaps easier to build a relationship with one's tutor in the withdrawal arrangement and to feel that one's difficulties are being taken seriously. But someone who helps in the classroom can more readily ensure that work is not missed and that the child is not treated so obviously as special. The helper or extra teacher can keep more children under her eye and can more easily coordinate and discuss work with the regular class teacher.

Reading out of the classroom

The main support arrangements that do withdraw children are Reading Recovery programmes. Because they are well established in some areas and because their impact is the subject of much discussion and research we include some detail at this point.

Reading Recovery is an early intervention strategy, developed by Marie Clay in New Zealand, designed to prevent reading failure in young children (six-year-olds). Children thought to be at risk are withdrawn from class and given one-to-one teaching daily for about half-an-hour over 12 to 20 weeks. The hope is that such intensive and early teaching will eliminate some of the enormous costs later, not only in financial terms but also in terms of pupil stress and poor prospects of progress later on. The characteristics of Reading Recovery are:

- intensive training of teachers (literacy methods, child development and children's books);
- high expectations conveyed to the child;
- a range of child-focused and meaning-based approaches;
- the linking of reading and writing;
- clear evidence given to the child of success.

Obviously a programme on this scale costs a lot but the evidence is that, of all the interventionist programmes, Reading Recovery is the only one which produces statistically significant effects which last (Pinnell *et al.* 1994). A typical Reading Recovery session as described by Jean Hudson (1992 pp. 239–41) goes through the following seven stages:

1. Rereading of two or more familiar books to practise reading skills and to develop reading fluency.
2. Practice in letter identification using plastic letters on a magnetic board.
3. Shared writing of a story to be read and reread.
4. Rearranging a cut-up story to provide many opportunities to study individual words and their structures.
5. Practice in analysing the sounds in words.
6. Introduction and attempted reading of at least one new book.
7. Individual variations depending on the child's needs, e.g. prediction, letter identification.

The clear benefits for children are:

- increased confidence that they will be able to read;
- an enthusiasm for books;
- a willingness to take risks and a corresponding reduction in the fear of failure;
- a wider range of strategies used;
- more independence;
- an early return to the normal work of the classroom.

The clear benefits for teachers and schools are:

- in-service training with clear practical outcomes;
- raised standards of literacy as Reading Recovery children are no longer held back;
- better monitoring of all children;
- easier planning as there is less differentiation to consider.

The criticisms that have been levelled against Reading Recovery are that:

- despite the range of approaches used, many children appear to believe that decoding is the only one that matters;
- it does not specify parental involvement;
- it deflects attention from other aspects of why children fail, e.g. poverty, shaky reading policy, poor teaching in the school, poor resources;
- class teachers may feel the responsibility is no longer theirs and abandon class and school attempts to improve the situation;
- it is expensive if children were going to improve anyway. Some children are late starters and there may be no serious reason to withdraw them at the age of six;
- if children are not 'successful' in the time allotted, they are passed on to, for example, an educational psychologist. This may or may not be useful, depending on the psychologist's interest in reading problems, expertise and time available.

At the time of writing, the government has stopped its share of funding for Reading Recovery programmes. This is despite early evidence that the programme is winning support here as it has in New Zealand, Australia, Canada and America. You may still meet Reading Recovery programmes in schools, however, as many local authorities are trying to finance teachers on courses and fund programmes in school.

Reading in the classroom

The Reading Recovery programme takes children out of the classroom in the early stages of reading but it offers principles for working with children, in Key Stages 1 and 2, within the classroom too. Key features of Reading Recovery – the volume of reading, the choice of appropriate texts, creating personal texts, the explicit discussion of strategies for getting at words, and the focus on what the child already knows – are all key aspects of appropriate provision for struggling readers.

There are programmes intended to provide in-class support for Key Stage 2 children (e.g. Clipson-Boyles 1998) and the *NLS* has published materials specifically for use with children in Years 3 and 4 who attained a level 2C or 1 in their Key Stage 1 SATs. These *Additional Literacy Support* materials (DfEE 1999d) are intended for use in the Literacy Hour and make use of close collaboration between the teacher and trained classroom assistants. The assistant runs three guided sessions each week and the teacher runs one. The focus is on reading, writing and phonics (making use of the *PIPs* games mentioned in Chapter 3).

Whether you are organising additional support programmes or not, there are still key principles that should guide your planning of in-class support and we look at these below.

Phonic and graphic knowledge, word recognition

Children who are over-reliant on the meaning of a text and do not use phonic knowledge in their reading will need the kind of careful teaching we discussed in 'Teaching Phonics' in Chapter 3 and you will need to revisit that section to support your planning in this area for struggling readers. Again we stress the importance of keeping such teaching firmly contextualised for the child. You will also find it helpful to reread

'Reading to the Teacher' which contains specific advice about ways of supporting children's decoding skills (among others) during a one-to-one reading session.

Work that you do in the context of the child's writing or during 'Shared Writing' (p. 69) can contribute to his or her graphic knowledge. You could use the shared writing of a story to demonstrate, for instance, past tense verb endings. In this extract from some writing with Year 1 children, the teacher took the opportunity to point out the consistently spelled though differently pronounced 'ed' endings as they arose in the shared composition: 'Red Riding Hood liv*ed* in a forest and every week she walk*ed* to her granny's cottage'.

In another example of work on graphic knowledge, a Year 3 class teacher wanted to target some work on plurals with a particular child as she had noticed him ignoring such word endings in his reading. She suggested he make a number book for a younger child (as part of a unit of work on bookmaking for different audiences). They planned the book together, firstly talking about the kind of items that would appeal to a younger child. Settling on the fruits from *Handa's Surprise* (Browne), the teacher wrote the list of fruits: banana, passion fruit, pineapple, guava, etc. Then they listed them again putting them into the traditional counting format: 1 banana, 2 passion fruits, 3 pineapples, 4 guavas . . . As she wrote each item the teacher asked the child 'How do I show there's more than one passion fruit, pineapple . . . ?' thus drawing his attention to the 's' ending in each case. You could of course carry out such an activity with either the whole class or a group of children.

For some children multi-sensory approaches to letter recognition work well: writing letters in the sand, trailing a finger over a letter cut out of sandpaper, feeling for wooden letters in a bag, having the letter written on your back, manipulating magnetic letters all make a positive contribution. Remember what we said about alphabet books in Chapter 2 and look out for interactive/multi-sensory examples or make your own. These can be made to meet the needs and interests of particular children: for instance, a football alphabet could be constructed by cutting the letters out of different coloured cloth representing different teams.

Children's word recognition skills will be supported by the 'Environmental Print' (Chapter 2) that you provide as well as by more specifically tailored activities. These might include: cloze procedures; name dominoes (which some teachers extend to topic words); a version of pelmanism (maybe based on book characters: wolf, pig, house, sticks, straw, etc.); class-made dictionaries (e.g. of favourite foods); short personal lists of words to learn that the children select themselves from their writing or from a favourite book.

A particularly useful activity for developing word recognition is one in which sentences are cut up and reassembled by the child. It works in this way. Take a book that the child knows well, for example *Not Now Bernard* (McKee), and either read it to the child or read it together. Then take a memorable page such as '"Not now, Bernard," said his mother'. The child watches as you write this out on a strip of paper and cut it up into the six words. Then the child reassembles the words matching them to the printed page. The activity can be developed either at this point or in a subsequent session by asking the child to rearrange the words without the support of the book. You could then provide additional nouns (e.g. other children's names, 'father', 'monster') and use these to generate new sentences: '"Not now, Sunil," said his mother';

'"Not now, Miles," said his father'. This activity works well because it keeps the words contextualised for the child and draws attention to one-to-one correspondence. It also encourages children to draw upon the structure of the sentence itself, the syntax, which children need to use when employing grammatical knowledge. It is to this key skill that we now turn.

Grammatical awareness and contextual understanding

Children who are over-reliant on the letters and words and lose the meaning of what they are reading will need support in developing grammatical awareness and contextual understanding.

These children are using graphic-phonic strategies well enough, so it is important that you work to strengthen the other areas. Then the fine-tuning of the decoding that has to go on can be made more rapidly. This, after all, is our aim with poor readers; we want rapid and automatic orchestration of all the cue-systems.

We pay particular attention to contextual understanding through our later points in this chapter about familiarity with texts and stories (the big shapes again), so we will spend some time now considering grammatical awareness. To explore this we return to an example from the miscue analysis we presented in the last chapter (pp. 124–5). We will consider possible responses to it in two teaching contexts: with the individual child and with the whole class.

In the passage, N misreads, 'I shall be a detective. I shall walk around and find some terrible crime going on' as 'I shall be a detective. I shall walk around and find some trouble crime going on'. She does not self-correct the miscue. In English the juxtaposition of these two nouns, 'trouble' and 'crime', is syntactically impossible and most readers would do a double take at this point, checking, among other things, the punctuation, the graphic arrangement ('terrible/trouble') and the general meaning of the sentence. What are you going to do to teach N to use such a range of strategies? Obviously, encourage her to have another run at the sentence; if she gets it right this time you could end the session by discussing the grapho-phonic differences between the two words. If she repeats the miscue you would need to read the sentence back to her correctly and ask her to identify the difference. You would want to talk to her about the importance of using context and of whether the sentence makes sense. This is something that you could reinforce when she later makes a similar mistake in the sentence, 'She remembered an arrow' which she reads as 'She remind an arrow'. In this case she does self-correct so you could ask her, 'How did you know that it was "remembered" and not "remind"?' If her answer only refers to the grapho-phonic differences, encourage her to reflect on the fact that she made it make sense.

As well as the work you do in one-to-one reading sessions like this on reminding children to reread and to read ahead, you could also model thought processes out loud when you are working with the whole class in shared reading and shared writing sessions. You might, for instance, say 'I'm going to read ahead now and see if that helps me with this word'. Another context for developing such whole-class awareness can arise as you prepare children for sessions when they are going to read with a younger child (see 'Reading Partners' in Chapter 3). One teacher gave her Year 5 class quite specific lessons in this. In groups they discussed questions (on 'prompt' cards) that were specifically designed to increase understanding about using the different cue-systems in reading. The teacher's intention here was twofold: she wanted to develop the quality of the interactions in the reading partnerships by giving her older class some effective strategies for supporting their younger partners, and she also wanted to take the opportunity to make such strategies very clear for the struggling readers in her class. For instance, one card asked the question, 'What would you do if your reading partner was trying to read "the pumpkin seed grew a pumpkin sprout" and she read it as "the pumpkin seed green a pumpkin sprout"?' (from *Pumpkin Pumpkin* by Jeanne Titherington). The children were able to verbalise that their pupil would need to see that the sentence disintegrated because 'green' did not fit; in other words, it was syntactically inappropriate. They also said that they would draw their pupil's attention to the ending of the word 'grew' and show how it was different from the ending of the word 'green'. After accepting the children's suggestions, the teacher added her own which included suggesting that they ask their pupil to reread the sentence. All the suggestions were collated on to a class list entitled 'Ways of Helping our Reading Partners'. In this way awareness and reading ability grow hand in hand.

Texts

The question of which books to have in the classroom is explored in general terms in Chapter 2. We will try to make points more specifically related to children with difficulties, though if the books are valuable for such children they should be valuable for all.

Margaret Meek (1991) speaks of the struggling reader's 'misalignment' with the text. Undoubtedly many children are given texts to read that for one reason or another are neither attractive nor supportive to them. Maybe they never encounter anybody remotely like themselves. We know of an older poor reader from a black family who angrily rejected any more of the 'Little Tim' books (Edward Ardizzone) which have all the middle-class assumptions of their time of writing (pre- and post-World War 2). Many children's books assume a readership that is comfortably off, middle-class, white, two-parented and amply grandparented. Eventually this may alienate those children who already feel marginalised and unsure of their place in this activity of reading. Conversely, and ironically, children may feel that they never have books that take them beyond their immediate environment. (A reading scheme designed especially for working-class inner-city children, 'Nippers', was found to be less popular with its intended audience than the 'exotic' 'Peter and Jane' Ladybird books.) What is probably essential is that the books have emotional truth. Children need to glimpse in them something of how they have felt and feel about life and its ways.

Many older readers are convinced that animal characters are babyish and will feel demeaned by a diet of such books (unless the teacher seeks out and promotes the more subtle examples, such as *The True Story of the Three Little Pigs* (Scieszka and Smith) or *Tusk Tusk* (McKee 1978) or *Fred* (Simmonds). Sadly, there is, in some schools, a prejudice against picture books for older children despite the vast numbers of such books that are suitable throughout the age range. In our view, illustrated texts not only welcome the child to the book and give clues about and a context for the written text, they also teach essential lessons about character, plot, setting and theme. They can add a sophistication to the whole book that keeps an older but less experienced reader involved. You might think that a picture book where the text and the illustrations seem to contradict each other or where the narrator seems unaware of what is going on in the picture, would be the last thing a struggling reader needs, but books such as those by Anthony Browne and Pat Hutchins bestow the pleasure of being 'in the know', and that superior feeling is rewarding enough to make the child return to the book to experience the pleasure again. Rereading is when the most important reading lessons are learned.

If we accept the idea that readers with difficulties have simply not had enough exposure to text then we will want to make sure that they have access to books they care about. The use of narrative texts in schools for early readers has a long and honourable history. In many ways the chronological, time-based ordering of events centring around characters is perhaps quite close to how we all see life. Thus, narrative texts present fewer disjunctions and difficulties to those coming new to reading. This is not to say that non-narrative texts will not be sought out, especially by older boys, but you will need to provide even more support for the reading of non-fiction if your pupil is not to be downcast by the textual challenges.

We have stressed in Chapters 2 and 3 that rhyming texts are the texts that children quickly learn off by heart and which give enormous, almost sensual, pleasure. Texts in verse or picture books of well-known songs have a secret support system: children find themselves able to read almost by magic as the rhyme reduces the possibilities. The fact that rhyming texts strengthen appreciation of onset and rime, so important to literacy development, makes them of central importance for the struggling reader. Ideally, all children would have experienced rhyme in nursery rhymes and songs before school; this is not always the case and it is not easy to share nursery rhymes with a reluctant nine-year-old. Fortunately, there are many rhyming texts, often in picture books, that are suitable, engaging and thought provoking, and which, in a pleasurable way, aid phonological awareness and reveal how our written language encodes the rhymes. Collections of poems by Michael Rosen, Allan Ahlberg, Kit Wright, Charles Causley and the subversive Roald Dahl yield many witty and accessible poems for you to share and enjoy with less experienced readers. When you want to move into classic poetry seek out, in the first instance, ballads and narrative poems as these provide the support of story.

Many children who find reading a problem will turn to humour very willingly; it gives a purpose to the struggle. The Ahlbergs, Jill Murphy, Quentin Blake and Tony Ross consistently come near the top of favourite author/illustrators in this respect. Look out also for the work of Colin McNaughton and Nicholas Allen. Emily Rodda's *Power and Glory* (illustrated by Geoff Kelly) is a very successful, humorous text to share with struggling readers. The child narrator is playing a computer game which has its full share of ogres, witches, goblins and monsters and the robust and well-paced text is repeated as the narrator restarts the game after endless family interruptions. Because the repetition is intrinsic to the whole construction of the story, there is nothing patronising about it for your struggling reader and much painless consolidating of sight words will be going on. In addition, he or she may well be the first person in the class to realise that the illustrations of the computer characters mirror the different family members.

Traditional tales make good reading for the struggler because, unless they are very inexperienced, they know 'how they go'. It is worth seeking out retellings from around the world; John Steptoe's *Mufaro's Beautiful Daughters*, for instance, is the Cinderella story set in Zimbabwe. Once readers have a store of these texts they will enjoy books which play around with traditional tales, such as many picture books by Tony Ross and the Ahlbergs or *Snow White in New York* (French). James Marshall's witty and streetwise retellings of traditional tales also have great appeal.

Finally, a word on comics is in order. Many children would love to belong to the 'club' that reads comics and they may well want to read such texts with you in class. They are not always easy to read aloud together: which bit do you look at first? do you read every bit of print? in which order? Comics and perhaps comic strip books such as Raymond Briggs' *Father Christmas* are probably best for poring over in private; there are reading lessons to be learned within and children are seldom 'just' looking at the pictures. We should not dismiss their efforts if they seem to be directed towards comics more than towards other texts for a limited period.

We have given thought to the role of told stories in Chapter 3. For poor readers, the lessening of tension involved in listening to a story is usually such that they can relax and reflect on some of the most significant reading lessons. They can start to contemplate and store in their minds narrative conventions such as openings, endings, characters, settings and the ups and downs of events in the plot, and they can begin to glimpse the pleasures of story and of language: all features of written narrative but in this mode supported by eye contact, facial expression and intonation. They can hold their own in classroom discussions that may follow. In our experience, some of the best comments on story and some of the best retellings have come from those who are still struggling with the print on the page. The told story gives them confidence and understanding of story conventions, and, with appropriate support, this eventually feeds into reading ability.

PARENTAL INVOLVEMENT

One of the relatively under-explored areas in education is what parents actually do at home when they are enlisted to help with their child's reading in a PACT scheme. As we said in Chapter 3 we know that, in various monitored projects, most children whose parents read with them and listened to them made greater progress than those children whose parents were not involved. What has been less appreciated is that some children whose parents had received insufficient guidance and resources did not make progress and that those children were usually the very ones most in need of extra help (see Toomey 1993 for a full discussion of this). We suggest that if, as we hope, you are seeking to enlist parental involvement with your poor readers, it is important to talk regularly with the parents to ensure that you share the same views of what works for the child. You should recognise that the older the child the harder it is to sustain parental contact over reading, but the more imperative it actually is to do so.

CONCLUSIONS

It may appear that our view of the poor reader contains a protective element. In your experience, the poor reader may be a tricky, disruptive boy (most of the children with literacy difficulties are boys) who rejects all your efforts and whose attention span is of seconds not minutes. But our feeling is that no child does not want to read. Angry, rejecting behaviour when it comes to reading lessons is a symptom of the grave realisation that fills the child of his incompetence in an area that society considers so essential and that he can see brings so much pleasure, knowledge and satisfaction to those around him. The anger is compounded by the evidence that it is so easy for some of his classmates. Most children with difficulties have missed vital early literacy experiences, have been confused by information that lets them down and have been allowed to slip through countless nets, ranging from inadequate resources to badly managed classrooms. We have stressed that collusion with defeatism or unconditional acceptance of the reader's low opinion of himself is not helpful, but a situation where we blame the victim is unforgivable. There is a great deal that can be done to help the poor reader, especially if it is done early enough. We are confident that if you can use some of the advice given here then your sullen/terrified/indifferent/aggressive child will start to experience success and you will know the rewards of helping him to become a reader.

At the beginning of your career, listening to a stumbling beginner may seem monotonous and unrewarding, but we hope you can draw inspiration from this book so that your increasing knowledge and repertoire of approaches, activities and strategies will enable you to respond creatively to your pupils' struggles and to hear their reading with a fresh ear. The message of this chapter, and of the book as a whole, is that as a teacher of reading you need to be fully informed about reading processes and practice. You will then be free to enjoy your teaching and to respond constructively to all your pupils' varying and multiple needs.

Further reading

Bentley, D. and Reid, D. (1995) *Supporting Struggling Readers*. Widnes: UKRA.

Martin, T. (1989) *The Strugglers: Working with Children who Fail to Learn to Read*. Milton Keynes: Open University Press.

Moss, G. (1995) *The Basics of Special Needs: A Routledge/SPECIAL CHILDREN Survival Guide for the Classroom Teacher*. London: Questions Publishing Company/ Routledge.

Ott, P. (1997) *How to Detect and Manage Dyslexia, A Reference and Resource Manual*. Oxford: Heinemann Educational Publishers.

References

Adams, M. J. (1990) *Beginning to Read: The New Phonics in Context*. Oxford: Heinemann.

Arnold, H. (1982) *Listening to Children Reading*. Sevenoaks: Hodder & Stoughton.

Avery, G. (1995) 'The Beginnings of Children's Reading', in Hunt, P. (ed.) *Children's Literature: An Illustrated History*. Oxford: Oxford University Press.

Barrs, M. and Laycock, E. (eds) (1989) *Testing Reading*. London: CLPE.

Barrs, M. and Pigeon, S. (eds) (1998) *Boys and Reading*. London: CLPE.

Barrs, M. and Thomas, A. (eds) (1991) *The Reading Book*. London: CLPE.

Barrs, M. *et al.* (1988) *The Primary Language Record Handbook for Teachers*. London: CLPE.

Beard, R. (1987) *Developing Reading 3–13*. Sevenoaks: Hodder & Stoughton.

Bennett, J. (1979) *Learning to Read with Picture Books*. Stroud: Thimble Press.

Bentley, D. and Reid, D. (1995) *Supporting Struggling Readers*. Widnes: United Kingdom Reading Association.

Brice-Heath, S. (1983) *Ways With Words*. Cambridge: Cambridge University Press.

Bromley, H. (1996) 'Reading Revolution at Story Time', *Primary English Magazine* **1**(2).

Bryant, P. and Bradley, L. (1985) *Children's Reading Problems*. Oxford: Blackwell.

Bussis, A. *et al.* (1985) *Inquiry into Meaning: An Investigation of Learning to Read*. Hillsdale, NJ: Lawrence Erlbaum Associates.

Campbell, R. (1993) *Miscue Analysis in the Classroom*. Royston: UKRA.

Cato, V. and Whetton, C. (1991) *NFER Enquiry into Evidence of Standards of Reading of 7 year old Children*. London: DES/HMSO.

Clark, M. (1976) *Young Fluent Readers*. London: Heinemann.

Clay, M. (1979a) *Sand: The Concepts About Print Test*. London: Heinemann.

Clay, M. (1979b) *Stones: The Concepts About Print Test*. London: Heinemann.

Clay, M. (1979c) *The Early Detection of Reading Difficulties (2nd edn)*. Auckland: Heinemann.

Clay, M. (1985) *The Early Detection of Reading Difficulties (3rd edn)*. Auckland: Heinemann.

Clipson-Boyles, S. *et al.* (1998) *The Catch Up Project*. Oxford: Oxford Brookes University.

Crystal, D. (1987) *Cambridge Encyclopedia of Language*. Cambridge: Cambridge University Press.

DES (1967) *Children and Their Primary Schools* (The Plowden Report). London: HMSO.

DES (1975) *A Language for Life* (The Bullock Report). London: HMSO.

DES (1978) *Special Educational Needs* (The Warnock Report). London: HMSO.

DES (1987) *Report of the Task Group on Assessment and Testing* (TGAT). London: HMSO.

DES (1992) *Curriculum Organisation and Classroom Practice in Primary Schools.* London: DES.

DfE (1994) *Code of Practice on the Identification and Assessment of Special Educational Needs.* London: Central Office of Information.

DfE (1995) *English in the National Curriculum.* London: HMSO.

DfEE (1998a) *The National Literacy Strategy Framework for Teaching.* London: DfEE.

DfEE (1998b) *Teaching: High Status, High Standards (Circular number 4/98).* London: DfEE.

DfEE/QCA (1999a) *English, The National Curriculum for England.* London: DfEE.

DfEE (1999b) *The National Literacy Strategy, Phonics: Progression in Phonics.* London: DfEE.

DfEE/QCA (1999c) *Early Learning Goals.* London: DfEE/QCA.

DfEE (1999d) *The National Literacy Strategy Additional Literacy Support Module.* London: DfEE.

DfEE (1999e) *The National Literacy Strategy Spelling Bank.* London: DfEE/QCA (2000) Curriculum Guidance for the Foundation Stage London: DfEE/QCA.

Diack, H. (1965) *In Spite of the Alphabet: A Study of the Teaching of Reading.* London: Chatto and Windus.

Edwards, V. (1998) *The Power of Babel, Teaching and Learning in Multilingual Classrooms.* Stoke-on-Trent: Trentham Books.

Fry, D. (1985) *Children Talk about Books: Seeing Themselves as Readers.* Milton Keynes: Open University Press.

Goodman, K. (1973) 'Miscues: Windows on the Reading Process', in Goodman, K. (ed.) *Miscue Analysis: Application to Reading Instruction.* Urbana, Ill.: ERIC Clearing House on Reading and Communication, NCTE.

Goodman, Y. (1987) 'A Kid Watching Guide: Evaluation for Whole Language Classrooms', Gnosis **10**.

Goodwin, P. (ed.) (1999) *The Literate Classroom.* London: David Fulton Publishers.

Goswami, U. (1995) 'Rhyme in Children's Early Reading', in Beard, R. (ed.) *Rhyme, reading and writing.* London: Hodder & Stoughton.

Goswami, U. (1996) *Rhyme and Analogy Teacher's Guide.* Oxford: Oxford University Press.

Goswami, U. and Bryant, P. (1991) *Phonological Skills and Learning to Read.* Hillsdale, NJ: Lawrence Erlbaum Associates.

Gregory, E. (1989) 'Do English Eat Octopus?' *English in Education* **23**(3).

Gregory, E. (1996) *Making Sense of a New World.* London: Paul Chapman Publishing.

Grey, D. (1999) *The Internet in Schools.* London: Cassell.

Hall, N. (1987) *The Emergence of Literacy.* Sevenoaks: Edward Arnold.

Her Majesty's Inspectorate (1991) *The Teaching and Learning of Reading in Primary Schools.* London: HMSO.

Hester, H. (1983) *Stories in the Multilingual Primary Classroom: Supporting Children's Learning of English as a Second Language.* London: ILEA.

Holdaway, D. (1979) *The Foundations of Literacy.* Sydney: Ashton Scholastic.

House of Commons Education, Science and Arts Committee (1990) *Standards of Reading in Primary Schools* (Select Committee Report). London: HMSO.

Hudson, J. (1992) 'Reading Delays', in Harrison, C. and Coles, M. (eds) *The Reading for Real Handbook*. London: Routledge and Kegan Paul.

Johns, L. (1992/3) 'Transforming the Library', *Language Matters*.

Laycock, E. (1989) 'Testing Reading – an investigation', in Barrs, M. and Laycock, E. (eds) *Testing Reading*. London: CLPE.

Leask, M. and Meadows, J. (2000) *Teaching and Learning with ICT in the Primary School*. London: Routledge/Falmer.

Mayor, B. (1988) 'What Does It Mean to Be Bilingual?', in Mercer, N. (ed.) *Language and Literacy from an Educational Perspective Vol.1*. Milton Keynes: Open University Press.

McKay, D. (ed.) (1970) *Breakthrough to Literacy*. Harlow: Longman.

Meek, M. (1988) *How Texts Teach What Readers Learn*. Stroud: Thimble Press.

Meek, M. (1991) *On Being Literate*. London: Bodley Head.

Meek, M. *et al.* (eds) (1977) *The Cool Web*. London: Bodley Head.

Millard, E. (1997) *Differently Literate: Boys, Girls and the Schooling of Literacy*. London: Falmer Press.

Minns, H. (1990) *Read it to me Now!* London: Virago.

Moon, C. (published yearly) *Individualised Reading*. Reading, Berkshire: Reading and Language Information Centre.

Moon. C. (1984) 'Making use of Miscues When Children Read Aloud', in *Children Reading to their Teachers*. Sheffield: NATE.

Morgan, R. (1976) 'Paired Reading Tuition: A Preliminary Report on a Technique for Cases of Reading Deficit', in *Child Care Health and Development* **2**.

National Writing Project (1989) *Becoming A Writer*. Surrey: Thomas Nelson.

Neate, B. (1992) *Finding Out About Finding Out: A Practical Guide to Children's Information Books*. Sevenoaks: Hodder & Stoughton/UKRA.

OFSTED (1993) *Boys and English*. London: OFSTED.

OFSTED (1996) *The Teaching of Reading in 45 Inner London Primary Schools*. London: OFSTED.

Pinnell, G. *et al.* (1994) 'Comparing instructional models for the literacy education of high risk first graders', *Reading Research Quarterly* **29**(1).

Reid, G. (1998) *Dyslexia: a Practitioner's Handbook*. Chichester: Wiley.

Schools Curriculum and Assessment Authority (1995) *Planning the Curriculum at Key Stages 1 & 2*. London: SCAA.

Schools Curriculum and Assessment Authority (1996) *Desirable Outcomes for Children's Learning on Entering Compulsory Education*. London: SCAA.

Sheridan C. (1982) *Introduction to Miscue Analysis*. Australia: Western Australia College of Advanced Education.

Singleton, C. (1996) *COPS 1 Cognitive Profiling System*. Nottingham: Chameleon Education Ltd.

Skinner, B. (1953) *Science and Human Behaviour*. Basingstoke: Macmillan.

Smith, F. (1978) *Reading*. Cambridge: Cambridge University Press.

Southgate, V. and Arnold, H. (1981) *Extending Beginning Reading*. London: Heinemann, for the Schools Council.

Stierer, B. and Bloom, D. (1994) *Reading Words*. Sheffield: NATE.

Tolkien, J. (1964) *Tree and Leaf.* London: Allen and Unwin.

Toomey, D. (1993) 'Parents Hearing their Children Read: a Review. Rethinking the Lessons of the Haringey Project', *Educational Research* **35**(3).

Topping, K. and Wolfendale, S. (eds) (1985) *Parental Involvement in Reading.* London: Croom Helm.

Vygotsky, L. (1978) *Mind in Society.* Cambridge, Mass.: Harvard University Press.

Wasik, B. and Slavin, R. (1993) 'Preventing Early Reading Failure with One-to-one Tutoring: a Review of Five Programs', *Reading Research Quarterly* **28**(2).

Waterland, L. (1985) *Read With Me.* Stroud: Thimble Press.

Weaver, C. (1980) *Psycholinguistics and Reading: From Process to Practice.* Boston, Mass.: Little, Brown and Co.

Wells, G. (1987) *The Meaning Makers.* London: Hodder & Stoughton.

Wiles, S. (1985) 'Language and Learning in Multi-Ethnic Classrooms: Strategies for Supporting Bilingual Students', in Wells, G. and Nicholls, J. (eds) *Language and Learning: An Interactional Perspective.* London: The Falmer Press.

Reading tests

Bookbinder, G. (1976) *Salford Sentence Reading Test.* Sevenoaks: Hodder & Stoughton.

Godfrey Thomson Unit (1977–1981) *Edinburgh Reading Test.* London: Hodder & Stoughton.

McLeod, J. and Unwin, D. (1970) *GAP Reading Comprehension Test.* London: Heinemann.

Neale, M. (Christophers, U. and Whetton, C. British adaptors and standardisers) (1988) *Neale Analysis of Reading Ability, Revised British Edition.* Windsor: NFER Nelson.

Schonell, F. and F. (1942, restandardised 1972) *Schonell Graded Word Reading Test.* Harlow: Oliver and Boyd.

Vincent, D. and De La Mare, M. (1986) *Effective Reading Tests (ERT).* Basingstoke: Macmillan.

Watts, A. (1948) *Holborn Reading Scale.* London: Harrap.

Young, D. (1980) *Group Reading Test.* London: Hodder & Stoughton.

CHILDREN'S BOOKS

Agard, J. and Nicholls, G. (1994) *A Caribbean Dozen.* London: Walker Books.

Ahlberg, A. and J. (1978) *Each Peach Pear Plum.* London: Kestrel/Viking.

Ahlberg A. and J. (1980) *Mrs Wobble the Waitress.* Harmondsworth: Picture Puffin.

Ahlberg, A. and J. (1986) *The Jolly Postman.* London: Kestrel/Viking.

Ahlberg, A and J. (1988) *Starting School.* London: Viking.

Ahlberg, A. and J. (1995) *The Jolly Pocket Postman.* London: Heinemann.

Anderson, R. (1984) *The War Orphan.* Oxford: Oxford University Press.

Ardizzone, E. (1936) *Little Tim and the Brave Sea Captain.* Oxford: Oxford University Press.

Armitage, R. and D. (1977) *The Lighthouse Keeper's Lunch.* Auckland: Scholastic.

Barber, A. and Bayley, N. (1990) *The Mousehole Cat.* London: Walker Books.

Berry, J. (ed.) (1995) *Classic Poems to Read Aloud.* London: Kingfisher.

Biet, P. and Bloom, B. (1998) *The Cultivated Wolf.* London: Siphano Press.

Binch, C. (1998) *Since Dad Left.* London: Frances Lincoln.

Blake, Q. (1968) *Patrick.* London: Jonathan Cape.

Blake, Q. (1980) *Mr Magnolia.* London: Jonathan Cape.

Blake, Q. (1999) *Fantastic Daisy Artichoke.* London: Jonathan Cape.

Branford, H. (1997) *Fire, Bed and Bone.* London: Walker Books.

Breinburg, P. and Lloyd, E. (1973) *My Brother Sean.* London: Bodley Head.

Briggs, R. (1973) *Father Christmas.* London: Hamish Hamilton.

Brown, J. (1974) *Flat Stanley.* Leicester: Methuen.

Brown, R. (1981) *A Dark Dark Tale.* London: Andersen.

Browne, A. (1983) *Gorilla.* London: Julia MacRae Books.

Browne, A. (1986) *Piggybook.* London: Julia MacRae Books.

Browne, A. (1998) *Voices in the Park.* London: Doubleday.

Browne, A. and Carroll, L. (1988) *Alice's Adventures in Wonderland.* London: Julia MacRae Books.

Browne, E. (1994) *Handa's Surprise.* London: Walker Books.

Browning, R. and Amstutz, A. (1993) *The Pied Piper of Hamelin.* London: Orchard Books.

Burningham, J. (1970) *Mr Gumpy's Outing.* London: Jonathan Cape.

Burningham, J. (1978) *Would You Rather?* London: Jonathan Cape.

Burningham, J. (1984) *Granpa.* London: Jonathan Cape.

Burningham, J. (1989) *Oi! Get off our Train!* London: Jonathan Cape.

Burningham, J. (1991) *Aldo.* London: Jonathan Cape.

Cameron, A. (1982) *The Julian Stories.* London: Gollancz.

Cameron, A. (1992) *Julian, Dream Doctor.* London: Transworld (Yearling Books).

Campbell, R. (1985) *Dear Zoo.* London: Picture Puffin.

Carle, E. (1970) *The Very Hungry Caterpillar.* London: Hamish Hamilton.

Cave, K. (1998) *W is for World.* London: Frances Lincoln in association with Oxfam.

Cooper, H. (1998) *Pumpkin Soup.* London: Transworld Publishers.

Counsel, J. and Dinan, C. (1984) *But Martin!* London: Faber and Faber.

Cousins, L. (1990) *Maisie Goes Swimming.* London: Walker Books.

Cross, G. (1992) *The Great Elephant Chase.* Harmondsworth: Puffin Books.

Fine, A. (1989a) *Bill's New Frock.* London: Mammoth.

Fine, A. (1989b) *Goggle Eyes.* London: Hamish Hamilton.

Fine, A. (1993) *The Angel of Nitshill Road.* London: Mammoth.

Fitzhugh, L. (1976) *Nobody's Family is Going to Change.* London: Gollancz.

Flournoy, V. and Pinkney, J. (1985) *The Patchwork Quilt.* London: Bodley Head.

Foreman, M. (1987) *Ben's Baby.* London: Andersen Press.

French, F. (1986) *Snow White in New York.* Oxford: Oxford University Press.

Graham, H. (1996) *The Boy and his Bear.* Leamington Spa: Scholastic.

Hastings, S. and Wijngaard, J. (1981) *Sir Gawain and the Green Knight.* London: Walker Books.

Hayes, S. and Craig, H. (1986) *This is the Bear.* London: Walker Books.

Heapy, T. (1997) *Korky Paul, Biography of an Illustrator.* Oxford: Heinemann Educational Publishers.

Hedderwick, M. (1986) *Katie Morag and the Troublesome Ted.* London: Bodley Head.

Heide, F. and Gorey, E. (1971) *The Shrinking of Treehorn.* New York: Holiday House.

Hoffman, M. and Binch, C. (1991) *Amazing Grace.* London: Frances Lincoln.

Hughes, S. (1977) *Dogger.* London: Bodley Head.

Hughes, T. (1968) *The Iron Man*. London: Faber and Faber.

Hutchins, P. (1969) *Rosie's Walk*. London: Bodley Head.

Hutchins, P. (1972) *Titch*. London: Bodley Head.

Hutchins, P. (1983) *You'll Soon Grow Into Them Titch*. London: Bodley Head.

Inkpen, M. and Butterworth, N. (1992) *Jasper's Beanstalk*. Sevenoaks: Hodder & Stoughton.

Kemp, G. (1977) *The Turbulent Term of Tyke Tiler*. Harmondsworth: Penguin.

King-Smith, D. (1978) *The Fox Busters*. Harmondsworth: Puffin Books.

King-Smith, D. (1983) *The Sheep Pig*. London: Gollancz.

Koch, K. and Farrell, K. (1985) *Talking to the Sun*. New York: Metropolitan Museum of Art.

Laird, E. (1991) *Kiss the Dust*. London: Heinemann.

Loewen, V. and Pearson, D. (1997) *The Best Book for Terry Lee*. London: Kingscourt.

Lloyd, E. (1982) *Nandy's Bedtime*. London: Bodley Head.

Lobel, A. (1973) *Frog and Toad*. Tadworth: World's Work.

MacAfee, A. and Browne, A. (1984) *The Visitors who Came to Stay*. London: Hamish Hamilton.

MacCauley, D. (1988) *The Way Things Work*. London: Dorling Kindersley.

Magorian, M. and Ormerod, J. (1992) *Jump!* London: Walker Books.

Marshall, J. (1987) *Red Riding Hood*. New York: Dial Books.

Mayer, M. (1994) *Arthur's Teacher Trouble*. Gravesend: Broderbund.

McCaughrean, G. (1995) *Golden Myths and Legends of the World*. London: Orion.

McKee, D. (1968) *Elmer*. London: Dobson Books Ltd.

McKee, D. (1978) *Tusk Tusk*. London: Andersen Press.

McKee, D. (1980) *Not Now Bernard*. London: Andersen Press.

Minarik, E. and Sendak, M. (1965) *Little Bear*. Tadworth: World's Work.

Morpurgo, M. (1995) *The Dancing Bear*. London: Collins.

Murphy, J. (1980) *Peace At Last*. London: Walker Books.

Murphy, J. (1983) *Whatever Next?* London: Macmillan.

Murphy, J. (1986) *Five Minutes Peace*. London: Walker Books.

Murphy, J. (1987) *All in One Piece*. London: Walker Books.

Murphy, J. (1989) *A Piece of Cake*. London: Walker Books.

Patten, B. (ed.) (1997) *The Puffin Book of Utterly Brilliant Poetry*. London: Viking.

Paul, K. and Thomas, V. (1987) *Winnie the Witch*. Oxford: Oxford University Press.

Prater, J. (1993) *Once Upon a Time*. London: Walker Books.

Provensen, A. and M. (1984) *Leonardo da Vinci*. London: Hutchinson.

Pullman, P. (1995) *Northern Lights*. Leamington Spa: Scholastic.

Pullman, P. (1996) *Clockwork or All Wound Up*. London: Doubleday.

Rodda, E. and Kelly, G. (1994) *Power and Glory*. St Leonards, Australia: Allen and Unwin.

Rosen, M. (ed.) (1991) *A World of Poetry*. London: Kingfisher.

Rosen, M. and Oxenbury, H. (1989) *We're Going on a Bear Hunt*. London: Walker Books.

Ross, T. (1985) *The Boy Who Cried Wolf*. London: Andersen Press.

Ross, T. (1986) *I Want my Potty!* London: Andersen Press.

Ross, T. (1987a) *Stone Soup*. London: Andersen Press.

Ross, T. (1987b) *Oscar Got the Blame*. London: Andersen Press.

Ross, T. (1991) *A Fairy Tale*. London: Andersen Press.

Rowling, J. K. (1997) *Harry Potter and the Philosopher's Stone*. London: Bloomsbury.

Scieszka, J. and Smith, L. (1989) *The True Story of the Three Little Pigs*. New York: Viking Penguin.

Scieszka, J. and Smith, L. (1992) *The Stinky Cheese Man and Other Fairly Stupid Tales*. London: Viking.

Sendak, M. (1963) *Where the Wild Things Are*. London: Bodley Head.

Seuss, Dr (1957) *The Cat in the Hat Comes Back*. New York: Random House.

Simmonds, P. (1987) *Fred*. London: Jonathan Cape.

Steptoe, J. (1988) *Mufaro's Beautiful Daughters*. London: Hamish Hamilton.

Storr, C. (1976) 'Lew, the fabulous detective', in Jackson, D. and Pepper, D. (eds) *The Yellow Story House*. Oxford: Oxford University Press.

Sutton, E. and Dodd, L. (1973) *My Cat Likes to Hide in Boxes*. London: Hamish Hamilton.

Titherington, J. (1986) *Pumpkin Pumpkin*. London: Julia MacRae Books.

Trivizas, E. and Oxenbury, H. (1993) *The Three Little Wolves and the Big Bad Pig*. London: Heinemann.

Voake, C. (1999) *Charlotte Voake's Alphabet Adventure*. London: Jonathan Cape.

Waddell, M. and Firth, B. (1988) *Can't You Sleep Little Bear?* London: Walker Books.

Wade, G. (1986) *Curtis the Hip-Hop Cat*. London: Macmillan.

Watanabe, S. (1979) *How Do I Put it On?* London: Bodley Head.

Webb, K. (ed.) (1979) *I Like this Poem*. Harmondsworth: Puffin.

Wells, R. (1973) *Noisy Nora*. New York: Dial Press.

Westall, R. (1992) *Gulf*. London: Methuen.

White, E. B. (1952) *Charlotte's Web*. London: Hamish Hamilton.

Wilder, L. Ingalls (1932) *Little House in the Big Woods*. London: Methuen.

Wildsmith, B. (1989) *The Christmas Story*. Oxford: Oxford University Press.

Wilson, G. and Parkins, D. (1994) *Prowlpuss*. London: Walker Books.

Wood, A. J. and Allen, H. (1992) *Errata*. Dorking: Templar Co.

Wormell, C. (1990) *An Alphabet of Animals*. London: Collins.

Books in series

(no dates given as these cover a range)

'Banana Books'. London: Heinemann.

Blyton, E. 'Famous Five'. London: Hodder & Stoughton.

'Jets'. London: Harper Collins.

Lane, S. and Kemp, M. 'Take Part'. London: Ward Lock.

Martin, A. 'The Babysitters' Club'. Leamington Spa: Hippo/Scholastic.

'Spirals'. Cheltenham: Stanley Thornes.

'Superchamp Books'. London: Heinemann.

Reading schemes

'All Aboard' (1994) Aylesbury: Ginn.
'Bangers and Mash' (1975) Harlow: Longman.
'Cambridge Reading' (1996) Cambridge: Cambridge University Press.
'Keywords' (1976) Loughborough: Ladybird.
'Letterland' (1973) London: Collins.
'New Reading 360' (1994) Aylesbury: Ginn.
'Nippers' (1968) London: Macmillan Education.
'One, Two, Three and Away' (1966) Glasgow: Collins.
'Oxford Reading Tree' (1985) Oxford: Oxford University Press.
'Story Chest' (1981) London: Kingscourt.

CD-ROMs

Arthur's Teacher Trouble Broderbund
Dr Seuss's ABC Living Books
Look! Hear! Talking Topics Sherston Software
My First Incredible Amazing Dictionary Dorling Kindersley
The Mystery of Hyphen-Hall Aircom Education
Nursery Rhyme Time Sherston Software
Oxford Children's Encyclopedia OUP
Oxford Reading Tree Rhyme and Analogy Sherston Software
Ridiculous Rhymes Sherston Software
Spot's Busy Day Europress
Teacher's Cupboard Sherston Software
Web Workshop Iona Software

Author index

Adams, M. J. 5, 13
Ager, R. 52
Arnold, H. 109, 121
Avery, G. 2

Barrs, M. *et al.* 31, 121, 134
Barrs, M. and Laycock, E. 129, 153
Barrs, M. and Pigeon, S. 8, 16
Barrs, M. and Thomas, A. 4, 5, 16
Barton, B. 68
Barton, B. and Booth, D. 79
Beard, R. 9, 16
Bennett, J. 10
Bentley, D. and Reid, D. 150
Branston, P. and Provis, M. 112
Brice-Heath, S. 7, 109
Bromley, H. 67
Brown, M. and Williams, A. 28
Bryant, P. and Bradley, L. 12
Bussis, A., Chittenden, E., Amarel, M. and
    Klausner, E 5, 82
Byrom, G. 52

Campbell, A. 33
Campbell, R. 59, 63, 109, 121
Carter, J. 58, 59
Cato, V. and Whetton, C. 10
Chambers, A. 59
Clark, H. 28
Clark, M. 6
Clay, M. 116, 117, 118, 127, 143
Clipson-Boyles, S. 82, 144
Collins, F. Y. 79
Crystal, D. 11, 84

Daniels, G. 33
Diack, H. 2

Dombey, H. and Moustafa, M. 93
Dombey, H. and Robinson, M. 104

Edwards, V. 16
Evans, J. 31

Fenwick, J. 63
Fincham, L. 54
Fry, D. 33

Gipps, C. 136
Goodman, K. 4
Goodman, Y. 117
Goodwin, P. 82
Goswami, U. 11, 13
Goswami, U. and Bryant, P. 12, 13
Graham, J. 76
Graham, J. and Kelly, A. 72, 93
Grainger, T. 79
Gregory, E. 8, 109
Grey, D. 52
Grugeon, E. and Gardner, P. 79
Guppy, P. and Hughes, M. 136

Hall, N. 18, 47, 57
Hannon, P. 112
Hardy, B. 78
Hendy, L. 82
Hester, H. 8
Holdaway, D. 6, 27, 28, 69, 70
Howe, A. and Johnson, J. 79
Hudson, J. 143

Johns, L. 53
Johnson, P. 46, 47

Kelly, A. 93

Kropp, P. and Cooling, W.   26

Laycock, L.   31, 72
Laycock, L. and Washtell, A.   93
Layton, L.   93
Leask, M. and Meadows, J.   51, 52

Mallett, M.   101
Marriott, S.
Martin, T.   150
Maybin, J. and Mercer, N.   104
Mayor, B.   8
McKay, D.   3
Medwell, J.   52
Meek, M.   8, 78, 147
Meek, M., Warlow, A. and Barton, G.
Millard, E.   8, 16, 76
Minns, H.   7, 109
Moon, C.   10, 121
Morgan, R.   110
Moss, G.   150

Neate, B.   98
Nutbrown, C.   136

Ott, P.   150

Palmer, S.   93
Pennac, D.   68
Perera, K.   34
Pinnell, G. *et al.*   143
Pinsent, P.   26
Powling, C. and Styles, M.   26

Reid, G.   141

Sanger, J.   112
Sheridan C.   121
Singleton, C.   141, 150
Skinner, B.   2
Simms, L.   77
Smith, F.   4
Smith, V.   101
Southgate, V. *et al.*   63
Stierer, B. and Bloom, D.   128
Stones, R.   26
Styles, M.   82

Teale, W. H.   68
Thomas, B. and Williams, R.   52
Thomas, H.   76
Thompson, G. B. and Nicholson, T.   93

Tolkien, J.   32, 72
Toomey, D.   149
Topping, K. and Wolfendale, S.   110
Toye, N. and Prendiville, F.   82
Trelease, J.   68

Vygotsky, L.   64

Washtell, A.   72
Washtell, A. and Laycock, L.   93
Wasik, B. and Slavin, R.   139
Waterland, L.   10
Watson, V.   33
Weaver, C.   4
Wells, G.   20, 60
Wiles, S.   7
Wray, D. and Lewis, M.   101

CHILDREN'S BOOKS

Agard, J. and Nicholls, G.   59
Ahlberg A. and J.   23, 24, 27, 30, 77, 94, 106, 148
Aiken, J.   20
Allen, N.   148
Amstutz, A.   74
Ardizzone, E.   147
Armitage, R. and D.   27, 58
Ashley, B.   24, 32

Barber, A. and Bayley, N.   48
Berry, J.   59
Biet, P. and Bloom, B.   vi, 58
Binch, C.   24
Blackman, M.   24
Blake, Q.   45, 48, 89, 90, 148
Blyton, E.   19, 31
Branford, H.   94
Briggs, R.   11, 48, 149
Brown, J.   22
Brown, R.   30
Browne, A.   24, 30, 45, 64, 148
Browne, A. and Carroll, L.   64
Browne, E.   9, 103, 145
Browning, R. and Amstutz, A.   74
Burningham, J.   28, 48, 66, 81, 89, 107

Cameron, A.   29, 32
Campbell, R.   29
Carle, E.   29, 68
Causley, C.   75, 148
Cave, K.   91

Cole, B.   23
Cooper, H.   29
Cousins, L.   29
Cross, G.   68
Crossley-Holland, K.   20

Dahl, R.   148

Fine, A.   24, 48, 73
Fitzhugh, L.   24
Flournoy, V. and Pinkney, J.   29
Foreman, M.   43, 44
French, F.   45, 149

Garland, S.   8
Graham, H.   75
Grimm brothers   23

Hastings, S. and Wijngaard, J.   30
Hawkins, C. and J.   13
Hayes, S. and Craig, H.   66
Heapy, T.   27
Hedderwick, M.   48
Heide, F. and Gorey, E.   32
Hill, E.   31
Hoffman, M. and Binch, C.   49
Hughes, S.   8, 66, 80
Hughes, T.   48, 66, 79
Hutchins, P.   30, 32, 71, 80, 89, 119, 148

Inkpen, M. and Butterworth, N.   29, 99

Keeping, C.   24
Kemp, G.   116
King-Smith, D.   32, 67, 73
Koch, K. and Farrell, K.   59

Laird, E.   24
Lane, S. and Kemp, M.   22
Lively, P.   33
Lobel, A.   32
Loewen, V. and Pearson, D.   45
Lurie, A.   23

MacAfee, A. and Browne, A.   43
Magorian, M. and Ormerod, J.   34
Marshall, J.   149
Mayer, M.   50
McCaughrean, G.   21, 100
McKee, D.   27, 32, 43, 145, 147

McNaughton, C.   148
Minarik, E. and Sendak, M.   32
Morpurgo, M.   74, 116
Murphy, J.   29, 32, 43, 99, 148

Nicholl, H. and Pienkowski, J.   31

Patten, B.   59, 75
Paul, K. and Thomas, V.   107
Pearce, P.
Prater, J.   30
Provensen, A. and M.   29
Pullman, P.   21, 73

Riordan, J.   23
Rodda, E. and Kelly, G.   148
Rosen, M.   59, 148, 149
Rosen, M. and Oxenbury, H.   30
Ross, T.   22, 23, 27, 43, 45, 65, 104, 148
Rowling, J. K.   19, 32

Scieszka, J. and Smith, L.   23, 30, 147
Sendak, M.   6, 43
Seuss, Dr   32, 50
Simmonds, P.   147
Steptoe, J.   149
Storr, C.   124
Sutton, E. and Dodd, L.   30

Tennyson, A. L.   71
Titherington, J.   147
Trivizas, E. and Oxenbury, H.   27

Voake, C.   87

Waddell, M. and Firth, B.   6, 32, 58
Wade, G.   46
Walsh, J. P.   21
Watanabe, S.   43
Wells, R.   43
Westall, R.   24
White, E. B.   73
Wilder, L. Ingalls.   32
Wildsmith, B.   30
Wilson, G. and Parkins, D.   30
Wilson, J.   21
Wood, A. J. and Allen, H.   98
Wormell, C.   87
Wright, K.   148

Subject index

Additional Learning Support materials   90, 144
All Aboard   37
alliteration   12, 20, 30, 87, 91
alphabet   18
   alphabetic method   1
   alphabetic knowledge   87, 91
analogy   13, 86
analytic phonics   14, 82, 91
'apprenticeship' approach   104
assessment   **113–136**
attainment targets   14
authors
   display   58, 75
   favourite   19, 32, 58
   visits   53–4

Bangers and Mash   36
baseline assessment   127
bedtime story   6, 69
behaviourism   2
bibliographic cue-system   5
Big Books/enlarged texts   18, **27–8**, 34, 45, 60,
   68–9, 70–1, 87, 88, 142
'big shapes'   5–6, 10, 14, 50, 65, 77, 86, 146
bilingual children   3, **7–8**, 43, 46, 64, 69, 77,
   110, 115, 116, 134
blend   9, 11, 85, 86, 91
book
   blurb 74, 96, 114, 138
   core books   17, 28–31
   corner   31, 55–8, 75
   -making   18, 45–7, 54
   reviews   76
   shops   53–4, 142
boys   8, 21, 22, 23–4, 26, 45, 59, 80, 94, 101,
   110, 149–50
Breakthrough to Literacy   2

Bullock Report   109

Cambridge Reading   39
cassettes   19, 20, 31, 34, 49, 73, 86, 138
CD-ROMs   18, 34, **49–50**, 86, 87, 95, 99, 100,
   101
children's interests   25, 115
choosing a book   24–6
CLPE   4, 5, 104
classification   55
   Dewey system   52–3
class reader   72–6
classroom assistants   116, 144
cloze procedure   97, 98, 145
cluster   83, 91
   consonant   84
Code of Practice   139, 140
colour coding   10, 26, 55
comics   23, 25, 149
computers   49–52, 142
concepts of print   116
consonant   11, 84, 91, 92
   cluster   91
   digraph   83, 92
   phoneme   12
contents page (information books)   22, 69, 98, 138
context cues/contextual understanding   8, 15,
   20, 100, 107, 146–7
controlled vocabulary   2
COPS   141
core books   17, 28–31
criterion referencing   135
cue-systems   5, 8, 9, 15, 82, 90
cultural diversity   7, 24, 109, 115
Curriculum Guidance for the Foundation Stage
   14
curve of distribution   135

decoding   2, 9, 26, 71, 82, 83, 100, 106, 137, 145

Desirable Outcomes for Children's Learning   14

developmental writing   6

Dewey system   52–3

diagnostic assessment   135

digraph   92

    consonant   83, 84, 92

    split   83, 90, 93

    vowel   83, 93

diphthong   92

directionality   116

drama   79–82, 138

dual-language books   44–5

dyslexia   140–1

Early Learning Goals   14, 127

early literacy   6–7

Edinburgh Reading Test   128, 130

Effective Reading Test   129, 130

e-mail   52

emergent writing   6

English as an Additional Language (EAL)   3,
    7–8, 43, 46, 64, 69, 77, 110, 115, 116, 134

enlarged texts/Big Books   **27–8**, 34, 45, 60,
    68–9, 70–1, 87–8, 142

environmental print   8, 18, 47, 145

equal opportunities   9, 20, 23–4, 43–5, 131, 147

ERIC   61–3, 114

fiction/narrative/story   20–1, 78, 95–6, 148

figurative language   20, 100

flashcards   2

formative assessment   135, 140

freeze-framing   81

games   34, 86, 87, 89, 91, 101, 145

Gap Test   128, 130

gender   8, 21, 22, 23, 45, 59, 80, 101, 110

genre   34, 17, 63, 64, 66, 67, 108, 132,

Gestalt theory   3, 4

girls   8, 20, 23–4

glossary   22, 69, 98, 99

grammatical/syntactical knowledge   15, 107,
    146–7

grapheme   11, 12, 13, 92

graphic

    cues   5

    knowledge   15, 82–93, 106

grapho-phonic cue-system   5, 8, 15, **82–93**

group/guided reading   21, 33, 46, 73, 90,
    94–101

guided/group reading   21, 33, 46, 73, 90, **94–101**

HMI   10, 33

Holborn Reading Test   128, 130

homograph   84

homophone   91

horn book   1, 9

hot-seating   81

House of Commons Select Committee   10

ICT   11, **47–52**

    cassettes   19, 20, 31, 34, 49, 138

    CD-ROMs   18, 34, 49–50, 86, 87, 95, 99, 100,
      101

    computers   49–52, 142

    film   20

    internet   51–2, 95

    television   18, 23, 48, 53, 138, 142

    video   20, 34, 48

illustrations   6, 9, 20, 27, 28, **30**, 33, 45, 75, 147,
    148

inclusion   139, 142

independent group work   90, 100

index   22, 69, 98

Individual Education Plan (IEP)   140, 141

individual needs   12–13, 69, 73, 101–2, **137–50**

individualised reading   10, 34

Initial Teaching Alphabet (ITA)   2

internet   **51–2**, 95

intonation   65, 108, 149

'invented spelling'   13

key words   2

labelling   47

language experience   3

learning styles   **5**, 26, 82, 138

Letterland   35

letter-sound correspondence   11, 12

libraries   52–4, 65

Literacy Hour   **15**, 18, 27, 28, 46, 60, 68, 72, 89,
    94, 95

literature circles   95

London Reading Test   130

look and say   2, 9

metalanguage   70, 85, 87

miscue-analysis   4, 89, 117, **121–7**, 129, 135,
    140, 141–2, 146

miscues   107, 117, 118, 131, 146

monosyllabic words   92

mother tongue   8, 49

motivation   25

multi-sensory approaches   145

names   47, 87
narrative/story/fiction   20–1, 78, 80, 95–6, 148
National Curriculum   4, 5, 12, **14–15**, 17, 18,
19, 21, 22, 25, 26, 33, 34, 45, 55, 66, 74, 128,
139, 142
National Grid for Learning   51
National Literacy Strategy   4, 11, 14, **15**, 18, 19,
20, 21, 22, 33, 34, 55, 60, 61, 66, 67, 82, 84, 85,
89, 90, 91, 94, 96, 116
National Writing Project   6
Neale Analysis   129, 130
New Reading   38
non-narrative texts   18, 22–3, 50, 55, 66, 67, 72,
80, 82, 98–9, 148
norm referencing   135
novelty books; see texts – interactive
nursery rhymes   13, 50, 86, 148

OFSTED   8, 33, 61, 94, 105
one-to-one correspondence   106, 117
1,2,3 and Away   42
onset and rime   13, 71, 86, 92, 148
overhead projector (OHP)   69, 70
Oxford Reading Tree   26, 41

PACT   109–112, 149
parents   109–112, 116, 140, 141, 149
phoneme   5, 11–14, 82–93
consonant   12
phonemic awareness   11–14, 15, 92, 70
phonemic system   83–4
vowel   12
phonetics   11, 92
phonics
analytic   14, 82, 91
approach   2, 5, **11–14**, 15
knowledge   **82–93**, 106, 120, 144–6
progression   84
rules   11
synthetic   11, 82, 93
teaching   **82–93**
terminology   85, 91–3
phonological awareness   **11–14**, 15, 86, 91, 92,
140
PIPs materials   83, 86, 89, 144
planning   60–61
play   6, 47, 81, 138
plays   21–2, 94
poetry   **21**, 51, 58, 97–8
polysyllabic words   92
prefix   84, 92
Primary Language Record   121, 134, 141

Programmes of Study   14
psycholinguistics   4–5
'publishing'   45–6

reading
age   127–8, 135
aloud   58, 60, **63–8**, 73, 100, 115, 138
conference   102, 104, 115, 141
ladder   10, 26
-like behaviour   6, 28, 105
logs   95
paired   101, 110
partners   **101–4**, 142, 146–7
policies   10, 46, 102
process   **4–6**
programmes   9, 33
quotient; see reading age
range   19–24, 63, 64, 66
'readiness'   7, 85
Reading Recovery Programme   139, 141,
143–4
records   25, 133–4, 138
resources   **17–59**
routines   **60–112**
schemes   9, 10, 18, 26, 33–42, 55
sustained   61–3, 72
tests   127–9, 135
'real books'   10
rhyme   12–13, 21, 70, 86, 87, 88, 91
rime and onset   13, 71, 86, 92, 148
role play   6, 47, 58, 79–82, 138
running record   89, **117–120**, 131, 140, 141–2

Salford Reading Test   128, 130
SATs   117, 131–133
Key Stage 1   131–2
Key Stage 2   132–3
scan   98, 134, 138
Schonell Graded Reading Test   128, 130
Schools' Library Service   52, 54
scripts   7, 8, 43
'searchlights'   15, 82, 90
'secondary worlds'   72, 81
segment   11, 12, 13, 14, 86, 92
self-correction   108, 120, 125, 138
semantic cue-system   5, 20, 120
SENCO   140, 141
sentence level work   15
sentence maker   3
series books   31–3, 53
shared reading   46, 68–9, 70–1, 100, 142
shared writing   69, 71–2, 142

silent letters   84, 93
single language books   43
skim   98
'smaller units'   5–6, 7, 10, 14, 50
Special Educational Needs (SEN)   3, 135, 139
specific learning difficulties   141
spelling   13, 84
Spelling Bank   91
SQUIRT   61–3
Story Chest   26, 40
story/fiction/narrative   20–1, 78, 80, 95–6, 148
story-telling   76–9, 80
story-time   63–8
struggling readers   12–13, 69, 73, 101–2,
   137–50
sub-headings   22, 98
subject knowledge   15
suffix   84, 93
summative assessment   135
syllable   87, 88, 93
syntactic cue–system   5, 8, 125
synthetic phonics   11, 14, 82, 93

taped books   49, 73
target setting   133–4, 140
TV programmes   18, 23, 48, 53, 138, 142
terminology   15
texts   19–46, 147–9
   affective   20, 29
   and teaching reading   9–11
   dual-language   18, 44–5

interactive   20, 29
narrative   20–1, 78, 80, 95–6, 148
non-narrative   18, 22–3, 50, 55, 66, 67, 72, 80,
   82, 98–9, 148
traditional   23–4, 27, 67, 78, 148–9
translated   18, 24, 43, 44, 46
text level work   15
TGAT Report   113
thought-tracking   81

USSR   61–3

videos   19, 20, 34, 48
Virtual Teachers' Centre (VTC)   51
vowel   11, 84, 92
   digraph   83, 93
   long   89, 92
   medial   84
   phoneme   12, 83, 84, 89
   short   92

Warnock Report   139, 142
websites   51–2
whole language   3
word level work   15
World Wide Web   51–2
writing-like behaviour   6

Young's Reading Test   128, 130

zone of proximal development   64, 102